common core
Performance
Coach™

English Language Arts

Performance Coach, English Language Arts, Grade 7   338NASE   ISBN-13: 978-1-62362-845-1   B
Cover Image: © Thinkstock

Triumph Learning® 136 Madison Avenue, 7th Floor, New York, NY 10016

CONTENTS

Standards

RL.7.1, RL.7.2, RL.7.3, RL.7.6, L.7.4.a

RL.7.4, RL.7.5, L.7.5, L.7.5.a, L.7.5.c

RL.7.3, RL.7.4, RL.7.5, L.7.4.a, L.7.5.a

RL.7.2, RL.7.4, RL.7.6, L.7.4, L.7.4.b, L.7.5.a

RI.7.1, RI.7.2, RI.7.4, RI.7.5, RI.7.6, L.7.4.b, RH.6–8.2, RH.6–8.7, RST.6–8.1, RST.6–8.2, RST.6–8.7

RI.7.4, RI.7.5, RI.7.6, RI.7.8, RI.7.9, RH.6–8.8

RI.7.5, RI.7.6, L.7.6, RH.6–8.1, RH.6–8.2, RH.6–8.3, RH.6–8.4, RH.6–8.5, RH.6–8.6, RH.6–8.7, RH.6–8.9, RH.6–8.10

RI.7.5, RI.7.6, L.7.6, RST.6–8.1, RST.6–8.3, RST.6–8.4, RST.6–8.5, RST.6–8.6, RST.6–8.7, RST.6–8.8, RST.6–8.9, RST.6–8.10

RI.7.2, RI.7.3, RI.7.9, L.7.6, RH.6–8.2, RST.6–8.1, RST.6–8.2

RL.7.1, RL.7.3, RL.7.9, RI.7.2, RI.7.9, L.7.5.b

Standards

W.7.1.a–e, W.7.2.a–e, W.7.3.a, W.7.3.c, W.7.3.e, W.7.4, W.7.5, L.7.1.a

RL.7.1, RL.7.2, RL.7.3, RL.7.4, RL.7.6, W.7.9, W.7.9.a, L.7.1.c

W.7.3.a–e, L.7.2.a

W.7.7, W.7.8, W.7.9, L.7.2

W.7.2.a–f, L.7.1

W.7.1.a–c, W.7.1.e, W.7.9.b, L.7.1.b

W.7.5, L.7.1, L.7.2, L.7.3

SL.7.2, L.7.4.c, L.7.4.d

SL.7.2, SL.7.3

DEAR STUDENT

Welcome to *Performance Coach*!

We made this book to help you strengthen your reading, writing, and listening skills. These skills are important to have for every subject you study this year, not just English Language Arts.

Each lesson in this book has three parts:

GETTING THE IDEA ①

Review some of the basic concepts and skills you've already learned.

② COACHED EXAMPLE

Read a passage or two, then answer a set of questions. Don't worry—the questions have hints that will help you!

LESSON PRACTICE ③

Now you're on your own! This part contains a longer passage and additional questions to answer.

 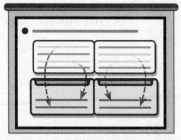

There are many different types of test items in *Performance Coach*. For some, you will have to choose more than one answer. For others, you will write out your answer. You will also see items that ask you to match words and phrases, put events in order, or complete a graphic organizer. Many items have more than one part. Be sure to read the directions carefully so you know how to answer each item.

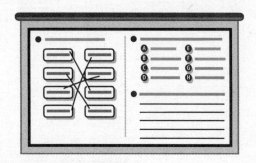

HAVE A GREAT YEAR!

Sincerely,
TRIUMPH LEARNING

STRAND 1

Working with Literature

RL.7.1, RL.7.2, RL.7.3, RL.7.6, L.7.4.a

Fiction

① GETTING THE IDEA

The term **fiction** describes stories that are created by an author. Although the stories may be based on true events, the author adds elements from his or her imagination.

Type of Fiction	What It's Like
contemporary fiction	takes place in the present day
historical fiction	takes place in the past; uses details about the history of the time
science fiction	about science and technology of the future; may be set in the future or in space
fable	a short story with a moral or lesson
myth	a traditional story from a certain place; may give reasons for how something was created or how it works

Every piece of fiction has the following elements, or parts: character(s), setting, plot, point of view, and theme.

Characters

Each character has traits and motivations. The author reveals a character's **traits**, or qualities, through the character's thoughts, dialogue, and action. When drawing conclusions about a character's traits, it's also important to notice how a character reacts to other characters and events.

Motivations are the needs and goals of a character. The motivations of the characters drive the action of the plot. For example, if a character is motivated to move far away from home, he or she might work hard to save money for a plane ticket. The actions he or she takes to serve this motivation will be the building blocks for plot events and will most likely reveal the character's traits—for example, a hardworking, independent nature.

Setting

The **setting** is the place where a story happens and the time period (past, present, or future) in which the action takes place. A story may have many settings and move from one place to another, or even move backward and forward in time. An author may state the setting clearly or just give clues about it through description. For clues to a story's location, look for details about the landscapes and buildings. For clues to its time period, look for details about technology and how characters dress and speak.

Where a story takes place influences the plot. For example, if a story is set in the future on a colony on Mars, the author must create events that could only occur there. The setting can also influence the characters' actions or development. Suppose that a story took place on a deserted island after a plane crash. Through this setting, a character might recognize his or her strength and ability to survive.

An author may or may not state the story's setting. To recognize it, readers may have to make inferences from details in the text. Read this example.

> Pradeep woke up with a large bump on his head, feeling groggy. The air in this place was dark and damp. The rock walls had moss growing on them.

By thinking about the underlined details, the reader can infer that Pradeep is in a cave.

Plot

The **plot** of a story is its series of events. Read the following story outline. Think about how the character's motivation drives the action of the plot.

> Ty is determined to win the lead in the school play. Every night he stays up late practicing his audition song. He spends so much time practicing that he doesn't get very much sleep and doesn't eat properly, and he begins to neglect his schoolwork. Finally, the day before auditions, he comes down with the flu.

Ty's motivation is that he wants a part in the play. His actions reveal that one of his traits is obsessiveness. These motivations and traits drive the plot: because of them, Ty finds himself getting sick right before auditions.

Theme

The **theme** of a story is the message or lesson that the author wants to share with the reader. The theme isn't often stated in the story, but readers can infer it by taking a close look at the characters' actions as well as the series of events in the story. Readers can then **draw conclusions** about the theme. What theme might a reader infer from the story about Ty? How do his actions lead you to a conclusion about the effects of obsession?

Point of View

Stories are told from the point of view of a **narrator**. A **first-person narrator** is a character in the story who looks at events and other characters from his or her point of view. This narrator uses the first-person pronoun *I* to tell the reader what he or she did, said, and thought throughout the events of the story. A first-person narrator usually doesn't know what the other characters are thinking and can't tell about events he or she hasn't personally witnessed or heard about.

A **third-person omniscient narrator** is all-knowing. The narrator knows everything about the characters, events, and setting of the story. An author might use this kind of narrator to present characters who see events from different points of view. The reader can then compare and contrast different versions of the same event.

Another choice is a **third-person limited narrator**. A third-person limited narrator focuses on narrating the experiences of one character in the third person, using the character's name and the third-person pronoun *he* or *she*. This type of narrator can make judgments about the character and share them with the reader, or narrate events from a character's life that a character might be unlikely to share in the first person, such as painful details from his or her past. Below is an example of how Ty's story might read if it had a third-person limited narrator.

> Ty shrugged off the warnings from his mother about how he should be spending more time studying or eating breakfast. *Who needs breakfast?* he thought. He had a part to win, and he wasn't going to distract himself with anything else.

The narrator above is limited to narrating Ty's experiences. If this piece had a third-person omniscient narrator, it might also go into detail about the mother's thoughts on Ty's behavior. Here, they are filtered through Ty's experience; the narrator can tell only what other characters have said, not what they think or feel.

Language Spotlight • Context Clues

Context clues are words in a sentence that help you understand the meaning of an unfamiliar word. When you read a word you don't know, look at the other words in the surrounding sentences for clues. Read the sentences below. The underlined words are clues to the meaning of *acclaim*.

> Renata longed to be a star as a country singer. Her <u>dreams of fame</u> came true when she won a television contest for singers and <u>turned the judges and the audience into instant fans</u>. Renata enjoyed national acclaim as country music magazines <u>praised</u> her soulful voice.

How do the clue words help you understand the meaning of the word *acclaim*? Use a dictionary to verify the meaning of the word.

Read the passage.

A New Beginning

My name is Henry Knox, and I was a child of eight in 1815 when my family was transported to Australia. Jeremiah Knox, my father, was imprisoned for stealing food to feed our family. Before that, my parents had lost their farm and came to London hoping for work in the factories, but there was little employment to be found. In desperation, my father stole food to ensure our survival. After a few months in prison, my father was put on a dreaded prison ship to Australia, a land halfway around the world to which convicts were sent to labor. My mother chose to go with him and, of course, I had to join her.

I cannot recall the horror of the journey, which lasted eight months, without trembling. We were crowded with hundreds of other men, women, and children in the airless hull of the ship. Some men spent the whole journey in chains, but my father was not one of them, as he had a calm and dignified temperament. We were often sick from the poor food, the horrific smells, and the rough seas. Some died on the journey.

We felt great relief when the ship docked in the harbor at New South Wales, a prison colony where convicts and their families were under the rule of British soldiers. Our relief at being on solid ground was short-lived. My father was sent with other convicts to labor at building roads. His sentence was for seven years of hard labor, but we were sustained by the hope that at the end of that time, he would be freed and our family reunited. My mother was sent to a factory, where she labored in textile mills for twelve to fourteen hours a day. Since she was not a convict, she was paid a small wage for her labor. We lived in crowded conditions but were able to obtain adequate food.

After four years, my father was given a ticket of leave for good behavior. He obtained a job working for a landowner on a large farm. I was now thirteen years old and well acquainted with hard work. Along with my mother, all three of us labored on the farm for the next five years, saving as much money as we could. My father rose to the position of farm manager and was entrusted by the owner with important responsibilities.

After five years, my father was able to buy a small plot of land. He and I built a simple house to live in, and in this way I learned carpentry skills. We worked hard to make our farm <u>profitable</u> and in time were able to hire convicts who had recently been freed to work the land with us. My father bought more land with his profits and became a respectable member of the community. I took on more and more carpentry work until I could earn a living at my trade.

After five more years, I was now twenty-three years of age and earning a decent living, so I asked the fair and clever daughter of our nearest neighbor to be my wife. Sally accepted, and we built our own house and carpentry shop with both our families' help. We had seven children and have led a very comfortable life. Although I endured a harsh childhood with much work and little education, I am glad that fate led us to Australia, where we have prospered. My children have had the opportunity to attend school and seem destined to rise in society. Perhaps someday, one of my descendants will bring great honor to our family and our new homeland.

Answer the following questions.

 This question has two parts. First, answer Part A. Then, answer Part B.

Part A

Underline **three** phrases or sentences in the passage about setting—both the time period and the locations—that let you know it is a piece of historical fiction.

Part B

How does the setting in the passage affect the plot?

_____

_____

_____

_____

_____

> **Hint** Remember that historical fiction takes place in the past and uses historical details of the time. Where does this passage take place? What does it tell the reader about life in that time and place? How does the action in the passage relate to the setting?

2 The following question has two parts. First, answer Part A. Then, answer Part B.

Part A

Identify the point of view of this passage and tell how you know.

_____

_____

Part B

Describe how the passage might have been different if it were told from Jeremiah Knox's point of view.

_____

_____

Hint Notice whose thoughts and feelings you learn about in this passage and which narrator is telling about them. Use these clues to answer Part A. Use what you know about Henry's father and the events of the passage to answer Part B.

3 Reread these sentences from the passage.

> **We worked hard to make our farm <u>profitable</u> and in time were able to hire convicts who had recently been freed to work the land with us. My father bought more land with his profits and became a respectable member of the community. I took on more and more carpentry work until I could earn a living at my trade.**

Use context clues to figure out the meaning of _profitable_ and write it on the line below. Then circle a word or phrase you used as a clue to the meaning.

_____

Hint Sometimes a context clue may be a word with the same root as the unknown word. Look for a word similar to the word _profitable_ in this passage. The meaning of that word can help you figure out the meaning of the word _profitable_.

4 A reader wants to cite textual evidence to support the theme written in the chart below. Write in at least **two** details about the passage's characters or plot that could provide support for the reader's inference about the theme.

Inference about Theme	Textual Evidence
If a good, hardworking person is given a chance, he or she can succeed.	

Hint Think about how Henry and his father and mother change their lives in Australia. What evidence do you see in the passage that they've succeeded at their goals? What does each character do to become successful?

Use the Reading Guide to help you understand the passage.

Underground Scientists Save the Day

Reading Guide

What clues does the author give about the setting of this passage?

Do the events take place now or at a different time?

What is the conflict, and what happens as a result of this conflict?

For weeks, teenager Jim Chang had been cooped up in his family's house, forced inside by the piles of garbage that now blocked every single street of his town. His family had only eaten food that was airdropped by government helicopters, and Jim was left with nothing to do but read online news articles about the garbage crisis, looking for some shred of hope that this would all be over soon. So far, he hadn't had much luck with that. "Garbage Chokes Farmland," proclaimed one headline. "Government Refuses to Spend Money on Garbage Research," screamed another.

The garbage problem had been caused by a number of factors, and it had been getting worse for years. Ignoring warnings about a coming garbage crisis, Earth's people continued to make more and more waste. They used their new electronic devices for only a few months before throwing them away. They stopped cooking entirely and started eating all their ready-made meals out of plastic containers. Metals and plastics piled up with regular trash and food waste until there was no longer anywhere to put it all.

Soon, the problem got even worse. Waste disposal companies took over farmland, threatening the farmers if they didn't leave. The companies charged high fees for removing people's garbage and then dumped it, killing crops. The heads of the waste disposal companies were now Earth's wealthiest and most powerful residents. Even some of Earth's governments feared standing up to them.

Instead of spending money on research to solve the garbage crisis, the government had started airdropping food to stranded families like Jim's. In big cities, where the garbage smell was the worst, they had even started pumping oxygen into peoples' homes, so no one would have to go outside.

This absence of government <u>funding</u> was a particular problem for Jim's parents, Molly and Clifford. Both were scientists studying the garbage crisis, but their lab had recently been closed due to lack of money. Before that, they'd been working on a solution that involved transforming plastics into soil.

Look for pronouns that can help you figure out the point of view in this passage.

What kind of narrator is telling this story?

Whose thoughts and feelings do you learn about in this section?

How does the setting change in this section? How does the change in setting affect the plot?

Since then, they'd continued their work at home. They worked into the night under florescent lights, analyzing soil samples. Every day they looked more exhausted, and Jim wished there was something he could do to help.

Then one day, he woke up early to find his parents at the kitchen table. They were talking excitedly.

"Jim, we have news," Molly exclaimed. "We're going underground."

"When we say *underground*, we mean it," Clifford added. "Our rescuers should be digging a hole through our living room floor in, oh, an hour, and taking us through a tunnel to the lab. It's the only way out of here."

"Wait, what lab? And what rescuers?" Jim sputtered. "Mom, Dad, what's going on?"

Molly and Clifford explained that they'd banded together with other concerned scientists around the world, and they'd recently found a very wealthy sponsor for their research.

"He used to own a waste disposal company," Molly explained. "But he had a change of heart and came to regret making money by ruining Earth's farmland. He bought a building that was supposed to be used for garbage disposal, but he actually used it to build a lab for us. It's super-secret, so we couldn't tell you until now. If the waste disposal companies find out, they'll take our land again."

Two hours later, Jim and his parents arrived at the new lab.

At the lab, Jim finally felt like he was doing something to help. After long days of work, when the scientists went to sleep for a few short hours, Jim scrubbed the equipment and got it ready for the next day. He frequently traveled through the tunnels back to his old home to collect airdropped food.

But despite his help, work at the lab was frustrating. Months passed with no solution. After a particularly infuriating day, when a promising test suddenly failed, the scientists called a meeting.

"Every day without a solution is another day we risk being discovered," Clifford worried.

"I was convinced that last test would work. What a waste of time!" Dr. Ellis, one of the scientists, moaned.

Reading Guide

How does Jim's discovery contribute to the scientists' solution?

What do the scientists do to test the discovery?

How is the conflict resolved?

Jim didn't want to interrupt, so he focused on his latest task: organizing a shelf full of bacteria samples, each in its own plastic container. As he moved the containers to clean the shelf underneath them, Jim noticed that one had sprung a leak.

"Dad, Mom!" Jim called. "Sorry to interrupt, but I have a bit of a hazardous situation here. One of the containers is leaking all over!"

"Step away and sanitize your hands," Clifford ordered as he donned a protective suit and face mask to examine the container.

"This is no ordinary leak," Clifford shouted, his voice muffled behind his mask. "The bacteria has completely eaten through the plastic! This is amazing!"

The scientists immediately began experimenting with the bacteria. Dr. Ellis tested it on hundreds of plastic samples, which all melted. Dr. Ellis also tested the bacteria on plant life, and the team discovered that the waste from the plastic-eating bacteria was actually good for soil. Huge vegetables could grow in it, and lab rats that ate the vegetables thrived. Then, taking a risk, two scientists volunteered to test the vegetables themselves. Both were unharmed.

At that point, the scientists presented the discovery to their sponsor. The former landfill owner used his wealth and power to get the attention of several governments. Soon, the scientists' method was worldwide news.

Five years later, the world's garbage had been cut in half. The scientists attended an awards ceremony, where they won a prize for their research. They all insisted that Jim attend.

"Without Jim's cleaning skills," Molly said in their acceptance speech, "we might still be drowning in trash!"

Answer the following questions.

1 Below are three statements giving possible themes for this passage.

Possible Themes
Discoveries can come from unexpected places.
Government funding is usually unnecessary.
It's best to quit while you're ahead.

Part A

Underline the theme above that is supported by evidence in the passage.

Part B

Write a piece of evidence from the passage to support the theme you chose.

_____

_____

2 Reread the following sentences from the passage.

> **This absence of government funding was a particular problem for Jim's parents, Molly and Clifford. Both were scientists studying the garbage crisis, but their lab had recently been closed due to lack of money.**

Based on the context clues in this passage, what does the word underline{funding} mean?

A. the act of doing scientific research

B. the act of supplying money

C. the act of building a lab

D. the act of studying a crisis

3 Reread this paragraph from the passage.

> **At the lab, Jim finally felt like he was doing something to help. After long days of work, when the scientists went to sleep for a few short hours, Jim scrubbed the equipment and got it ready for the next day. He frequently traveled through the tunnels back to his old home to collect airdropped food.**

How does the narrator use the setting of the lab to develop Jim's character in this section? Write your answer on the lines below.

_____

_____

_____

_____

4 Write **two** details from the passage that the author uses to develop the central idea that teamwork is important.

_____

_____

_____

_____

5 The following question has two parts. First, answer Part A. Then, answer Part B.

Part A

Read the following sentences from the passage.

> Since then, they'd continued their work at home. They worked into the night under florescent lights, analyzing soil samples. Every day they looked more exhausted, and Jim wished there was something he could do to help.

How does the author use the sentences to develop the point of view?

A. The author uses first-person point of view in this section to show Jim's feelings about wanting to help his parents.

B. The author uses third-person omniscient point of view in this section to show how Jim's parents feel about their work.

C. The author uses third-person limited point of view in this section to show Jim's feelings about wanting to help his parents.

D. The author uses third-person omniscient point of view in this section to show the different perspectives of Jim and his parents.

Part B

How would the passage be different if it were told from Molly's first-person point of view?

_____

_____

_____

_____

_____

6 Using textual evidence from the passage, explain how the setting of "Underground Scientists Save the Day" contributes to the events of its plot. In your answer, be sure to describe the setting of the passage and provide a brief plot summary.

Write your answer on the lines below.

_____

_____

_____

_____

_____

_____

_____

_____

_____

_____

_____

_____

_____

_____

RL.7.4, RL.7.5, L.7.5, L.7.5.a, L.7.5.c

Poetry

1 GETTING THE IDEA

A **poem** is a type of writing in which the poet chooses and arranges words to create a strong feeling through meaning, sound, and rhythm.

Structure of Poetry

A simple way to recognize a poem is by its structure. Poetry has certain structural elements that are different from prose.

- Every poem has **lines**, which are rows of words. Unlike sentences, lines in a poem do not always follow rules of capitalization and punctuation.

- Lines in a poem are often broken up into **stanzas**, or groups of lines set apart by spaces. Stanzas are somewhat like paragraphs in prose. Each stanza fits into the overall structure of a poem. Poets may use more than one stanza to develop their ideas or theme. They may also break lines and stanzas in unusual places to get the reader's attention or to create a certain effect.

Sounds of Poetry

Poetry is meant to be read aloud, so poets play with the sounds of words to create a certain effect.

- **Rhyme** describes words with the same ending sound. Many poems have lines that end with words that rhyme. Usually a poem has a **rhyme scheme**. The ending of certain lines rhyme with each other. Rhyme schemes are shown by a sequence of letters, such as *abab*. An *abab* rhyme scheme stands for a four-line stanza in which lines 1 and 3 rhyme (*a*) and lines 2 and 4 rhyme (*b*).

- **Rhythm** creates the "beat" of the poem. It is the pattern of stressed and unstressed syllables in a line of poetry.

- **Meter** is a recurring pattern of stressed and unstressed syllables.

- **Repetition** is the repeating of words or lines in poetry. Repetition may help to unify a poem or to reinforce the meaning or theme.

- **Alliteration** is the repetition of an initial consonant sound.

Read Alan L. Strang's poem "The Storm." What is its rhyme scheme? What are its rhythm and meter?

> The rough old Mr. Storm
> Is whirling, swirling past
> He makes the treetops bow their heads
> And trembles at his blast.
>
> He never stops to think
> Of the damage he may do,
> He's always rushing in and out
> And hitting, batting you.

Figurative Language

Poets use **figurative language**, or figures of speech, to create word pictures, or images. Their word choices affect the meaning and **tone** of a poem. This chart shows some common figures of speech. Which ones can you find in "The Storm" above?

Figure of Speech	Definition	Example	Meaning
simile	a comparison that uses *like* or *as*	The lake was as smooth as glass.	The lake is compared to glass.
metaphor	a comparison that does not use *like* or *as*	Mia remembers everything; her mind is a steel trap.	Mia's mind is compared to a steel trap.
personification	the assigning of human qualities to a nonliving thing	The sun smiled on our picnic.	The sun was warm as if it were smiling.
symbolism	the use of an image or thing to stand for something else	Lindsay wore black to the funeral.	The color black often stands for death.
allusion	a reference to another work, such as the Bible or mythology	It rained so much that I thought we'd have to build an ark.	In the Bible, Noah builds an ark to save animals from a flood.

Point of View, Theme, and Tone

Point of view is the position or outlook from which the speaker tells a story or observes something. The **speaker** in a poem is like the narrator of a story; he or she is the voice of the poem, which may be the voice of the poet or that of another person or character.

Often, the speaker in a poem reflects on a topic and reveals the poem's theme. The **theme** is the central idea that a poem explores.

The speaker's voice has a certain tone. The **tone** is the mood the poem creates for the reader. The tone of a poem may be playful, angry, melancholy—and it can change as the speaker's reflection on a topic moves in a different direction.

Forms of Poetry

The form of a poem often adds to its meaning. Many forms of poetry follow certain rules of structure, rhyme, and sometimes topic.

Form	Definition
lyric poem	a short poem that is like a song
ode	a poem that has two or more stanzas with similar structures
haiku	a very short poem with seventeen syllables in three lines; usually about nature
sonnet	a poem that has fourteen lines with ten to twelve syllables per line; first eight lines develop one idea, last six lines question that idea
ballad	a short poem with stanzas of two to four lines and a refrain that repeats; tells a story
free verse	a poem that does not follow any rules of rhythm or rhyme

Language Spotlight • Denotations and Connotations

Poets rely on both the denotations and connotations of words to convey meaning. Their choice of words can affect the tone of a poem.

- **Denotations** are the dictionary definitions of words. For example, both *hideous* and *homely* mean "having an unpleasant appearance."
- **Connotations** are meanings suggested or implied by a word, separate from its dictionary definition. The connotation of *hideous* is terribly ugly. A movie monster may be hideous. The connotation of *homely* is plain and drab. Unfashionable clothing may be homely.

Would you rather have a pet that was *hideous* or *homely*? Why?

Read the poems.

Pretty Words

by Elinor Wylie

Poets make pets of pretty, docile words:
I love smooth words, like gold-enameled fish
Which circle slowly with a silken swish,
And tender ones, like downy-feathered birds:
5   Words shy and dappled, deep-eyed deer in herds,
Come to my hand, and playful if I wish,
Or purring softly at a silver disk,
Blue Persian kittens, fed on cream and curds.

I love bright words, words up and singing early;
10 Words that are luminous in the dark, and sing;
Warm lazy words, white cattle under trees;
I love words opalescent, cool, and pearly,
Like midsummer moths, and honied words like bees,
Gilded and sticky, with a little sting.

The Fruit Garden Path

by Amy Lowell

The path runs straight between the flowering rows,
A moonlit path, hemmed in by beds of bloom,
Where phlox and marigolds dispute for room
With tall, red dahlias and the briar rose.
5   'Tis reckless prodigality which throws
Into the night these wafts of rich perfume
Which sweep across the garden like a plume.
Over the trees a single bright star glows.
Dear garden of my childhood, here my years
10 Have run away like little grains of sand;
The moments of my life, its hopes and fears
Have all found utterance here, where now I stand;
My eyes ache with the weight of unshed tears,
You are my home, do you not understand?

Answer the following questions.

1 This question has three parts.

Part A

Which is true about **both** "Pretty Words" and "The Fruit Garden Path"? Circle **all** that apply.

A. Lines 1–4 and 5–8 have an *abba* rhyme scheme.

B. Both stanzas of each poem have the same rhyme scheme.

C. Each stanza has the same number of lines.

D. Each poem has 14 lines.

Part B

Based on your answer in Part A, what type of poems are these?

A. odes

B. sonnets

C. ballads

D. free verse

Part C

In Part B you identified the form of both poems. How does knowing their form help you understand their meaning?

_____

_____

> **Hint** What do you know about the structure and rhyme of each form of poetry? Poets use different forms of poetry to create different meanings.

2 Read the lines from "Pretty Words" in each choice. Then, match each line to the kind of figurative language it shows.

A. Poets make pets of pretty, docile words	**1.** personification
B. I love smooth words, like gold-enameled fish	**2.** metaphor
C. I love bright words, words up and singing early	**3.** simile

> **Hint** Personification, metaphor, and simile are kinds of figurative language. What do you know about how each one creates a different kind of image?

3 The following question has two parts. First, answer Part A. Then, answer Part B.

Part A

What is the tone of "Pretty Words"?

A. angry

B. somber

C. reflective

D. celebratory

Part B

The poet uses repetition to help establish the tone you identified in Part A. Circle at least **two** lines that show this repetition.

Hint Remember that the tone of a poem is related to its mood. What is the mood of "Pretty Words"?

4 The following question has two parts. First, answer Part A. Then, answer Part B.

Part A

At what point does the tone of "The Fruit Garden Path" change?

A. line 5

B. line 8

C. line 9

D. line 11

Part B

Which sentence supports the answer in Part A? Choose **all** that apply.

A. The poet describes the garden to the reader and then turns and sorrowfully speaks to the garden directly.

B. The poet uses an allusion to explain why the garden upsets her.

C. The poet changes the rhyme scheme.

D. The poet develops only one idea in this poem.

Hint Where does the language change to show a new idea? How is this change also reflected in the structure of the poem?

Use the Reading Guide to help you understand the poem.

The Death of the Old Year

by Alfred Tennyson

Reading Guide

Who is the speaker in this poem?

What effect does the poet's word choice have on the tone of the poem?

What figures of speech does the poet use? How do you identify them?

Full knee-deep lies the winter snow,
And the winter winds are wearily sighing:
Toll ye the church-bell sad and slow,
And tread softly and speak low,
5   For the old year lies a-dying.
     Old year, you must not die;
     You came to us so readily,
     You lived with us so steadily,
     Old year, you shall not die.

10 He lieth still: he doth not move:
He will not see the dawn of day.
He hath no other life above.
He gave me a friend, and a true truelove,
And the New-year will take 'em away.
15   Old year, you must not go;
       So long as you have been with us,
       Such joy as you have seen with us,
       Old year, you shall not go.

He froth'd his bumpers[1] to the brim;
20 A jollier year we shall not see.
But tho' his eyes are waxing dim,
And tho' his foes speak ill of him,
He was a friend to me.
     Old year, you shall not die;
25   We did so laugh and cry with you,
     I've half a mind to die with you,
     Old year, if you must die.

[1] **bumper:** a brimming cup or glass

How does the poet feel about the old year? How do you know?

How is each stanza organized? How does the organization of the stanzas help you understand the poem?

He was full of joke and jest,
But all his merry quips are o'er.
30 To see him die across the waste
His son and heir doth ride post-haste,
But he'll be dead before.
    Every one for his own.
    The night is starry and cold, my friend,
35   And the New-year blithe and bold, my friend,
    Comes up to take his own.

How hard he breathes! over the snow
I heard just now the crowing cock.
The shadows flicker to and fro:
40 The cricket chirps: the light burns low:
'Tis nearly twelve o'clock.
    Shake hands, before you die.
    Old year, we'll dearly rue for you:
    What is it we can do for you?
45   Speak out before you die.

His face is growing sharp and thin.
Alack! our friend is gone.
Close up his eyes: tie up his chin:
Step from the corpse, and let him in
50 That standeth there alone,
    And waiteth at the door.
    There's a new foot on the floor, my friend,
    And a new face at the door, my friend,
    A new face at the door.

Answer the following questions.

1 This question has two parts. First, answer Part A. Then, answer Part B.

Part A

What does the dying old friend personify in this poem?

A. winter snow

B. church bells

C. a starry cold night

D. the old year

Part B

Which line from the poem supports the answer to Part A?

A. Toll ye the church-bells sad and slow

B. For the old year lies a-dying

C. Full knee-deep lies the winter snow

D. The night is starry and cold, my friend

2 The following question has two parts. First, answer Part A. Then, answer Part B.

Part A

Read the line from the poem.

And the winter winds are wearily sighing:

What figure of speech does the poet use in this line? Circle **all** that apply.

A. simile

B. metaphor

C. personification

D. alliteration

Part B

What imagery does your answer to Part A create? How does this add meaning to the poem? Write two to three sentences to explain your answer.

_____

_____

_____

3 Read the lines from the poem and the directions that follow.

> **To see him die, across the waste**
> **His son and heir doth ride post-haste,**

In Greek mythology, the old king Kronos was replaced by his young son Zeus. Select the sentence that **best** explains why the poet uses this allusion in the lines above.

- **A.** The old king is like the old year.
- **B.** The son is the new year.
- **C.** Both the son in the poem and Zeus rode horses.
- **D.** The son's coming to replace the old king is a metaphor for the new year coming to replace the old year.

4 Read the lines from the poem and the directions that follow.

> **How hard he breathes! over the snow**
> **I heard just now the crowing cock.**
> **The shadows flicker to and fro:**
> **The cricket chirps: the light burns low:**
> **'Tis nearly twelve o'clock.**

Using details from the poem, write a word that has the same denotation as flicker. Then think about the connotations of the word flicker. Why did the poet choose flicker rather than another word with a similar definition? Use details from the poem to support your answer.

Write your answer on the lines provided.

_____

_____

_____

_____

5 Read the stanzas from the poem and the directions that follow.

Full knee-deep lies the winter snow,
And the winter winds are wearily sighing:
Toll ye the church-bell sad and slow,
And tread softly and speak low,
For the old year lies a-dying.
    Old year, you must not die;
    You came to us so readily,
    You lived with us so steadily,
    Old year, you shall not die.

He lieth still: he doth not move:
He will not see the dawn of day.
He hath no other life above.
He gave me a friend, and a true truelove,
And the New-year will take 'em away.
    Old year, you must not go;
    So long as you have been with us,
    Such joy as you have seen with us,
    Old year, you shall not go.

Look at the structure of the stanzas. Why are they indented this way? How does the structure reflect important details about the poem and add to its meaning? Write two or three sentences on the lines below.

_____

_____

_____

_____

6 The poem "The Death of the Old Year" is an extended metaphor in which the end of a year is compared to the dying of an old man. Write one or two paragraphs to explain how Tennyson expands and extends this metaphor throughout the poem to describe an old year ending and a new one beginning. Be sure to include lines from the poem to support your answer.

Write your answer on the lines provided.

_____

_____

_____

_____

_____

_____

_____

_____

_____

_____

_____

_____

_____

_____

_____

_____

_____

Drama

Drama is a story that is written to be performed by actors for an audience. It may be a film, a television show, or a stage play. Most of a drama is told through the characters' words. The rest of the story is told through the characters' actions. Dramas also have distinct elements and a unique format. These elements include the following.

Elements of Drama	Definition
cast of characters	the performers in a drama
act	the main divisions of a drama
scene	the smaller divisions within an act
setting	the place and time where the action takes place
dialogue	the lines spoken by the characters
stage directions	the directions telling characters how to speak or act; directions telling how sound, lighting, and props are used

Setting

In a drama, the **setting** is a brief description of the time and place and any other factors that directly affect the characters or the plot. For example, five friends spending a relaxing weekend in a mountain cabin might have very different experiences than the same five friends trapped by a snowstorm in the same mountain cabin. In this way, the setting creates the **mood**, or the atmosphere, of the drama. A setting might make a character relaxed, cheerful, anxious, fearful, or angry.

Plot

All good stories have a **plot**, or a series of events where the characters try to solve a problem or attain a goal. In a drama, the plot unfolds over the course of one or more acts. Acts and scenes usually show a change in setting, in the characters, or in the plot. Critical incidents in the plot can move the action forward, trigger a character to make a decision, or do both. The snowstorm mentioned above, for example, might make the friends argue about waiting to be rescued or attempting to make it down the mountain on their own.

A typical plot has the following structure.

- The **exposition** introduces the characters, setting, and conflict.

- The **rising action** includes the plot events that lead to the climax.

- The **climax** is the turning point in the plot when the conflict is at its highest.

- The **falling action** is the part of the plot that leads to the resolution.

- The **resolution** is how the conflict is or is not resolved.

Dialogue

The lines spoken between two or more people in a drama are called **dialogue**. Most of what you learn about the characters comes from what they say, how they say it, and how other characters respond. Dialogue can move the plot forward, trigger a character's response, or cause the action to move to a different setting. In addition to revealing aspects of a character's personality, dialogue can provide clues to a character's education, background, or nationality.

Like any conversation, dialogue contains figures of speech. An **idiom** is a common phrase that has a different meaning than the meaning of its individual words. An **adage** or **proverb** is an old saying that expresses an accepted truth about life. Many fables have morals that are adages, such as "Slow and steady wins the race."

Read the sample dialogue below. Underline the idioms and circle the adages.

> PAT: Uh-oh. (*frowns*) I can tell by the look on your face the game didn't go well.
>
> LIV: (*sighs*) It was bad, Pat. The pitcher was the best, and even he was all thumbs.
>
> PAT: Hey, don't worry. If you win the next two games, you still have a shot at the division championship.
>
> LIV: (*forces a smile*) And that's why Coach doubled our practices. He actually said, "Practice makes perfect."
>
> PAT: (*laughs*) Well, no pain, no gain.
>
> LIV: (*tosses ball in air, catches it*) That's for sure. Come on. You can walk me to practice.

Based on this dialogue, what can you infer about Pat and Liv?

Point of View

Dialogue also reveals a character's point of view or perspective. An author can use several devices to help an audience understand a character's point of view and explore the characters' thoughts and feelings.

- A **monologue** is a speech given by one actor.

- A **soliloquy** is a speech in which a character reveals his or her thoughts and feelings to the audience but not to the other characters.

- An **aside** is a comment made to the audience that is not heard by the other characters.

- **Dramatic irony** is created when the audience knows more than one or more of the characters do.

- **Verbal irony** is when a character says the opposite of what he or she really means. Depending on the context, it may show sarcasm or humor.

Theme

The **theme** is the central message the author wants to convey to readers. It may be a statement about life or the way the world works. In a drama, the theme is often alluded to in the title and at the beginning of the play. Look for ways in which the characters respond to other characters, the setting, and the events to reveal aspects of the theme. Repeated phrases, details, or symbols may also help identify the theme.

Putting It All Together

When you read a drama, pay attention to all its parts. Use details in the dialogue and stage directions to make inferences about the characters' traits and feelings. Think about how the setting affects the characters and the plot. Look for clues in the stage directions that tell how characters act or how lighting, sound, and props are used.

Language Spotlight • Antiquated Language

When you read traditional dramas or modern dramas set in the past, you will most likely encounter antiquated language. **Antiquated language** is language that was used in the past. The words *thou* and *thee*, for example, are antiquated words for the pronoun *you*. When you see an antiquated word or phrase, use context clues to help you figure out its meaning. Think about how the word or phrase is used in the sentence. Is it a noun, a verb, or a pronoun?

Read the sample passage below from the play *Julius Caesar* by William Shakespeare. Underline the antiquated words. Can you figure out what the words mean?

BRUTUS: A soothsayer bids you beware the ides of March.

CAESAR: Set him before me; let me see his face.

CASSIUS: Fellow, come from the throng; look upon Caesar.

CAESAR: What say'st thou to me now? Speak once again.

SOOTHSAYER: Beware the ides of March.

Read the play.

excerpted from

Julius Caesar

by William Shakespeare

When Julius Caesar returns to Rome after a great victory, the Roman citizens want to crown him king. Fearing Caesar's popularity, a group of men, among them Brutus, conspire to discredit and murder him. In the following scene, Caesar's friend, Antony, is allowed to speak at Caesar's funeral—as long as he doesn't criticize the conspirators.

Cast of Characters

ANTONY, military commander, loyal friend of Caesar
FIRST CITIZEN
SECOND CITIZEN
THIRD CITIZEN
FOURTH CITIZEN

Act III, SCENE 2

The Forum. Enter Antony and others, with Caesar's body.

FIRST CITIZEN: Stay, ho! and let us hear Mark Antony.

THIRD CITIZEN: Let him go up into the public chair;
We'll hear him. Noble Antony, go up. . . .

FOURTH CITIZEN: 'Twere best he speak no harm of Brutus here.

FIRST CITIZEN: This Caesar was a tyrant.

THIRD CITIZEN: Nay, that's certain:
We are blest that Rome is rid of him.

SECOND CITIZEN: Peace! let us hear what Antony can say.

ANTONY: You gentle Romans,—

CITIZENS: Peace, ho! let us hear him.

ANTONY: Friends, Romans, countrymen, lend me your ears;
I come to bury Caesar, not to praise him.
The evil that men do lives after them;
The good is oft interred with their bones;
So let it be with Caesar. The noble Brutus
Hath told you Caesar was ambitious:
If it were so, it was a grievous fault,

And grievously hath Caesar answer'd it.
Here, under leave of Brutus and the rest—
For Brutus is an honorable man;
So are they all, all honorable men—
Come I to speak in Caesar's funeral.
He was my friend, faithful and just to me:
But Brutus says he was ambitious;
And Brutus is an honorable man.
He hath brought many captives home to Rome
Whose ransoms did the general coffers fill:
Did this in Caesar seem ambitious?
When that the poor have cried, Caesar hath wept:
Ambition should be made of sterner stuff:
Yet Brutus says he was ambitious;
And Brutus is an honorable man.
You all did see that on the Lupercal
I thrice presented him a kingly crown,
Which he did thrice refuse: was this ambition?
Yet Brutus says he was ambitious;
And, sure, he is an honorable man.
I speak not to disprove what Brutus spoke,
But here I am to speak what I do know.
You all did love him once, not without cause:
What cause withholds you then, to mourn for him?
O judgment! thou art fled to brutish beasts,
And men have lost their reason. Bear with me;
My heart is in the coffin there with Caesar,
And I must pause till it come back to me.

FIRST CITIZEN: Methinks there is much reason in his sayings.

SECOND CITIZEN: If thou consider rightly of the matter,
Caesar has had great wrong.

THIRD CITIZEN: Has he, masters?
I fear there will a worse come in his place.

FOURTH CITIZEN: Mark'd ye his words? He would not take the crown;
Therefore 'tis certain he was not ambitious.

Answer the following questions.

1 Read the dialogue from the drama in each choice. Then, match the underlined word or words to its modern equivalent on the right.

A. 'Twere best he speak no harm of Brutus here.	**1.** you marked
B. The noble Brutus hath told you Caesar was ambitious.	**2.** fair with
C. He was my friend, faithful and just to me.	**3.** I think
D. I thrice presented him a kingly crown.	**4.** three times
E. Methinks there is much reason in his sayings.	**5.** has
F. Mark'd ye his words?	**6.** it would be

> **Hint** Use context clues to help you figure out the meaning of antiquated language. Deciding if the word is a noun, verb, or other part of speech can also help you infer its meaning.

2 The following question has two parts. First, answer Part A. Then, answer Part B.

Part A

What device does the author use to help the citizens and audience understand how Antony feels about Caesar?

A. monologue

B. soliloquy

C. aside

D. dialogue

Part B

What effect does Antony's speech have on the citizens?

A. The citizens begin to think that Caesar was wrong.

B. The citizens begin to question Brutus's opinion of Caesar.

C. The citizens begin to think Brutus is ambitious.

D. The citizens begin to realize Antony was Caesar's friend.

> **Hint** To answer Part A, remember that playwrights have different techniques they can use to convey a character's thoughts and feelings. To answer Part B, think about how the citizens respond to Antony's speech.

3 Explain how Antony uses verbal irony to make a point about both Brutus and Caesar.

Write your answer on the lines provided.

_____

_____

_____

_____

> **Hint** Remember that with verbal irony, speakers say the opposite of what they really mean. Think closely about what Antony says and why he says it.

4 A student made the following claim about the play.

Claim
The time and location of the setting have a big influence on the plot of the play.

What is the importance of the setting to the play? How does it shape the events of the plot?

_____

_____

_____

_____

> **Hint** Think about how the setting affects the events of the plot. Would Antony's speech have the same effect if he gave it at a different time or place?

Use the Reading Guide to help you understand the play.

Ferndale Park

Reading Guide

Think about the structure of the play. What happens when a scene changes?

What is the conflict in the play? How do you know?

Cast of Characters

GUS COSTAS, Walking Society President
MODERATOR, woman, mid 30s
BEN REYES, condo developer
BRENNA FELMAN, middle-school student
MAYOR DIXON
TOWNSPEOPLE: parents, students, residents

Act I, Scene 1

Town hall meeting room. Several chairs and a podium are in front; seated are Brenna Felman, Ben Reyes, Mayor Dixon, and Moderator. Gus Costas is at podium. Townspeople are seated along the sides, facing the podium.

GUS: . . . And that's why the Walking Society doesn't want the condo to be built.

(*applause as Gus returns to seat; Moderator takes podium.*)

MODERATOR: Well, thank you very much, Mr. Costas. (*looks at her notes*) We've heard from Mayor Dixon, and now Gus Costas on behalf of the Walking Society. Next on the agenda is Mr. Reyes, the developer of ABC Condos. Mr. Reyes. . . .

Act I, Scene 2

(*applause as Ben Reyes takes the podium*)

BEN: (*adjusts glasses to look at notes, raises head*) Thank you for inviting me here this evening. It's gracious of you to come and hear me out. (*nods to townspeople on each side*)
I know some of you are troubled by my company's proposed condominiums, but just think of what the town will get in exchange for a rather small, tired old park.

(*pauses dramatically; then booms*) The plans are glorious! A new condo . . . ten stories high! With sixty brand-spanking-new units . . . fully furnished! (*gestures with hands*) And wait, there's more. A fully-equipped modern gym that anyone can join, a rooftop patio with a built-in barbeque and an outdoor garden.

Reading Guide

Where does Brenna use repetition in her speech? Why do you think she does that?

How does Brenna express her point of view about the park?

(*Several townspeople nod and smile.*)

BEN: (*takes off his glasses; lowers voice, confidentially*) We have had many, many people stop by our temporary offices to look at the plans. Some of your own townspeople are chomping at the bit to buy in. Not to mention some interested city folk!

(*Several townspeople nod in agreement; mild applause.*)

BEN: (*puts on his glasses*) In my view, out with the old and in with the new—the old Ferndale Park in exchange for the new Parkview Condos. Just think how the town will benefit from the construction. It will new bring jobs and new residents with money to spend. (*gestures to townspeople*) You will all benefit. Think of this when you cast your vote. Thank you.

(*bows slightly, smiles, and returns to his seat to applause; Moderator takes podium.*)

MODERATOR: Thank you, Mr. Reyes. (*looks at her notes*) And now, last but not least, we have Brenna Felman, a seventh grader from Ferndale Middle School, speaking on behalf of Ferndale's students. (*looks at Brenna*) Brenna, the podium is yours.

Act I, Scene 3

(*applause as Brenna takes the podium*)

BRENNA: (*nods and smiles*) Hello, everyone. I am honored to be here tonight on behalf of Ferndale's students. (*looks down*) Forgive me if I'm a little nervous.

(*Townspeople murmur sympathetically.*)

BRENNA: (*looks up*) I shouldn't be nervous speaking to you. I've known you all my life, and you love this town as much as I do.

(*Townspeople applaud.*)

BRENNA: And if you think we should go along with what Mr. Reyes proposes, well, I'll support you. After all, Mr. Reyes (*waves toward Reyes*) certainly seems to know what's best for our town . . . even though he doesn't live here. Here we are, listening to him, applauding him, and agreeing with him. Maybe he does know what's best for us. Maybe he should decide what happens to Ferndale Park.

Reading Guide

The climax of a play is when the plot events reach a turning point. At what point do you think the conflict reaches a turning point?

Why do you think the author ends the play without telling us what happens?

What do you think the townspeople will do? What textual evidence supports your answer?

After all, who knows better than Mr. Reyes how much we use the park? How us kids (*nods to classmates*) rollerblade and skateboard around the green. How we look forward to family movie nights under the stars or the farmer's market on Saturdays. Who would know better than Mr. Reyes how often we attend little league games, fly kites in the field, or play on the playground?

(*Several townspeople begin to mutter.*)

BRENNA: Maybe Mr. Reyes is right about the condos being more important. After all, who knows better than Mr. Reyes that school clubs, scout troops, and volunteers maintain that tired, old park all year? That every morning, our seniors gather there for tai chi exercises or that our war veterans meet to play checkers on the green. Who would know better than him? (*points to Mr. Reyes*)

(*Townspeople mutter more loudly.*)

BRENNA: It's not like we know what's best at all. We just live here. No, it's probably best to listen to Mr. Reyes. After all, I'm sure he has our best interests at heart. I'm sure he knows more about this town than you . . . (*points to random person*) or you . . . (*points to second person*) or you. . . . (*points to third person*) Doesn't he? Thank you, very much.

(*Audience stands and applauds; curtain closes.*)

Answer the following questions.

1 Consider the organization of the play. Why does the author divide the play into three scenes? Choose **all** that apply.

A. to feature a different character and his or her thoughts

B. to develop the conflict and move the townspeople to action

C. to give the moderator a chance to share her views

D. to discuss the benefits of replacing the park with condos

2 How does Brenna use repetition to her advantage?

A. to tell about the events held in the park

B. to point out that Mr. Reyes doesn't live in the town

C. to ask similar questions that the townspeople can't answer

D. to imply that Mr. Reyes knows better before citing how the park is used

3 Read the dialogue from the play in each choice. Then, match the dialogue to the type of figurative language on the right.

A. Some of your own townspeople are chomping at the bit to buy in.	**1.** verbal irony
	2. idiom
	3. metaphor
B. In my view, out with the old and in with the new.	**4.** simile
	5. adage
C. Maybe he does know what's best for us.	**6.** repetition

4 Explain the role of the setting in the play and how it contributes to the actions of the characters and the development of the plot.

_____

_____

_____

5 The following question has two parts. First, answer Part A. Then, answer Part B.

Part A

How do the characters interact in the play?

A. The main characters engage in a spirited discussion.

B. The main characters deliver speeches with reactions from the townspeople.

C. The main characters take turns speaking about the town to each other.

D. The main characters interact with the townspeople.

Part B

How does the answer you chose for Part A affect the plot of the play?

_____

_____

_____

6 Compare and contrast Brenna from *Ferndale Park* to Antony from *Julius Caesar*. Explain the goal of each character's monologue and whether or not the characters accomplished their goals. Then identify a common theme between the plays.

Write you answer on the lines provided.

Analyze Literature

1 GETTING THE IDEA --

There are many ways to **analyze** literature. You can focus on different parts of a single text, or you can compare one text to another. When you look at two texts, you can compare and contrast how they approach elements like characters, point of view, setting, theme, plot, and style. You can also compare and contrast the form and structure of two types of texts, such as a poem and a short story.

Compare and Contrast Text Types

Different types of literature include stories, poems, and plays. When you compare and contrast different types of texts, you look at how the structure of a text affects how it tells a story or expresses a theme.

The same topic or theme may be expressed differently in different types of texts. For example, a poem might use rhyme and simile to express a theme in few words. A story might express the same theme using description, character development, and dialogue.

The two passages below deliver the same scene, but one is from a poem and one is from a story. What differences in structure do you notice between the two texts? What is different about how they create a sensory image?

from **Seed-Time and Harvest**
by John Greenleaf Whittier

As o'er his furrowed fields which lie
Beneath a coldly dropping sky,
Yet chill with winter's melted snow,
The husbandman goes forth to sow

The spring day was cloudy with the chill of winter still in the air. The farmer set out with his bag of seeds toward his furrowed fields.

Compare and Contrast Theme

The **theme** of a story, play, or poem is the message an author wants readers to take away from the text. Two texts might have the same theme—such as the importance of hard work—but the authors may have different ways of getting this theme across. Different types of texts may have different ways of hinting at theme. A story may make the theme clear through the characters' actions and dialogue, while the theme of a poem may come out through its language.

Read the poem and story excerpt below. What theme do they both express? How does the text structure affect how the theme is expressed?

First Fig

by Edna St. Vincent Millay

My candle burns at both ends;
    It will not last the night;
But ah, my foes, and oh, my friends—
    It gives a lovely light!

"Eric, I have to go," said Ryan. "I have soccer practice. Then I'm going to drama club. Then I have to study for the math test."

"When do you sleep?" asked Eric. "You do so much! You're going to burn out one of these days."

"Maybe," said Ryan, "but I'm having a great time!"

Compare and Contrast Points of View

When you compare and contrast texts for **point of view**, determine the narrator of a story or the speaker of a poem. To compare points of view in two different texts, look at whose thoughts and feelings the reader knows about. Characters in a story may tell their thoughts and feelings in first-person point of view, or an outside narrator may use third-person point of view to show the characters' thoughts and feelings. A poem may also have a first-person or third-person point of view. Think about how the choice of point of view affects a story or poem. Ask yourself, "If this had a different point of view, how would the story or poem be different?"

Compare and Contrast Author's Style

Every author has his or her own style. **Style** often comes through in an author's language and sentence structure. It affects the tone and mood of a text, and how readers react to it. Here are some style differences you may see in two texts:

- formal language versus casual language

- antiquated language versus modern language

- humorous writing versus serious writing

- rhyming words versus non-rhyming words

- short, simple sentences versus long sentences with figures of speech

Look for Allusions

Allusions are references to texts, events, places, or people. Authors use them to draw on past events or stories that readers are likely familiar with. Readers can then make connections between what is alluded to and the ideas in the text. For example, a story character may be described as having the Midas touch. This allusion comes from a Greek myth in which everything Midas touched turned to gold. It means that the character makes a lot of money in anything attempted.

Comparing and Contrasting Checklist

These questions can help you begin to compare and contrast texts:

- What type of text is it? What kind of language does the answer use?

- What is the theme? How does the text structure affect the treatment of the theme or topic?

- What is the plot, or what topics does the author write about?

- What is the point of view? How does this point of view influence what the readers learn about the characters or speaker?

Language Spotlight • Multiple-Meaning Words

Multiple-meaning words are words that have more than one meaning. Read the following sentence and look at the word *quarter*.

Ali was so hungry he ate a quarter of the pizza.

You know that *quarter* can have different meanings, so you can use any or all of the following strategies to determine which meaning the word has in the sentence.

- Use the overall meaning of a sentence or paragraph as a clue. You can tell from the context of the sentence that a *quarter* is a part of the pizza.

- Use a word's position or function in a sentence as a clue. In this sentence *quarter* is used as a noun.

- Use Greek or Latin roots as clues. You can use the Latin root *quart*, which means *fourth*, to figure out that *quarter* means a part that is a fourth.

- Verify your definition of the word by checking a dictionary. The dictionary gives one definition of *quarter* as one of four equal parts.

Try the strategies to determine the meanings of the underlined words in the following sentences.

People in service occupied a particular station in British society.

The committee tabled the discussion until the next meeting.

Read the poems.

Thanksgiving

by Ralph Waldo Emerson

For each new morning with its light,
For rest and shelter of the night,
For health and food,
For love and friends,
For everything Thy goodness sends.

Poem 655

by Emily Dickinson

Without this— there is nought[1]—
All other Riches be
As is the Twitter of a Bird—
Heard opposite the Sea—

5 I could not care— to gain
A lesser than the Whole—
For did not this include themself—
As Seams— include the Ball?

I wished a way might be
10 My Heart to subdivide—
'Twould[2] magnify— the Gratitude—
And not reduce— the Gold—

[1] **nought** nothing

[2] **twould** It would

Answer the following questions.

1 Which sentence is the **best** summary of the poem "Thanksgiving"?

    A. The poet gives thanks for all he has.

    B. The poet is thankful for food and shelter.

    C. The poet is celebrating Thanksgiving.

    D. The poet is grateful for love and friends.

Hint The details in the poem support the most important point. Think about the main point the poet wants to convey.

2 Write **two** sentences to summarize "Poem 655." Include a quote from the poem to support your answer.

_____

_____

_____

_____

Hint A summary includes only the most important ideas.

3 Which **best** states the theme of both poems?

    A. We should be grateful for what we have.

    B. Without love, there is nothing.

    C. Riches are not important.

    D. We should not want to gain less than the whole.

Hint What is the message that both poets want readers to take away from the poems? What words in the poems can help you figure this out?

4 The following question has two parts. First, answer Part A. Then, answer Part B.

Part A

Underline examples of repetition of sounds in "Thanksgiving" and "Poem 655," including rhyme, alliteration, and repeated words.

Part B

Compare and contrast the impact of rhyme and other repetitions of sound on meaning in the two poems.

_____

_____

_____

_____

_____

_____

_____

_____

Hint What is the meaning of each poem? How does the repetition of sounds affect the meaning? Is this the same for both poems?

Use the Reading Guide to help you understand the passage.

excerpted from

Another Case of Ingratitude

by John Reed

Reading Guide

Is the narrator a character from the passage, or someone outside of the action?

How does the author describe the sleeping man?

What is the setting? How does the setting affect the plot?

Walking late down Fifth Avenue, I saw him ahead of me, on the dim stretch of sidewalk between two arc-lights. It was biting cold. Head sunk between hunched-up shoulders, hands in his pockets, he shuffled along, never lifting his feet from the ground. Even as I watched him, he turned, as if in a daze, and leaned against the wall of a building, where he made an angle out of the wind. At first I thought it was shelter he sought, but as I drew nearer I discerned the unnatural stiffness of his legs, the way his cheek pressed against the cold stone, and the glimmer of light that played on his sunken, closed eyes. The man was asleep!

Asleep—the bitter wind searching his flimsy clothes and the holes in his shapeless shoes, upright against the hard wall, with his legs rigid. . . . There was something bestial in such gluttony of sleep.

I shook him by the shoulder. He slowly opened an eye, cringing as though he were often disturbed by rougher hands than mine, and gazed at me with hardly a trace of intelligence.

"What's the matter—sick?" I asked.

Faintly and dully he mumbled something, and at the same time stepped out as if to move away. I asked him what he said, bending close to hear.

"No sleep for two nights," came the thick voice. "Nothing to eat for three days." He stood there obediently under the touch of my hand, swaying a little, staring vacantly at me with eyes that hung listlessly between opening and shutting.

"Well, come on," I said, "we'll go get something to eat, and I'll fix you up with a bed." Docilely he followed me, stumbling along like a man in a dream, falling forward and then balancing himself with a step. From time to time his thick lips gave utterance to husky, irrelevant words and phrases. "Got to sleep waking around," he said again and again. "They keep moving me on."

Reading Guide

How does the narrator describe the man before and then after eating?

What are the differences in the man's behavior?

How does the author use dialogue to reveal information about the characters?

I took his arm and guided him into the white door of an all-night lunchroom. I sat him at a table where he dropped into a dead sleep. I set before him roast beef, and mashed potatoes, and two ham sandwiches, and a cup of coffee, and bread and butter, and a big piece of pie. And then I woke him up. He looked up at me with a dawning meaning in his expression. The look of humble gratitude, love, devotion, was almost canine in its intensity. . . . I sat back and watched him eat.

At first he went at it awkwardly, as if he had lost the habit. Mechanically he employed little tricks of table manners—perhaps his mother had taught them to him. He fumblingly changed knife and fork from right hand to left, and then put down his knife and took a dainty piece of bread in his left hand; removed the spoon from his coffee cup before he drank, and spread butter thinly and painstakingly on his bread. His motions were so somnambulistic that I had a strange feeling of looking on a previous incarnation of the man.

As the dinner progressed, a marvelous change took place. The warmth and nourishment, heating and feeding his thin blood, flooded the nerve centers of that starving body; a quick flush mounted to his cheeks, every part of him started widely awake, his eyes glowed. The little niceties of manner dropped away as if they had never been. He slopped his bread roughly in the gravy, and thrust huge knife-loads of food into his mouth. The coffee vanished in great gulps. He became an individual instead of a descendant: where there had been a beast, a spirit lived; he was a man!

The metamorphosis was so exciting that I could hardly wait to learn more about him. I held in, however, until he finished his dinner. . . .

"How much will it cost you for a bed—a quarter?" I asked.

"Yeh," he answered. "T'anks!"

He sat looking rather nervously at the table. . . . It was my opportunity.

"What's the matter—no work?"

How does the man react to the narrator's questioning? What does this reveal about him?

Why does the man's point of view surprise the narrator?

How does the passage end? Why?

He looked me in the eye for the first time since dinner had begun, in a surprised manner. "Sure," he said briefly. I noticed, with somewhat of a shock, that his eyes were gray, whereas I had thought them brown.

"What's your job?"

He didn't answer for a moment. "Bricklayer," he grunted. What was the matter with the man?

"Where do you come from?"

Même jeu[1]. "Albany."

"Been here long?"

"Say," said my guest, leaning over. "What do you think I am, a phonygraft[2]?"

For a moment I was speechless with surprise. "Why, I was only asking to make conversation," I said feebly.

"Naw, you wasn't. You thought just because you give me a handout, I'd do a sob-story all over you. What right you got to ask me all them questions? I know you fellers. Just because you got money you think you can buy me with a meal. . . ."

"Nonsense!" I cried. "I do this perfectly unselfishly. What do you think I got out of feeding you?"

"You get all you want," he smiled. "Come on now, don't it make you feel good all over to save a poor starvin' bum's life? You're pure and holy for a week!"

"Well, you're a strange specimen," I said angrily. "I don't believe you've got a bit of gratitude in you."

"Gratitude!" said he easily. "What for? I'm thanking my luck, not you—see? I might as well 'a been as any other bum. You see," he leaned across the table, "you just had to save somebody tonight. I understand. . . ."

Whereupon I left that ungrateful bricklayer. . . .

[1] *Même jeu* French for *same game*

[2] **phonygraft** dialect for *phonograph*, a device that plays recorded music and speech

Answer the following questions.

1 Write a summary of the passage. Include a description of its structure and the most important elements.

_____

_____

_____

_____

_____

_____

2 The following question has two parts. First, answer Part A. Then, answer Part B.

Part A

Read the following sentence from the passage.

> **He slowly opened an eye, cringing as though he were often disturbed by rougher hands than mine, and gazed at me with hardly a trace of intelligence.**

Which is the **best** definition for the word rougher as it is used in the passage?

A. coarser

B. harsher

C. more difficult

D. more incomplete

Part B

Which strategies did you use to determine the meaning of rougher? Circle **all** that apply.

A. used the overall meaning of a sentence or paragraph as a clue

B. used the word's position or function in a sentence as a clue

C. used Greek or Latin affixes and roots as clues

D. consulted a dictionary

3 How does the author contrast the points of view of the narrator and the man? How do these points of view help convey the theme of the passage? Cite evidence from the passage to support your answer.

_____

_____

_____

_____

_____

Answer the following questions about the poems and the passage in this lesson.

4 Which statement **best** compares the points of view of "Poem 655" and "Another Case of Ingratitude"?

- **A.** Both use first-person point of view.
- **B.** Both use third-person point of view.
- **C.** "Poem 655" uses first person and "Another Case of Ingratitude" uses third person.
- **D.** "Poem 655" uses third person and "Another Case of Ingratitude" uses first person.

5 Which of the following are true statements about how "Poem 655" and "Another Case of Ingratitude" are alike? Choose **all** that apply.

- **A.** Both use similes to create images.
- **B.** Both use comparisons with animals.
- **C.** Both use dialogue between two characters.
- **D.** Both have a speaker/narrator who believes gratitude is important.
- **E.** Both use old-fashioned language to express lofty ideals.

6 Both "Thanksgiving" and "Another Case of Ingratitude" explore the theme of gratitude in very different ways. Write an essay in which you analyze and compare how these texts develop this theme. Be sure to cite textual evidence and draw inferences from each text to support your analysis.

Write your answer on the lines provided.

_____

_____

_____

_____

_____

_____

_____

_____

_____

_____

_____

_____

_____

_____

_____

_____

_____

Read the passage.

A Joint Effort

"What do you want to do this summer?" Brenda asked.

"We could build a glider like they use in the war and push it off the bluff," Frank suggested. "I'd like to see how far I could glide in it."

"I don't imagine your mom would get behind that project," Brenda said, chuckling. "What about something a little more gratifying—something we could do to contribute to the war effort?"

Frank and Brenda were just out of school for the summer and were sitting on a brick wall outside Woolworth's. The United States had entered World War II six months earlier, and the country was engaged in a massive war mobilization program. The effort involved not only recruiting thousands of people for the armed services, but also persuading people on the home front to participate in any way they could.

"Well . . . I guess we could do something," Frank hesitated, wondering where this was headed. "But I don't want to spend my vacation cutting up sheets for bandages."

"My mom is putting in twelve hour days at the airplane factory," Brenda said, "and your mom's treating injured soldiers at the VA hospital. Both our dads are overseas fighting. Aren't you interested in doing something to help us get this war over with?"

"Well, yes, of course," Frank answered defensively, "but we're just kids and we've worked hard all year. Is it really so horrible to take the summer off and have some fun?"

"I know!" Brenda said, apparently not having heard any of Frank's excuses. "The city council is sponsoring a scrap metal drive, and whoever collects the most by the Fourth of July—that's you and me of course—gets a pair of tickets to a Cardinals game."

That got Frank's attention, as Brenda knew it would, because he was a huge baseball fan. Still, he wavered, "I don't know, Bren. It seems like a lot of work."

"C'mon, Frank," Brenda pleaded. "You know I can't do this without you. It's too big a job for one person, but with the two of us working together, I'll bet we could win the tickets—and help a lot of soldiers at the same time."

"Okay," Frank said. "Since you've obviously been thinking about this, how are we going to do it?"

"I figure the most important thing is to locate the scrap and put in a claim on it before anyone else can obtain it," Brenda said, "because with so many people looking, it'll be tough to find the good stuff later on."

"So we just collect it and pile it up at some convenient point," Frank chimed in, "and then we can take it all to the scrap recycling center later."

"Between the two of us," Brenda said, "we've got family all over this part of town. We can pile the stuff in their backyards so we don't have to haul it so far, which will give us more time for collecting."

So the two headed home to find every piece of old metal junk they could uncover. Then they <u>combed</u> the backyards of neighbors, scoured empty lots across town, and checked in at the local junkyards. They piled the scrap in the backyards of family and friends who were glad to encourage the kids in their patriotic endeavor.

One mid-morning, a loud thumping on the front door rattled through Frank's house. He stumbled to the door and opened it for Brenda, who burst in with great excitement.

"C'mon, Frank, I've found the scrap to end all scrap out at Mr. Abington's house. We've got to get it out of there before someone else finds it."

"What is it?" Frank asked, but Brenda was already halfway down the driveway on her bike.

When they got to Mr. Abington's house, Brenda took him around back and opened up a garage door. Frank saw what all the excitement was about: a massive old rusted-up road grader sat in the garage. Brenda was beaming at him as Frank's jaw dropped and he stuttered, "How are we ever going to get that thing to the recycling station?"

"That's a problem, all right," said Mr. Abington, who'd just joined them. "It hasn't run in at least ten years, which is why I haven't gotten rid of it. Brenda said you'd take it away, so it's all yours."

"We can do this!" Brenda said as Frank flopped to the ground in disbelief. "And it'll ensure we win the tickets. Box seats!" she added, seeing the skeptical look on Frank's face.

So the two collectors began making their plans. Frank recalled that his older brother's friend Ned worked for a road construction company. At first, Ned was resistant, but relented when Frank and Brenda reminded him it was for the war effort. They headed over to the road construction company to talk to Ned's boss about borrowing a truck and flatbed trailer. "My dad and two uncles are in the war," Brenda pleaded when she saw Mr. Cabrina's face cloud over, "so this is personal for me. Please—we need your help." It was a tough sell, but in the end they even persuaded Mr. Cabrina to come along and supervise the loading and transportation.

The road grader made quite an impression at the scrap metal recycling center as they weighed it and checked it in under Brenda's and Frank's names. Later that week, Brenda recruited a cousin who had a pickup truck, while Frank got a friend's dad who had a trailer to help haul the scrap from all their collection points to the recycling center. On July 4, Frank and Brenda stood on the podium and accepted the mayor's official congratulations, and the baseball tickets.

Answer the following questions.

1 Read all parts of the question before responding.

Part A
From what point of view is the story told?

- **A.** Frank's first-person point of view
- **B.** Brenda's first-person point of view
- **C.** a limited point of view
- **D.** a third-person omniscient point of view

Part B
Underline two pieces of text evidence that helped you answer Part A.

Part C
Choose a point of view you did not select in Part A. Describe how the passage might be different if it were told from that point of view.

_____

_____

_____

_____

2 Read the following sentence from the passage.

> Then they **combed** the backyards of neighbors, scoured empty lots across town, and checked in at the local junkyards.

Which is the best definition of <u>combed</u> as it is used in the sentence?

- **A.** prepared
- **B.** searched
- **C.** explored
- **D.** untangled

3 This question has two parts. First, answer Part A. Then, answer Part B.

Part A

Read each description of Brenda in the box. Decide whether it is a character trait or a motivation. Write the description in the correct column.

help the war effort	motivator
good at planning	persuade others to help
patriotic	win the competition

Traits	Motivations

Part B

Choose one motivation from the right-hand column and explain how it is influenced by the setting of the passage. Cite text evidence in your answer.

_____

_____

_____

4 This question has two parts. First, answer Part A. Then, answer Part B.

Part A

Circle the theme below that is **most** developed in the passage.

Themes	Disagreeing never furthers a cause.
	Everyone has a responsibility during wartime.
	People can accomplish much by working together.
	The value of friendship cannot be overstated.

Part B

Circle three paragraphs from the passage that develop the theme you identified in Part A. Underline details in each paragraph that support the theme.

5 The following question has two parts. First, answer Part A. Then, answer Part B.

Part A

Read the following excerpt from the passage. Underline **three** setting details in the excerpt.

> **Frank and Brenda were just out of school for the summer and were sitting on a brick wall outside Woolworth's. The United States had entered World War II six months earlier, and the country was engaged in a massive war mobilization program. The effort involved not only recruiting thousands of people for the armed services, but also persuading people on the home front to participate in any way they could.**

Part B

Which setting detail in Part A has the **biggest** influence on the plot? Explain your answer using evidence from the passage.

_____

_____

_____

_____

Read the passage.

The Day We Flew!

Cast of Characters

ORVILLE WRIGHT

WILBUR WRIGHT, Orville's brother

JOHN T. DANIELS, a crew member at a nearby lifesaving station

FIVE OTHER STATION CREW MEMBERS

Act I, Scene 1

It is the morning of December 17, 1903, on a sandy strip of beach at Kitty Hawk, North Carolina. The Wright Flyer *sits on a single rail used as a runway. The engine is running. Orville and Wilbur Wright and the station crew members stand nearby talking. One, John T. Daniels, is eyeing a camera that has been set up.*

ORVILLE: (*looking back at the plane*) Cold morning for a flight, but I'm not going to complain.

WILBUR: (*shivering as he checks a machine*) You'll forget the cold once you're in the air. The weather seems good. Good, steady wind about 22 to 27 miles per hour according to the anemometer. Is that camera aimed for the takeoff?

ORVILLE: Yeah. You ready to snap the shutter, John?

JOHN: Yep. I just have to pick the right second. It ought to be a good one.

WILBUR: (*glancing over at the plane*) Everything looks set and the engine should be good and warmed up. Are you ready?

ORVILLE: (*enthusiastically*) Absolutely. I can't wait to see what this thing will do!

(*Orville climbs onto the center of the wing of the plane and lies down, gripping the controls in his hands. Wilbur steadies a wing while John stands beside the camera and another man stands at the rear of the plane ready to release it.*)

Act I, Scene 2

The men are rejoicing over the short but successful first attempt.

WILBUR: That was truly a great beginning, Orville.

ORVILLE: (*very excited*) What do you think, about 120 feet?

WILBUR: Yes, about that, and I think it must have lasted about 12 seconds. We didn't stop the watch quite on time. Too excited, I guess. What was your impression of the machine?

ORVILLE: (*still lively, gesturing enthusiastically*) It felt fantastic, better than the glider because of that little engine pumping away. It has good lift, too, like we expected, but it's hard to manage. The rudder seems to catch too much air and jerks the flyer around before I can react. It's probably something we can learn to handle, but I'd rather figure out how to fix it. Better safe than sorry, huh? (*to John*) Hey, Johnny, did you get that picture?

JOHN: (*smiling sheepishly*) I don't know. I think so, but I was so excited I don't remember for sure if I snapped the shutter.

WILBUR: I hope so. That takeoff couldn't have been any cleaner. We didn't need to worry about the tail hitting the truck as it jumped off. I'll have to think about that rudder, why it's proving difficult to manage. I'll see what I can do on the next attempt.

Act II, Scene 1

Two hours have passed. Orville, Wilbur, and the crew members carry the Wright Flyer *up from its third flight down the beach and set it down on the launch railing.*

WILBUR: (*breathless*) Whew! This flying machine gets heavier every time we have to haul it back.

ORVILLE: (*laughing*) That's because we have to haul it farther each time, and I'm happy for that. What did you say, 200 feet? That's pretty good, but we can do better.

WILBUR: (*analytically*) We're starting to get a better feel for the rudder control. I think the problem is that it's balanced too near the center, making it kind of unsteady. A little more wind hits it than we expect, and it just pushes that rudder too far one way or the other and we start veering off center. We'll adjust that later—for now, I'm happy with what we've accomplished. I think we've got one more flight in us, though.

ORVILLE: I agree, and we need a good one. We need to better what we can do with a glider, and so far we're not even close. C'mon, it's your turn. Give us that record flight to prove that this thing really is powered flight and not just gliding.

Act II, Scene 2

Farther down the beach, the Wright Flyer *has just landed. Wilbur climbs out of the flyer as the others run over excitedly.*

ORVILLE: (*leaping on his brother and hugging him*) That was a fantastic flight, Will. We did it! We flew today with a powered flying machine!

WILBUR: (*with a huge smile*) We sure did, brother. It's been a grand day. Say, how long was I in the air? Must've been a minute or so.

ORVILLE: Fifty-nine seconds exactly, and I figure it was about 900 feet.

WILBUR: That sounds right to me. We'll have to measure it exactly before we leave. (*looking closely at the flyer*) I hit the ground kind of hard there, and I think the rudder's pretty badly broken up. The main frame seems OK, though. I don't see a bit of damage to it. That's lucky.

JOHN: (*smiling happily*) You two are a fantastic team. No one else could have done this.

ORVILLE: (*still jubilant*) And we couldn't have done it today without all you fellows helping out and lugging that flyer all over the beach (*pausing, then suddenly solemn*). John, all of you that helped us out, this has been a historic occasion—I'm betting one of the most historic occasions of all time. Human beings have learned to fly today. This is just the start, but it's a great start.

WILBUR: Precisely, Orville. It's just the beginning.

Answer the questions.

6 This question has two parts. First, answer Part A. Then, answer Part B.

Part A

Based on Orville's and Wilbur's dialogue, what inference can you make about their characters?

   A. Orville is more enthusiastic, while Wilbur is more analytical.

   B. Orville is more stubborn, while Wilbur is more humorous.

   C. Orville is more outgoing, while Wilbur is more anxious.

   D. Orville is more scientific, while Wilbur is more confrontational.

Part B

Write two pieces of dialogue that support your answer to Part A.

_____

_____

_____

7 The following question has two parts. First, answer Part A. Then, answer Part B.

Part A

Underline a figure of speech in this excerpt from the play.

> **The rudder seems to catch too much air and jerks the flyer around before I can react. It's probably something we can learn to handle, but I'd rather figure out how to fix it. Better safe than sorry, huh?**

Part B

Which **best** describes the figure of speech you underlined in Part A?

   A. metaphor

   B. idiom

   C. adage

   D. personification

8 Choose the statement that **best** describes how the play is structured.

A. Act I, Scenes 1 and 2 describe how the Wright brothers prepare to fly the *Wright Flyer*; Act II, Scenes 1 and 2 describe their reaction to that flight.

B. Scene 1 in each act describes what happens before a flight; Scene 2 in each act describes the reaction to the flight in the previous scene.

C. Act I, Scenes 1 and 2 describe how the Wright brothers repair their plane; Act II, Scenes 1 and 2 describe how the plane was damaged.

D. Scene 1 in each act describes how the Wright brothers repair their plane, Scene 2 in each act describes how they prepare for a flight.

9 This question has two parts. First, answer Part A. Then, answer Part B.

Read this excerpt from the play.

> **ORVILLE: (*still jubilant*) And we couldn't have done it today without all you fellows helping out and lugging that flyer all over the beach (*pausing, then suddenly solemn*). John, all of you that helped us out, this has been a historic occasion—I'm betting one of the most historic occasions of all time. Human beings have learned to fly today. This is just the start, but it's a great start.**

Part A

Choose the device that **best** describes the excerpt.

A. verbal irony

B. stage direction

C. soliloquy

D. monologue

Part B

Explain how the dialogue in Part A is used to develop a theme of the play.

_____

_____

_____

Both passages you have read explore important historical events: World War II in "A Joint Effort" and the Wright brothers' first airplane flight in "The Day We Flew!" Write an essay in which you compare and contrast how each passage helps you better understand the historical event it describes. Include an analysis of how the characters react to the events, as well as a description of how the themes reflect the history that is taking place at the time. Remember to use textual evidence to support your ideas.

Write your answer on the lines provided.

STRAND 2

Working with Informational Texts

RI.7.1, RI.7.2, RI.7.4, RI.7.5, RI.7.6, L.7.4.b RH.6–8.2, RH.6–8.7, RST.6–8.1, RST.6–8.2, RST.6–8.7

Articles

① GETTING THE IDEA

Nonfiction is factual writing about real people, places, events, ideas, and things. It is often referred to as **informational text** because it informs readers about the real world.

Nonfiction Forms	Description
biography	tells the true story of a person's life
essay	shares the author's outlook or point of view
speech	presents a topic orally
textbook	gives factual information about a topic
letter or journal	gives a personal account of events
interview	shares a person's experiences, ideas, and opinions

An **article** is a common form of nonfiction. Nonfiction articles appear in newspapers, magazines, encyclopedias, and online. Every nonfiction article has one or more main ideas. The **main idea** is the central message the author wants to convey about a topic. The author develops the main idea with **supporting details**, such as facts, reasons, examples, statistics, and quotations. These details are arranged and presented in paragraphs, each of which has a main idea that backs up the main idea of the article. Both the main idea of an article and the main idea of a paragraph may be stated directly or implied through the supporting details.

Author's Purpose

The author's main purpose in writing a nonfiction article is to inform. Most nonfiction articles are presented objectively. The author uses formal language to present the facts in a neutral way, without expressing his or her point of view. The language and tone of the article changes, however, when the author's purpose is to inform as well as entertain a reader or persuade a reader to take some course of action. When writing to inform and entertain, an author may use informal language and speak directly to a reader. When writing to persuade, an author may pick and choose which facts and words he or she uses to persuade a reader to agree with his or her point of view.

Read the following passage. Draw a line under the two main ideas of the article. Think about how the statistics support both main ideas. The author uses formal language to support his or her purpose to inform the reader. Circle five words that set an objective tone to the article.

There are many sources of news today. Which reaches the most people? A couple of sources offer statistics on the subject. However, statistics can be misleading.

A recent Gallop poll generated statistics that support the idea that television is the most popular news source among adults in the United States. It is favored by 55 percent of the population. That is a 10 percent increase over the statistics gathered in 1957. The survey also found it was the most popular medium among the subgroups surveyed. Fifty percent of those in the eighteen to twenty-nine age group and 50 percent of those in the thirty to forty-nine age group relied mostly on television for news.

Another survey, however, generated different statistics resulting in a different conclusion. In that survey, once again, 55 percent of the adults noted television as their source of news. However, their numbers show that only 34 percent of people under thirty years of age relied on television news. This represents a drop of 16 percent since 2006. It also leads to the conclusion that television news watchers are older.

How can two surveys taken around the same time generate different statistics and conclusions? It's simple. They asked different questions. In the first survey, people were asked what they most relied on for news. In the second survey, they were asked what medium they had used the previous day for news. Different questions generate different responses. Different statistics result in different conclusions.

Both surveys lead to the conclusion that television is the most popular medium for news coverage. However, perhaps the greater thing learned from the surveys is to beware of floating statistics. The numbers alone will tell only part of the story.

Why does the author include the third paragraph? What does it provide to the rest of the article? How does it support one of the main ideas?

Text Structures

Authors write with their audience in mind. They carefully organize the facts and details in a way that makes sense. This organization is called **structure**. Text structure helps you connect ideas in a text and better understand how parts of the text relate to the whole article. Depending on the details that support a main idea, an article may have one overall structure and use different structures to organize details in the supporting paragraphs.

The following chart shows some common structures found in articles.

Structure	Description	Signal Words and Phrases
chronological/ sequence	organizes details in time order; may include dates, times, or numbered sequences	*before, during, after, next, then, finally, until, later, first, second, third, while, last*
compare and contrast	compares two or more people, things, ideas, or events to tell how they are similar and different	compare: *also, same as, like, similarly, in the same way* contrast: *however, but, unlike, in contrast, different from, in comparison*
problem and solution	states a problem and suggests one or more solutions	*question, answer, problem, solution, if . . . then, because*
cause and effect	relates two or more events by examining what happened and why	*because, then, since, as a result, thus, therefore, on account of, hence*

Revisit the passage about television news again. What signal words help you recognize the overall structure of the article?

Text and Graphic Features

Authors also use text and graphic features to organize information in an article. **Text features** include headings, bold and italic type, bulleted lists, captions, and sidebars. They help readers locate information quickly in a text. **Graphic features** present information visually. Some graphic features, such as tables and charts, consolidate information to present many facts in an organized way. Others, such as photographs, illustrations, and maps, expand on a main idea presented in the text.

Language Spotlight • Affixes and Roots

A **root** is a basic word unit from which other words are formed. Many English words come from Latin and Greek roots. For example, the word *geography* contains the roots *geo*, meaning "earth," and *graph*, meaning "to write." Some roots are complete words, such as *form*, meaning "shape." Most, however, are combined with other roots or word parts to form words. An **affix** is a letter or group of letters added to a word to create a new meaning. A **prefix** is an affix at the beginning of a word, and a **suffix** is an affix at the end of a word.

Use your knowledge of roots and affixes to define the underlined words below. Use a dictionary to verify the meaning.

Early telegrams were written much like modern-day tweets. Because the senders were charged per word, people learned how to communicate in brief phrases.

Read the passage.

Shark Tales

The word *shark* causes many swimmers to tremble, but should it? In reality, many of the stories people share about sharks are based on myths, not facts. Yet many of the truths about sharks are so strange they are difficult to believe.

Many frightening tales center on a shark clamping its sharp teeth into a victim. It is true that both the shark's upper and lower jaws move, which gives the shark a strong grip. However, people envision all sharks with sharp, pointed teeth capable of ripping through anything. Some sharks live up to this perception, but some have flat, boxy teeth, which they use to crush hard shells. Others have small teeth that are not useful for eating.

Another frequently held myth is that sharks are always vicious because they have many thousands of teeth. That myth is based on fact. Sharks aren't always vicious, but their teeth work much like a conveyer belt. When a tooth falls out the others rotate and a replacement tooth fills the space. They are not all there simultaneously, but in its lifetime a shark will have had tens of thousands of teeth!

One common misunderstanding about sharks is that they are people hunters. Sharks are predators, but they prefer fish, crustaceans, mollusks, plankton, krill, other sharks, and marine animals. Scientists think shark attacks on people are cases of mistaken identity; the shark assumes it is biting another mammal, like a seal. The truth is a person is more likely to be struck by lightning than to be attacked by a shark. In fact, although millions of sharks were killed by people in 2012, only seven people were killed by sharks worldwide.

Many people consider the presence of sharks detrimental to an area. However, sharks are a vital part of marine ecosystems. They help maintain a balance in the ecosystem by hunting mid-level predators, which helps maintain marine plant life. For example, sea turtles and dugongs, a species of sea mammals, eat sea grasses. Left unchecked, they could destroy an entire seabed. Tiger sharks eat some of the sea turtles and dugongs. This helps preserve some of the sea grasses and the other life forms that depend on them.

Sharks have existed on Earth for more than 400 million years and were here before the dinosaurs! A greater awareness among people of what is fact and what is fiction might help these creatures last another 400 million years.

Sharks—Fact and Fiction	
Idea	**Explanation**
Sharks have acute hearing.	**True**—Sharks can hear a fish swimming from a mile away.
Never go into the ocean with a cut. Even a single drop of blood will attract sharks.	**False**—A shark can smell a drop of blood in a million drops of water from a mile away. However, think of how many drops of water are in an ocean.
If you see a shark in the water, stay still. It will sense movement, but it can't see you.	**False**—A shark senses motion, but it also has excellent vision and can even distinguish colors. A shark's eyes have lenses that are up to seven times as powerful as a person's.
A shark could beat a person at a staring contest.	**True**—A shark's upper and lower eyelids are stationary, so a shark never blinks.
Sharks are smart.	**True**—Sharks can learn conditioned responses (behaviors that respond to specific stimuli) faster than cats or rabbits can.
Sharks are continuous eaters.	**False**—Sharks can fast for weeks between meals.
Sharks keep other sharks informed.	**True**—Sharks can't vocalize, but they do communicate through body language.

Answer the following questions.

1 Choose the **two** sentences that represent the central ideas in the passage.

   A. Sharks have tens of thousands of teeth.

   B. Many of people's ideas about sharks are not fact-based.

   C. Sharks use body language to communicate with each other.

   D. Some facts about sharks seem too strange to be true.

   E. Sharks are predators in a marine ecosystem.

> **Hint** The central ideas are what a passage is all about. The details support the main ideas. Read the details and think about what connects them.

2 How does the table support the information in the main body of the passage?

    A. by giving more examples of myths and facts about sharks

    B. by presenting a different point of view about shark dangers

    C. by separating the most important ideas from the detailed text

    D. by organizing the information in the body of the text in a new way

> **Hint** Read the title of the chart and the headings. They will tell you what kind of information you will find. Then read each entry. Think about how they relate to the text in the main body of the passage.

3 The following question has two parts. First, answer Part A. Then, answer Part B.

Part A

What is the author's point of view on sharks?

_____

_____

Part B

Which details reveal the author's point of view in the passage?

_____

_____

_____

_____

_____

> **Hint** To determine the author's point of view, look at the details the author chose to include.

4 Read the sentence from the passage and the dictionary entry. Then, answer the question that follows.

> **Some sharks live up to this perception, but some have flat, boxy teeth, which they use to crush hard shells.**

perception (*n*) the way a person thinks about something. Synonyms—*wisdom, insight, understanding, awareness*

Why did the author **most likely** choose to use the word perception instead of one of its synonyms? What is the connotation of the word in the sentence?

_____

_____

_____

> **Hint** Try reading the sentence again several times, substituting one of the synonyms each time. How do the different words affect the meaning of the sentence?

5 Read the sentence from the passage and the questions that follow.

> **However, people envision all sharks with sharp, pointed teeth capable of ripping through anything.**

Part A

Which shows the word envision broken into its root word and affixes?

A. envi/sion

B. en/vi/sion

C. en/vi/si/on

D. en/vis/ion

Part B

Use your knowledge of roots and affixes to determine the meaning of envision.

_____

_____

> **Hint** Think about what other words are built from the same root word. Determine what ties the meanings of those words together. Then look at the affixes. Think about how they change or focus the meaning of the root word.

Use the Reading Guide to help you understand the passage.

The Quest for Speed

Reading Guide

Draw a line under the sentences best supported by the photograph.

Why were early car makers less concerned about speed?

Which part of *proverbial* is the root word? What does *proverbial* mean?

For almost as long as there have been cars, there has been a desire to make them go faster. The earliest cars ran on steam, but by the 1800s engineers expanded their thinking. Some of the new designs still ran on steam, but others ran on electricity or gas. Speed wasn't at the top of the list of priorities for these early cars. Designers were more concerned with building engines that wouldn't explode, yet would attach to carriages. They worked to improve the basics, such as accelerators, brakes, and steering controls. It didn't take long, though, for the engineers' and the public's attention to turn to speed.

Gasoline Power

In 1885, Carl Benz made the Benz Patent Motor Car. It was a two-seater with a steel frame and three wheels. It looked much like an overgrown tricycle. The automobile had a single-cylinder gas-powered engine and at top speed could go nine miles per hour (mph). Benz received a patent for the car the following year, and the proverbial barn door was opened.

By 1910, it was common to see a car in the driveway of a home. People used their cars for both practical purposes and pleasure. Owning a car made it easier for people to work, shop, and visit family. Cars were still expensive, though, and that prohibited some families from owning one. In 1913, Henry Ford developed a new process to manufacture cars—the assembly line. The assembly line made it possible for car manufacturers to make cars faster and cheaper. This made the finished product cheaper for the public to buy. Ford sold more than fifteen million of his first assembly line car, the Model T.

Early cars were very basic and lacked modern-day safety features.

How did modern technology improve automotive engineering?

What is the purpose of all of the dates in the passage?

What is a production car? Which details support your definition?

The Need for Speed

People's attention soon turned to speed. Records show that in 1926 there was a car available, a Bentley, that could travel slightly more than sixty-two mph. Automotive engineers were bitten by the speed bug. Only three years later, there was a car that could double the speed of the 1926 Bentley. The engineers didn't stop there.

Expanding Concerns

By the mid-1970s, cars needed to be more than fast and affordable. They also needed to be safe, fuel efficient, and environmentally friendlier than in the past. Engineers worked to meet all of these goals. Today, supercomputers help engineers test crash safety, fuel efficiency, and aerodynamics before a model of the car is even produced. These supercomputers contribute greatly to the manufacturing of fast, safe, clean-running, and efficient cars. They also cut costs for the manufacturers and the public. Automotive engineers, however, discovered something decades ago about the people who test the limits of land speed— their budgets seem to be limitless.

Fastest Car?

Car buffs might be confused by the discrepancies they see between lists of the fastest cars. It is generally agreed that the term "fastest car" refers to the fastest production car. The definition of production car is not as clear. In general, people agree that the car must be driven as it was manufactured for street use; it cannot be modified for speed. Secondly, the car has to be available for sale to the general public. The "general public" is taken in the broadest of meanings, since the average car buyer cannot afford a car that sells for more than a million dollars. The phrase "available for sale" is a sticking point. There is no limitation currently on this point. Does a manufacturer have to make a certain number of these cars for sale for the model to be considered a production car? The Guinness World Records committee is working to refine the definition of "production car" and make it clearer.

Beyond what cars can be considered production cars, there is the question of what qualifies as a car's speed record. For example, on some lists the top position belongs to the Koenigsegg Agera R. Its manufacturers claim it can reach a top speed of 273 mph, but it hasn't been track-proven yet.

Reading Guide

What words or phrases in "Fastest Car?" signal the organizational structure of the section?

What is the difference between a claimed speed and a certified speed?

Which details in the passage support the idea that driving with or against the wind can affect speed?

On other lists, the top position belongs to the Bugatti Veyron Super Sport. This car's speed has been certified by Guinness at 267.8 mph. That speed was arrived at by averaging lap times on an oval track driving in both directions around the track. If the list is comprised of only certified speeds, the Bugatti will have first place.

In addition, people question lists because not only is there a difference between a claimed speed and a certified speed, but there are also differences among the certified speeds. Guinness certifies some of the cars, but other organizations also certify speeds. The conditions under which these varied groups verify the speeds can differ.

One thing car buffs and engineers can agree on: the quest for greater speeds will continue.

Speed Milestones

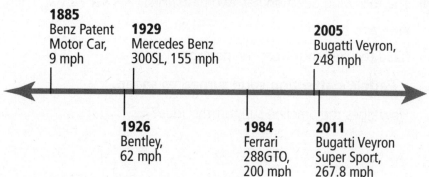

1885
Benz Patent Motor Car, 9 mph

1929
Mercedes Benz 300SL, 155 mph

2005
Bugatti Veyron, 248 mph

1926
Bentley, 62 mph

1984
Ferrari 288GTO, 200 mph

2011
Bugatti Veyron Super Sport, 267.8 mph

Answer the following questions.

1 Choose the **two** central ideas of the passage.

A. Cars have become safer, cleaner running, and faster over time.

B. The fastest cars are too expensive for the average person to buy.

C. The assembly line process made it possible for more people to buy cars.

D. People have used cars for both productivity and pleasure since the early 1900s.

E. Environmental concerns changed the way cars were designed and manufactured in the 1970s.

F. People need a clearer definition of "production car" and standard rules for certification before they can determine what is truly the fastest car.

2 The following question has two parts. First, answer Part A. Then, answer Part B.

Part A

Read the sentence from the passage.

People's attention soon turned to speed.

How does the timeline support this idea?

_____

_____

_____

Part B

The timeline does not include data for the Koenigsegg Agera R. What can be inferred about the author's point of view on speed records based on this exclusion?

_____

_____

_____

3 The following question has two parts. First, answer Part A. Then, answer Part B.

Part A

Read the sentence from the passage.

The phrase "available for sale" is a sticking point.

What does the phrase sticking point mean in the sentence?

A. a price that makers have to stay within

B. an issue that people disagree about

C. an idea that connects people

D. something that is needed

Part B

Describe the effect of using the phrase sticking point on the overall tone of the paragraph.

_____

_____

4 How does paragraph 4 of "Fastest Car?" contribute to the section as a whole?

_____

_____

5 Read all parts of the question before responding.

Part A

Read this sentence from the passage.

> **Today, supercomputers help engineers test crash safety, fuel efficiency, and aerodynamics before a model of the car is even produced.**

Which **two** roots help the reader understand the meaning of aerodynamics?

A. the root *aero*, meaning "air"

B the root *neo*, meaning "new"

C. the root *nom*, meaning "name"

D. the root *dyna*, meaning "power"

Part B

Based on the meaning of the roots you chose in Part A, what does aerodynamics mean?

A. new ways of making cars run cleanly

B names of vehicles with powerful engines

C. qualities that affect how an object moves through air

D. qualities that affect the appearance of objects in a vehicle

6 After reading the passage, a student predicts that cars will reach even higher speeds in the future. Explain why this is a reasonable prediction based on the text and graphic features. Cite several examples of textual and graphic evidence to support your explanation.

Write your response on the lines below.

_____

_____

_____

_____

_____

_____

_____

_____

_____

_____

_____

_____

_____

_____

_____

_____

_____

Persuasive Texts

❶ GETTING THE IDEA

A **persuasive text** attempts to persuade, or convince, readers to accept a certain view or take a specific action. Persuasive texts include speeches, arguments, editorials, letters to the editor, and opinion blog posts.

In persuasive writing, **point of view** refers to the author's unique set of ideas and opinions about a topic or issue. Most persuasive texts take the form of an **argument**, in which the author supports his or her position with logical reasoning and evidence.

Persuasive texts are often organized using the following structure.

- An **introduction**, which states the **claim**, or main point the writer is trying to make

- Supporting paragraphs with reasons and evidence

  Reasons are statements that tell readers why they should believe the claim. **Evidence** includes the facts, examples, or other data used to back up the reasons.

- Statement of opposing argument, with a rebuttal

- A **conclusion**, which restates the claim, summarizes the main points, and makes a concluding statement

Evaluating Argument

Identifying and evaluating reasons and evidence can help you determine how well an author supports a claim. Reasons and evidence should be clear, relevant, and directly connected to the claim. There also should be sufficient, or enough, evidence to show why readers should believe what the author is saying.

Irrelevant evidence, or evidence that is not directly connected to the claim, weakens the effectiveness of the author's claim. Look at the examples in the chart below. Compare and contrast the relevant and irrelevant evidence.

Reason	Reading at home helps children perform better in school.
Relevant Evidence	A recent study showed that children who read 30 minutes or more per night scored better on reading tests than children who read 20 minutes or less per night.
Irrelevant Evidence	Some children prefer fantasy stories over realistic fiction stories.

Now read the following paragraph. Identify the author's point of view. Circle the sentence that is a reason. Underline a sentence that gives relevant evidence, and draw a line through a sentence that gives irrelevant evidence.

> Taxpayers' money should no longer be used to fund public libraries. Brick-and-mortar libraries are no longer necessary because people can access books and research materials online. The first library was founded in the city of Philadelphia in 1731. Today, millions of books, and databases with journals and publications, are available over the Internet. A majority of active readers also have e-reading devices or smartphones on which they can read books.

Types of Evidence

A persuasive text may include many types of evidence, such as survey and research results and direct quotations. Other types of evidence include the following.

Type of Evidence	Example
example	For example, one library has cleared space for more computers because patrons are demanding more Internet access, not books.
case study	A study by the Information Policy & Access Center at the University of Maryland found that libraries can't keep up with the computer and Internet demand.
statistics	Nearly 78 percent of the U.S. population has Internet access at home.
expert opinions	A career librarian recently debated that libraries were designed to share resources. Now, these resources can be shared online.

Rebuttal to Opposing Argument

If an author presents only his or her perspective and ignores the other side of an issue, a text may be too one-sided and mislead readers. A good persuasive text includes information about the **opposing argument**, in which an author acknowledges that there is a view different from his or her own. However, the author will then provide a strong **rebuttal**, or **counterargument**, to refute it, effectively dismissing it with support for his or her own claim.

For example: *Although some people disagree with using taxpayer money to fund public libraries, taxpayers who use the library save money. For example, one family who borrows eight books and four DVDs each month can save as much as one thousand dollars a year.*

Persuasive Techniques

An author may use different **persuasive techniques** to create a certain response from the reader. These techniques generally appeal to the reader's emotions or sense of logic.

Technique	What It Does	Example
propaganda	information that is meant to stir up fear in readers	Under Sal Morgan's ineffective policies, the crime rate will rise.
bandwagon appeal	implies that "everyone is doing it"	A majority of citizens think Bill Sampson is the better candidate.
generalizations	makes a general statement that sounds authoritative	Everyone knows that our citizens cannot afford another tax increase.
stereotyping	a general statement about a group of people	That political party ignores the real issues citizens care about.

Author's Bias

Since a persuasive text gives opinions, sometimes the arguments presented may be **biased**. The author may distort the information presented to support a personal interest.

To evaluate for possible bias, ask: "What might the author gain from persuading people to change their views?" Most likely, this information will not be stated directly, and you will need to infer it from textual evidence.

Language Spotlight • Persuasive Language

Authors use persuasive language, to strengthen the impact of their argument. **Persuasive language** are words and phrases that affect how a reader thinks and feels.

Read the sentences below.

A vote for Sal Morgan is a vote for tyranny. Sal Morgan's recklessly dangerous agenda will destroy our city. If you care about our city's future, then you'll make the right choice and vote for Bill Sampson.

Which sentence includes the strongest persuasive language?

_____

Add another sentence with persuasive language to tell why Bill Sampson is the better candidate.

_____

Read the passage.

Heinrich Schliemann: Father of Archaeology

Heinrich Schliemann deserves to be recognized as the "father of archaeology." As a dedicated scholar with a passion for Homer's works, Schliemann devoted years to discovering and writing about ancient civilizations, including Troy. The field of archaeology was brought to life with his groundbreaking work. Thanks to Schliemann, many other history enthusiasts and scholars were inspired to pursue archaeology as a hobby or a profession. Schliemann truly was a pioneer in archaeology and should be acknowledged for his incredible contributions to the world.

In many ways, Schliemann was a genius. Although his first career was not as an archaeologist, he developed an interest in history and foreign cultures when he was just a child. No one can question his devotion to learning and studying new things. Skilled at learning new languages, Schliemann became fluent in thirteen languages, including ancient and modern Greek.

It is said that his first awareness of the city of Troy came from a history book his father gave him as a present. Later, he would read Homer's *The Iliad* and *The Odyssey*, and his fascination for the legendary city would increase even more. Homer's classic works tell epic stories about the events during and after the Trojan War. Most people assumed that like the Greek myths described in the tales, the city itself was also a myth. But Schliemann had faith in the city's existence and believed that the descriptions were too specific to be the stuff of fiction.

Even though some people claim Schliemann was motivated by greed, he cared more about the city of Troy than any person in history. At the age of forty-six, Schliemann decided to focus his life on archaeology and the pursuit of finding Homeric Troy. He had accumulated great wealth through his success as a businessman and decided to dedicate his time to this new career. Why would he need to look for treasure in an ancient city when he already had plenty of wealth? Rather, his interest was driven by a fascination with the mythic city he first loved as a child.

No one can doubt that Schliemann worked hard to accomplish his goals. He prepared for his exploration by visiting different countries and studying archaeology in Paris. Then, after theorizing about where the city of Troy actually was, he began to excavate. What he found in 1873 was evidence of an ancient city along with a collection of gold jewelry. Schliemann claimed that the city was the city of Troy and the gold was the treasure of Priam, a king mentioned in Homer's *The Iliad*.

These discoveries prove that Schliemann should be recognized as a great archaeologist. Despite any doubts that some scholars had about the city, the vast majority of the public accepted the idea that the discovered city was the real Troy.

Yet the discovery of Troy was just the beginning of Schliemann's greatness as an archaeologist. In the next ten years, he would continue to make discoveries, including another ancient city. Schliemann seemed to have a sixth sense of knowing where to dig for sites. Even modern archaeologists with advanced equipment rarely have the type of repeated success that Schliemann had.

Even though many modern archaeologists and scholars criticize Schliemann's approach as an archaeologist, they forget that he was excavating at a much earlier time. There were no universally accepted rules of excavation in the late 1800s. Schliemann's dig was also the first for a large, dry-land human-made mound on land. Considering these factors, Schliemann should be complimented, not insulted, for his archaeological work. He helped set the standard for what would and would not be accepted for fieldwork.

Schliemann truly paved the way for modern archaeology and should be recognized for his innovative techniques and the discovery of Troy. The field of archaeology, and the world, would not be the same had it not been for Schliemann's contributions as the father of archaeology.

Answer the following questions.

1 Which of the following **best** summarizes the author's claim?

 A. Heinrich Schliemann received much attention for his discoveries.

 B. Heinrich Schliemann was a gifted historian.

 C. Heinrich Schliemann should be recognized for his archaeological work.

 D. Heinrich Schliemann spoke many foreign languages.

 E. Heinrich Schliemann should not be criticized for his work.

> **Hint** Think about the main point the author is trying to make. Remember that an author usually states the claim in the introduction and reaffirms it in the conclusion.

2 Write two sentences from the passage that show examples of persuasive techniques.

_____

_____

_____

_____

> **Hint** Look for places in the text where the author makes general statements that sound authoritative but cannot be proved. Also, find a sentence where the author addresses the reader.

3 Read the following statement from the passage.

> **These discoveries prove that Schliemann should be recognized as a great archaeologist.**

Which of the following is **true** about this statement?

A. The author claims that Schliemann proved the existence of Troy.

B. The author uses false reasoning to make a statement that is not completely true.

C. Stereotyping is used to make a general statement about archaeologists.

D. The statement gives an expert opinion as evidence.

> **Hint** Look closely at the author's word choice in this sentence. Notice how the author uses certain words to exaggerate the argument so that it sounds factual and authoritative.

4 The following question has two parts. First, answer Part A. Then, answer Part B.

Part A

Which of the following statements shows how the author addresses the opposing argument?

A. Although his first career was not as an archaeologist, he developed an interest in history and foreign cultures when he was just a child.

B. Most people assumed that like the Greek myths described in the tales, the city itself was also a myth.

C. Even though many modern archaeologists and scholars criticize Schliemann's approach as an archaeologist, they forget that he was excavating at a much earlier time.

D. He helped set the standard for what would and would not be accepted for fieldwork.

Part B

Which of the following shows how the author offers a rebuttal to the opposing argument you chose in Part A?

A. It is said that his first awareness of the city of Troy came from a history book his father gave him as a present.

B. But Schliemann had faith in the city's existence and believed that the descriptions were too specific to be the stuff of fiction.

C. He prepared for his exploration by visiting different countries and studying archaeology in Paris.

D. There were no universally accepted rules of excavation in the late 1800s.

> **Hint** Remember that authors of persuasive texts generally acknowledge an opposing view and then offer information that refutes, or opposes, it. A rebuttal explains why the opposing view is unfair or inaccurate.

Use the Reading Guide to help you understand the passage.

Heinrich Schliemann: Archaeological Con Artist

Reading Guide

What is the author's claim?

Notice how the author uses strong adjectives and nouns to describe Schliemann. How does this affect the portrayal of Schliemann and what readers learn about him?

How does the author include expert opinions?

Heinrich Schliemann, the man who some call the father of archaeology, was more of a money-hungry treasure seeker than he was an archaeologist. Schliemann did dig at a site and find ruins of an ancient city. But his claims about this discovery were partially falsified and completely over-glorified. Not only did he not discover the real city of Troy from Homer's works, but he also demonstrated poor excavation practices and stole artifacts. Schliemann should not be remembered as anything but a villain. He deceived both the general public and the archaeological field.

First and foremost, an examination of many of Schliemann's claims will show that he was a pathological liar. Professors William Calder and David Traill investigated some of the statements about Schliemann's life and found that the man was a liar. Calder and Traill believe that Schliemann's early interest in archaeology was exaggerated and that he falsified information to obtain a U.S. citizenship.

However, most people can agree that Schliemann's interest in Troy was partly fueled by Homer's *The Iliad* and *The Odyssey*. And really, anyone who has any interest in Troy, even to this day, turns to those books to feed that curiosity. While popular opinion did view the city's existence as implausible, Schliemann was not the only person who believed it was real.

In fact, Schliemann did not even identify where to dig for the city. Although some accounts state that Schliemann closely studied Homer's writings to pinpoint the place to excavate for Troy, they are not accurate. Many other scholars had previously identified the site of Troy, including an English archaeologist named Frank Calvert. As the owner of part of the site, Calvert asserted that the ancient city of Troy was buried under a hill called Hisarlik. Then Schliemann simply used that information to choose the place where he would excavate. As a wealthy businessman, Schliemann had the necessary funds to put together an archaeological dig, albeit a rushed and haphazard one. His fortune allowed him to retire at a young age and pursue archaeology as an interesting hobby.

Look at the quote the author includes. How does this quote support the author's claim?

Why is there so much debate over Schliemann's discoveries?

What lies did Schliemann tell about "Priam's Treasure"?

Notice how the author acknowledges some claims from the opposing view but then refutes them with support for his or her own claim.

One expert on Schliemann, D. F. Easton, writes that Schliemann "came into archaeology in an intuitive rush, in a mid-life crisis, and the scholarship, reasoning, and excavation technique all had to be developed later." This is a perfect statement to describe Schliemann's leap into archaeology. His personal motivations trumped any desire to follow the appropriate procedures one should uphold as a scholar or archaeologist. Granted, the science of archaeology may have been new at the time of Schliemann's work, but he still made mistakes that were obviously unacceptable. Because he believed that Troy was at the bottom layers of the hill where he was digging, he just dug straight down without any regard for the layers he was plowing through. He did not carefully investigate the ruins he was sorting through, nor did he properly record his findings.

Although Schliemann later wrote several books about his discoveries, the information he included is highly debated. There is great disagreement over whether Schliemann accurately represented when and where he found certain ruins and treasures. One of the most controversial of Schliemann's findings is what he called "Priam's Treasure." Priam was a king from Homer's tales, and Schliemann assigned his name to a collection of jewelry and other valuable artifacts he found during one of his first digs. There is tremendous doubt over the information about the collection because Schliemann lied about it on several occasions. For one, his story changed later in his life to say the treasure was found on or inside the wall of Troy, when really it was found outside the wall. He also falsely claimed that his wife was there to witness the discovery. Later, pictures surfaced of his wife wearing some of the gold jewelry, but other reports from people who knew him and his wife confirmed that she was elsewhere at the time of the discovery.

Worst of all, Schliemann often lied about the date of the discovery, and he did this to cover up the thievery of some of the treasure. He smuggled some of his findings out of Turkey. The Turkish authorities were angered by this theft and brought a lawsuit against him.

Reading Guide

How does the author continue to recognize an opposing argument?

What makes the last paragraph a strong conclusion?

Look closely at the words used in the conclusion. What types of persuasive language and techniques does the author use?

Does the author sufficiently support the claim? Is the passage convincing?

In the years after Schliemann's discovery, other archaeologists continued to explore the excavation site. These archaeologists more properly identified and labeled the different layers of the site to correspond to different time periods in Troy's history. They also determined that the layer of Troy Schliemann found was not the Troy of Homer's tales. Rather, the ruins Schliemann uncovered were from an early time period many years before the Trojan War.

Although supporters of Schliemann may claim that he was a pioneer of archaeology who "discovered" Troy, perhaps they too have fallen for Schliemann's fabricated stories he spun to glorify himself. In reality, Schliemann was a liar, a con artist, and a thief. More importantly, he was not a skilled archaeologist who cared about studying and preserving history for the future. His shady practices of archaeology would not be tolerated in today's archaeological world, nor can they be excused because they occurred in a different time. Archaeological equipment and standards may have improved since the 1800s, but decent human behavior has always been the same. Lying, cheating, and stealing should not be excused for the sake of historical importance. Yes, Schliemann may have taken information from others and used his wealth to dig at the site of Troy, but beyond that, he deserves no recognition. If anything, his dishonest practices and writings should be used as an example of what not to do in the field of archaeology.

Answer the following questions.

1 Circle **three** sentences in the passage that show strong persuasive language.

2 Describe the structure the author uses to organize his or her argument. How do the paragraphs build on each other to provide support for the claim? Use details from the passage to support your response.

Write your answer on the lines below.

_____

_____

_____

_____

_____

_____

_____

3 Which of the following **best** support the author's view that Schliemann was a liar and a thief? Choose **all** that apply.

A. Granted, the science of archaeology may have been new at the time of Schliemann's work, but he still made mistakes that were obviously unacceptable.

B. For one, his story changed later in his life to say the treasure was found on or inside the wall of Troy, when really it was found outside the wall.

C. He smuggled some of his findings out of Turkey.

D. These archaeologists more properly identified and labeled the different layers of the site to correspond to different time periods in Troy's history.

E. More importantly, he was not a skilled archaeologist who cared about studying and preserving history for the future.

Answer the following questions about both passages in this lesson.

4 Evaluate and explain whether or not the author of "Heinrich Schliemann: Archaeological Con Artist" included sufficient evidence to support the claim. Use details from the passage to support your response.

Write your answer on the lines below.

_____

_____

_____

_____

_____

_____

5 The following question has two parts. First, answer Part A. Then, answer Part B.

Part A

Which sentences from "Heinrich Schliemann: Archaeological Con Artist" includes a statement about the opposing argument?

A. However, most people can agree that Schliemann's interest in Troy was partly fueled by Homer's *The Iliad* and *The Odyssey*.

B. Although some accounts state that Schliemann closely studied Homer's writings to pinpoint the place to excavate for Troy, they are not accurate.

C. Although Schliemann later wrote several books about his discoveries, the information he included is highly debated.

D. In the years after Schliemann's discovery, other archaeologists continued to explore the excavation site.

Part B

Which sentences from "Heinrich Schliemann: Father of Archaeology" relate to the opposing argument you chose in Part A? Choose **all** that apply.

A. Then, after theorizing about where the city of Troy actually was, he began to excavate.

B. In the next ten years, he would continue to make additional discoveries, including another ancient city.

C. Schliemann seemed to have a sixth sense of knowing where to dig for sites.

D. There were no universally accepted rules of excavation in the late 1800s.

6 The authors of "Heinrich Schliemann: Father of Archaeology" and "Heinrich Schliemann: Archaeological Con Artist" present very different views of Heinrich Schliemann. Analyze how each author presents a claim about Schliemann and the reasons and evidence used to support that claim. Compare and contrast the evidence provided in each passage and how each author interprets the facts related to Schliemann's life and work as an archaeologist. Use details from both passages to support your response.

Write your response on the lines below.

_____

_____

_____

_____

_____

_____

_____

_____

_____

_____

_____

_____

_____

_____

_____

_____

_____

Historical Texts

1 GETTING THE IDEA

Historical Text

Do you keep a journal? Journals are a type of historical text because they tell about life at a certain time and place. **Historical texts** are informational texts that tell about the past. They can inform, persuade, or do both. Letters, biographies, and newspaper stories are all examples of historical texts.

- A **speech** is a talk given to an audience. The speaker informs the audience about a topic or tries to persuade the audience to think or do something. Political, educational, and business leaders often give speeches. Dr. Martin Luther King Jr.'s "I Have a Dream" speech from the March on Washington for Jobs and Freedom is such a speech.

- A **pamphlet** is a short booklet that contains information on a topic. It might, for example, tell about a political candidate or explain the rules of driving.

- Government agencies create informational material in the form of **government documents**. These documents include forms, reports, court rulings, the Constitution, the Declaration of Independence, laws, and treaties.

Point of View

Historical documents are told from the writer's particular **point of view**. Point of view is the writer's position or way of thinking about a subject. Many factors can influence that perspective, such as age, background, life experiences, and when and where the writer lives. A writer reveals his or her point view about a topic by the facts and evidence that he or she includes in the text and by word choice. **Loaded**, or very emotional, **language**, for example, can also tell how an author feels about a subject.

Primary and Secondary Sources

Historical texts can be primary or secondary sources. A journal is a primary source because the person who wrote it saw or took part in the events. **Primary sources** are original records created during the time of the event. They are firsthand accounts and give an insider's view. Examples include journals, manuscripts, letters, speeches, paintings, photographs, and autobiographies.

A **secondary source** is written after the events occurred by someone who did not witness an event firsthand. Often, secondary sources evaluate and comment on the information in primary sources. Examples of secondary sources include biographies, textbooks, encyclopedias, and newspaper articles.

Consider these differences between primary and secondary sources. When reading historical texts, these clues can help you identify in which category a source belongs.

	Primary Source	Secondary Source
The author . . .	witnesses events firsthand	was not present
	speaks from personal experience	cites other sources
The author knows about the events or people from . . .	direct observation or experience	secondhand experience and/or primary sources
The materials are first written . . .	at the time of the event or as a recollection of the event	after the events occurred
The point of view is . . .	usually first person	usually third person

When you read primary and secondary sources on the same topic, you can compare and contrast the point of view. It is possible to see each author's perspective on the events and how the information is presented to the reader. Read the sample sources below. In each one, underline words or phrases that help you recognize the text as a primary or a secondary source.

> ### Dust Bowl in the 1930s and 1940s
> Over an eight-year period, millions of farmers were forced from their land because of the severe drought that hit the Great Plains states. With no rain for their crops, most lost everything they had. Because of years of dry land and dry soil, the winds easily picked up the soil and formed thick dust clouds.

> ### from Mabel Holmes's Diary (Kansas, March 16, 1935)
> Temp. went from 82 to 24 today. The dust wave blew all night, at times could not see, everything covered with dirt. Dried the clothes in the bathroom, got them ironed . . . Several deaths & accidents from the Dust storms, trains were late.

How do the words and phrases you underlined help you determine which type of source each text is? What differences do you notice between the two sources? How does the author's point of view affect how the information is presented?

Text Structures

Historical texts can include a lot of information, including dates, people, and places. Recognizing how the text is organized—its **structure**—can make it easier to remember and understand all of that information. The following three text structures are commonly used in historical texts.

A **sequence structure** presents ideas or events in the order they happen. It is useful in laying out the steps in a process because it shows how one step follows another. Dates, numbers, or signal words such as *first, next*, and *finally* can organize this structure. Biographies and government documents often use a sequence structure. How does the example below organize the steps in a process to apply for disaster relief?

1. Apply online at FEMA's Web site.

2. Have the following information available: Social Security number, description of losses, insurance information, address of damaged property, and telephone number.

3. An inspector will visit the damaged property and file your report.

4. If you are eligible, you will receive funds.

A **cause-and-effect structure** explains why something happens (cause) and what happens as a result (effect). In this structure, words such as *because, if . . . then, as a result, due to, therefore, since,* and *so* can signal the relationship. An article explaining how drought forced millions of people to leave the Midwest might use this structure.

A **compare-and-contrast structure** describes how two or more topics are alike or different. Signal words such as *similar, like, both, unlike, although, but,* and *however* are often used. A textbook might compare and contrast a city before and after a great fire.

Graphic Features

In historical texts, authors often include **graphic features** to help readers better understand the information presented.

- A **timeline** shows a sequence of events in the order they happened.

Dust Bowl (1931–1935)

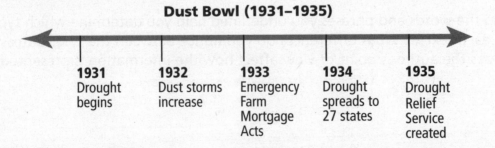

| 1931 | 1932 | 1933 | 1934 | 1935 |
| Drought begins | Dust storms increase | Emergency Farm Mortgage Acts | Drought spreads to 27 states | Drought Relief Service created |

- A **map** displays the location of things or places.

Dust Bowl Region

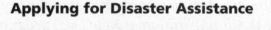

Severe wind erosion in 1935–1936

Most severe wind erosion in 1935–1938

- A **flowchart** shows steps in a process or how things relate to one another using arrows or connecting lines.

Applying for Disaster Assistance

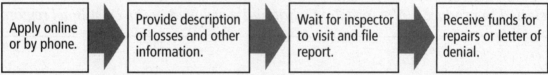

| Apply online or by phone. | → | Provide description of losses and other information. | → | Wait for inspector to visit and file report. | → | Receive funds for repairs or letter of denial. |

Language Spotlight • Domain-Specific Vocabulary

Some words in historical texts are **domain specific**, or have a specific meaning when used in history or social studies text. In a text about the Dust Bowl, for example, you might read *plague*, *migration*, or *drought*. You can use context clues or a reference to figure out the meaning of words that are unfamiliar.

Read the following sentences. Define the underlined words. Then, use a dictionary to verify their meaning.

During the 1930s, thousands of farms could no longer produce crops. In the Dust Bowl states, many farms went into foreclosure. People migrated to California to search for work. Unfortunately, steady employment was not to be found anywhere.

Read the passage.

Background Information about the Dust Bowl

> Starting in 1929, the United States plunged into the Great Depression. This time of high unemployment and low wages lasted through the 1930s into the 1940s. People found themselves jobless, penniless, hungry, and with little to look forward to. To add to the terrible economic times, the southern Great Plains suffered a prolonged and dangerous drought beginning in 1931 and lasting until 1939. The devastating results of so little rain were huge dust storms that swept through states like Kansas, Texas, Oklahoma, and New Mexico. The region became known as the Dust Bowl. Farmers had no means to cultivate crops or shield their cattle. People could not venture outside or breathe the air. Multitudes of families packed their meager belongings and headed to California, hoping to pick up the pieces of their lives.
>
> To document this near decade of tragedy, the government hired photographers and film directors to record images of the times. The program was part of the Resettlement Administration, a New Deal program. Pare Lorentz was selected to produce a film revealing what had developed in the Dust Bowl region.

excerpt from

"The Plow That Broke the Plains" *from* the Documentary Film Script

by Pare Lorentz

PROLOGUE
This is a record of land . . . of soil, rather than people
a story of the Great Plains: the 400,000,000 acres of windswept grasslands that spread up from the Texas Panhandle to Canada . . .
a high, treeless continent, without rivers, without streams . . .
a country of high winds, and sun . . . and of little rain . . .

CATTLE

First came the cattle . . . an unfenced range a thousand miles long . . .
an uncharted ocean of grass, the southern range for winter grazing
and the mountain plateaus for summer.
It was a cattleman's Paradise . . .
For a decade the world discovered the grasslands and poured cattle into
the plains.
The railroads brought markets to the edge of the plains . . .
land syndicates sprang up overnight and the cattle rolled into the West.

HOMESTEADERS

The railroad brought the world into the plains . . . new populations, new
needs crowded the last frontier.
Once again the plowman followed the herder and the pioneer came to the plains.
Make way for the plowman!
The first fence.
Progress came to the plain.
Two hundred miles from water, two hundred miles from home, but the land is
new. High winds and sun . . . a country without rivers and with little rain.
Settler, plow at your peril!

DROUGHT

A country without rivers . . . without streams . . . with little rain . . .
Once again the rains held off and the sun baked the earth.
This time no grass held moisture against the winds and the sun . . . this time
millions of acres of plowed land lay open to the sun.

DEVASTATION

Baked out—blown out—and broke!

Year in, year out, uncomplaining they fought

the worst drought in history . . . their stock choked to death on the barren land . . .

their homes were nightmares of swirling dust night and day.

Many went ahead of it—but many stayed

until stock, machinery, homes, credit, food, and even hope were gone.

On to the West!

Once again they headed for the setting sun.

Once again they headed West.

Last year in every summer month 50,000 people left the Great Plains and hit the

highways for the Pacific Coast, the last border.

Blown out—baked out—and broke . . .

nothing to stay for . . . nothing to hope for . . .

homeless, penniless and bewildered they joined the great army of the highways.

No place to go . . . and no place to stop.

Nothing to eat . . . nothing to do . . .

their homes on four wheels . . . their work a

desperate gamble for a day's labor in the fields along the highways . . .

The price of a sack of beans or a tank of gas.

All they ask is a chance to start over

and a chance for their children to eat

to have medical care, to have homes again.

50,000 a month!

The sun and winds wrote the most tragic chapter in American agriculture.

Answer the following questions.

1 This question has two parts. First, answer Part A. Then, answer Part B.

Part A

How is the section "Homesteaders" organized?

A. in time-order sequence

B. by cause and effect

C. by compare and contrast

D. by problem and solution

Part B

Explain your answer in Part A.

Write your answer on the lines below.

_____

_____

> **Hint** Look for words that tell whether the events are told in order, are compared, or explain how one event led to other events. If you can find any one of those relationships, you can then identify the structure.

2 Read these phrases from the passage and the question that follows.

**a high, treeless continent, without rivers, without streams . . .
a country of high winds, and sun . . . and of little rain . . .**

Why does the author use these phrases to describe the Great Plains?

A. to predict the outcome of storms

B. to explain that the area is unprotected from the effects of nature

C. to compare the region to areas with water

D. to provide background about the event that affects the area

> **Hint** The passage describes the land as exposed. Why would the author want the reader to know that information about the land?

3 How could a reader identify that the photograph in the text shows the Great Plains during the Dust Bowl era? What does the reader learn in the text that provides clues to figuring out where and when the photograph was taken?

Write your answer on the lines below.

_____

_____

Hint Look for clues in the text that describe what the land looks like. Do those clues match what you see in the photograph?

4 This question has two parts. First, answer Part A. Then, answer Part B.

Part A

What is "The Plow That Broke the Plains" mostly about?

A. what happened to the people of the Midwest in the 1930s

B. a record of the lands of the Great Plains in the 1930s

C. an explanation of the causes of the Great Depression

D. the story of why people moved to the Great Plains

Part B

Which line from the text **best** supports the answer in Part A?

A. This is a record of land . . . of soil, rather than people a story of the Great Plains.

B. The railroads brought markets to the edge of the plains . . .

C. Once again the rains held off and the sun baked the earth.

D. . . . land syndicates sprang up overnight and the cattle rolled into the West.

Hint The main idea of a text is often stated at the beginning or in a prologue.

Use the Reading Guide to help you understand the passage.

The Dust Bowl and the Government Rescue

Reading Guide

Summarize what happened in the Great Plains between 1931 and 1939.

Great Plains farmers did not just go back to their farms when they discovered that California was not the opportunity they had hoped for. Why not?

What role did the federal government play in helping farmers and others in the 1930s? Why did they get involved?

The Source of the Trouble

When wind and dry soil meet, dust sweeps across the land. This combination happened on a massive scale during the 1930s in the United States. From 1931 to 1939, little or no rain fell across the Great Plains. The drought and erosion created a "Dust Bowl" across more than 50 million acres of farmland in states that included New Mexico, Kansas, Texas, and Oklahoma.

With no rain, little soil, and dusty air, farmers were powerless and penniless. They became refugees of the environment. To escape the dust storms, which became known as "black blizzards," many of them moved from the Great Plains to farms in California and cities in the West. It is estimated that 2.5 million people left the Great Plains during this period. They hoped to begin again, but most found poor living conditions and little aid. Many cities tried to keep them out; few people or organizations helped them resettle.

Desperate Times

The displaced had nowhere to turn and could not go back. Their old farms were useless, and they had already spent what little money they had to travel west. It would take major measures in the form of laws, programs, and financial assistance by the federal government to assist the millions of people devastated by the Dust Bowl and repair the unprecedented environmental problems.

The Government Responds

In the early 1930s, the U.S. government under President Franklin Roosevelt began to implement a series of "New Deal" programs to help the country recover from the Great Depression. Since the wide-scale dust condition in the Great Plains had never occurred before, it was not clear what should be done to help correct it. Beginning around 1934, though, the federal government tried a number of New Deal–style measures to alleviate the problems.

Suppose the president vetoes a bill. How can it still become a law?

Reread the purposes of the Taylor Grazing Act and the Frazier-Lemke Farm Bankruptcy Act. How were they different?

How did the Federal Surplus Relief Corporation help Great Plains farmers?

The First Acts of the New Deal

The first of many New Deal maneuvers were laws passed to protect farmers and their land. Passing a law requires both the legislative and executive branches of the government, so both Congress and President Roosevelt were involved.

In 1934, Congress passed, and the president signed, the Taylor Grazing Act. It regulated grazing on publicly owned lands. That control stopped farmers from letting their animals overgraze as they had been and destroying farmlands. That same year, the Frazier-Lemke Farm Bankruptcy Act became law. It restricted banks from taking away farms from farmers who lacked the money to keep up with their payments.

How a Bill Becomes a Law

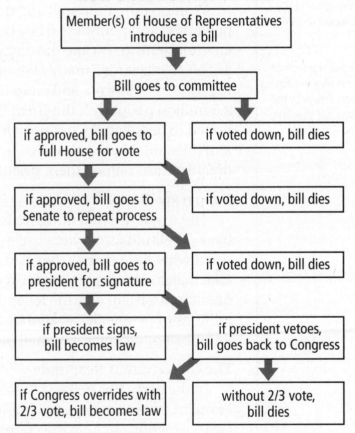

- Member(s) of House of Representatives introduces a bill
- Bill goes to committee
- if approved, bill goes to full House for vote
- if voted down, bill dies
- if approved, bill goes to Senate to repeat process
- if voted down, bill dies
- if approved, bill goes to president for signature
- if voted down, bill dies
- if president signs, bill becomes law
- if president vetoes, bill goes back to Congress
- if Congress overrides with 2/3 vote, bill becomes law
- without 2/3 vote, bill dies

How did the government spend $500 million through the Emergency Relief Appropriation Act?

Why was it important for the government to have soil conservation programs like the Soil Conservation Service?

1935: A Busy Year for the New Deal

Many additions were made to the New Deal in 1935. The Drought Relief Service, designed to oversee all programs related to the drought situation, bought cattle from failing farms. Sick cattle were destroyed. The rest were distributed by the Federal Surplus Relief Corporation as food all over the country. While some farmers were unhappy to lose their cattle, the act helped them avoid losing everything. They could not afford to keep the cattle, and the price the government paid was significantly higher than the farmers could get anywhere else.

On April 8, the president signed the Emergency Relief Appropriation Act. It authorized $500 million to create work-relief programs for drought victims and other people suffering through the depression. The Works Progress Administration, one of the most famous of all New Deal programs, started under this act. The idea was that the government would hire people—perhaps millions of them—for various jobs. The concept and scale of the program was unprecedented. It remains one of the largest public-assistance programs in American history.

Programs such as the Works Progress Administration helped people by providing jobs, loans, and other assistance.

Land Preservation

Although the new programs gave some relief to farmers, the land was getting worse. After another 850 million tons of topsoil were lost in the wind, a government report noted, "Unless something is done, the western plains will be as arid as the Arabian desert." Soil erosion needed to be stopped, so Congress created the Soil Conservation Service to teach improved farming methods. It taught farmers about crop rotation, which involves changing crops every few years so the soil has time to recharge its nutrients. They also learned about contour plowing with the curves of the land and strip cropping (planting different crops in alternating strips). Farmers who agreed to follow these methods received money from the government.

Reading Guide

Camps, like the Arvin Migratory Labor Camp, had an arrangement with people who lived there. What was it?

Consider the main points made in the conclusion. What do they suggest about the author's point of view regarding the New Deal? What phrases suggest that perspective?

Look at the timeline. Which year was the busiest for New Deal programs and legislation?

Other programs made efforts to protect the land from wind and erosion. The Prairie States Forestry Project, for example, worked with farmers to plant trees. Trees create a shield against the wind, and their roots hold soil in place.

Help in California

Great Plains farmers also received some help in California. In 1937, the Farm Security Administration opened places there for people to live. The first was the Arvin Migratory Labor Camp, and the federal government paid for its operation. It provided a place to live in exchange for work. The conditions were simple, mostly tents on wooden platforms, but improved on the desolate situation before. Twelve more camps opened after Arvin, and the people in the camps worked together to govern them. It was still difficult to find regular, daily work, and the wages were low, but over time the transplants from the Dust Bowl began to make a life for themselves beyond the Great Plains.

Conclusion

The 1930s were an unbelievably desperate time for Americans, particularly the farmers of the Great Plains. Without the enormous help of the U.S. government through New Deal programs, there is no telling how much more difficult those years would have been and how much more devastated the farmlands would have become. Even a partial summary of the New Deal gives an idea of the contribution the government made to ease the challenges faced during the terrible decade known as the Dust Bowl.

The Dust Bowl and the New Deal

1931
Drought,
Dust Bowl
begins

1934
Taylor Grazing Act
Frazier-Lemke Farm
Bankruptcy Act

1936
Soil
Conservation
Project

1937
Farm Security
Administration

1939
Drought ends

1935
Drought Relief Service
Federal Surplus Relief Corporation
Emergency Relief Appropriation Act
Works Progress Administration
Soil Conservation Service
Prairie States Forestry Project

1938
Dust storms lessen

Answer the following questions.

1 The text claims that people who fled the Great Plains to California did eventually receive some help from the federal government. Identify the evidence in the text that supports that idea.

Write your answer on the lines below.

_____

_____

_____

_____

2 The following question has two parts. First, answer Part A. Then, answer Part B.

Part A

What is a work-relief program?

A. any plan that makes a person's job easier

B. an office where people can apply for jobs

C. money people receive when they lose their jobs

D. a government program that pays people to work

Part B

Which sentence from the passage explains the meaning of work-relief in Part A?

A. It restricted banks from taking away farms from farmers who lacked the money to keep up with their payments.

B. The idea was that the government would hire people—perhaps millions of them—for various jobs.

C. While some farmers were unhappy to lose their cattle, the act helped them avoid losing everything.

D. Twelve more camps opened after Arvin, and the people in the camps worked together to govern them.

3 What does the author think about the New Deal and its role during the Dust Bowl? Would all people feel the same way? How can you tell that the author's perspective might be different from others?

Write your answer on the lines below.

_____

_____

4 How is "The Dust Bowl and the Government Rescue" structured?

  A. in time-order sequence

  B. by comparing and contrasting events

  C. as a list of problems and solution

  D. in a series of cause-and-effect paragraphs

5 The following steps in how a bill becomes a law are out of order. Write 1, 2, 3, 4, and 5 to put them in order from beginning to end.

☐	The full House of Representatives approves the bill.
☐	A representative introduces a bill.
☐	The president signs the bill.
☐	The Senate approves the bill.
☐	A House committee approves the bill.

6 Compare and contrast the primary source "The Plow That Broke the Plains" and the secondary source "The Dust Bowl and the Government Rescue." In what ways are the topic, structure, and author's point of view alike and different? Use details from both passages to support your answer.

Write your response on the lines below.

_____

_____

_____

_____

_____

_____

_____

_____

_____

_____

_____

_____

_____

_____

_____

_____

_____

_____

RI.7.5, RI.7.6, L.7.6, RST.6–8.1, RST.6–8.3, RST.6–8.4, RST.6–8.5, RST.6–8.6,
RST.6–8.7, RST.6–8.8, RST.6–8.9, RST.6–8.10

Scientific and Technical Texts

① GETTING THE IDEA

Two important types of nonfiction writing are scientific and technical texts.
Scientific texts explain a science topic, such as how the planets revolve around the
sun. Science magazine articles, experiments, and academic textbooks are examples
of scientific texts. **Technical texts** provide detailed information on a specific topic,
often about how to do something. User manuals, experiments, how-to guides,
instructions, brochures, and cookbooks are examples of technical texts.

Structure

Like most nonfiction texts, scientific and technical texts contain a lot of
information. Authors rely on text structure to organize all of the facts and details.
Organizing the text in a certain way makes it easier for the reader to understand
and remember the information. Some common text structures are **compare and
contrast**, **cause and effect**, and **problem and solution**. You may also see scientific
and technical texts use the following structures.

- A **sequence structure** presents ideas and concepts in a specific order.
  Numbered steps or time-order words, such as *first*, *next*, *before*, and *after*, can
  organize this structure. When a text explains a procedure or gives instructions,
  it is important to follow the steps in order. Following the steps of an
  experiment or directions in a manual out of order can make the results come
  out wrong.

  Underline the time-order words in this sample. Then, number the steps
  in order.

  First, prepare the terrarium by placing soil along the bottom of the
  container. Then, cover the soil with moss and other plants. Next, mist it
  with water from a spray bottle. Finally, cover the whole thing with mesh
  and secure the cover.

- A **whole-to-part structure** begins with a topic sentence or general idea, or the "whole." Facts and details are the "parts" that come next, explaining and supporting that idea.

> A volcano has many parts. The vent is the center opening in a volcanic mountain. If it is wide, it is called a crater. The opening extends the length of the volcano into a magma chamber below Earth's crust. That tunnel is called a pipe, or conduit.

- A **part-to-whole structure** is the reverse of a whole-to-part structure. Here, the facts and details lead to a main idea or concept.

> Recycling saves money. It reduces the amount of trash in landfills and makes us aware of the resources we use. These are all important reasons to start a recycling program at our school.

- A **spatial structure** describes things in terms of where they are. It uses location words such as *above, bottom, front, back, east,* and *southwest.* A user manual or a geographic guide may use this type of structure.

> A number of mountain ranges cover the United States. The farthest west is the Coast Range along the edge of California. The largest is the Rocky Mountains, which run through many western states like Montana, Wyoming, and Colorado. The Appalachian Mountains are in the East.

Graphic Features

A **graphic feature** is an image that helps the reader visualize information. Some graphic features explain the text. Others provide new information in a visual way. Scientific and technical texts use a variety of graphic features.

- A **flowchart** shows the steps in a process using lines or arrows to connect the steps. This flowchart shows the steps of the scientific method.

Scientific Method

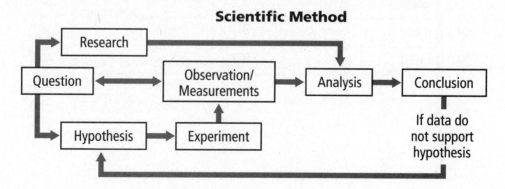

- A **diagram** is a drawing that shows the parts of something or how something works. This diagram shows sound waves in both loud and soft sounds.

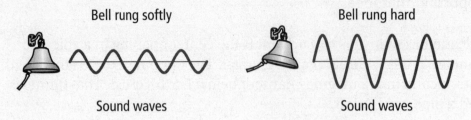

Bell rung softly

Sound waves

Bell rung hard

Sound waves

- A **graph** is a visual way to show data, or information given as numbers.

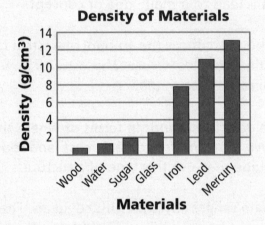

Density of Materials

- A **table** displays information in columns and rows. This table shows the information on the graph as a table.

Density of Materials

Materials	Density
Wood	1
Water	1.5
Sugar	2
Glass	3
Iron	8
Lead	9
Mercury	13

- A **model** is a picture or object that represents a real-life object. The real-life object is usually something too big, small, far away, hidden, or otherwise hard to see.

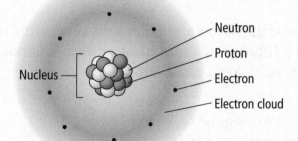

Language Spotlight • Symbols and Key Terms

Scientific and technical texts often contain symbols and key terms. A **symbol** is a picture or letter that represents a word or idea. In the expression +2°C, for example, the symbol "+" means *positive*, and the round symbol means *degrees*. The letter *C* stands for *Celsius*, which is a measurement scale for temperature. The word *Celsius* is a **key term** because it is an important science word.

Read this paragraph. Underline any key terms. Then, circle the symbols.

The experiment requires students to cool the H_2O to 32°F and then add 2 mL of NaCl to the container. There are many kinds of salts, but NaCl is sodium chloride, or common table salt.

What do the key terms and symbols you marked mean?

Read the passage.

Which Plants Can Tolerate Salt?

Some plants live near the ocean and other salty places and do well living in contact with salt water. Other plants cannot survive well in those conditions. This experiment explores which plants can tolerate salt.

Materials
- two healthy rugosa roses growing in soil
- two healthy begonia plants growing in soil
- water
- table salt (NaCl)
- watering cans and measuring cups
- camera (optional)

Procedure
1. Predict which plant or plants will tolerate salt water. Record your prediction and explain why you think that outcome will happen.
2. Create a saltwater mix in a watering can. Dissolve ¼ cup of salt for every 2 cups of cool water.
3. Set all four plants in a cool, sunny spot, such as by a window.

Rugosa Rose

Begonia

4. Water one begonia and one rugosa rose every third day with water only. Water one of each plant with the saltwater mix at the same time.
5. Observe the plants each week. Write, draw, and take photographs if possible to record your observations.

One student made notes about what she observed.

Data

Prediction: The plants that get plain water will do well. The plants that get salt water will not. I think so because I rarely see plants with flowers near the ocean.

Week	Rose 1 (plain water)	Begonia 1 (plain water)	Rose 2 (salt water)	Begonia 2 (salt water)
1	• many green leaves • roses in bloom	• many green leaves • flowers in bloom	• many green leaves • roses in bloom	• many green leaves • flowers in bloom
2	• many green leaves • roses in bloom	• many green leaves • flowers in bloom	• many green leaves • roses in bloom	• leaves lighter green • white spots on leaves • flowers wilting
3	• many green leaves • roses in bloom • new flowers	• many green leaves • flowers in bloom	• many green leaves • roses in bloom • new flowers	• white leaves • mostly wilted flowers
4	• many green leaves • new roses in bloom • new flowers	• many green leaves • new flowers in bloom	• many green leaves • new roses in bloom • new flowers	• shriveled leaves • dead flowers

Analysis

At the start of the experiment, all four plants looked healthy. They had green leaves and plenty of flowers. Both control plants, the ones that got plain water, were equally healthy or healthier four weeks later. In week 4, they had the same green leaves and flowers in bloom. They even had a few new flowers.

The plants that received salt water did not have equal results. The rugosa rose did just as well with salt water as the one with plain water. It had as many green leaves, roses in bloom, and new flowers. The begonia that got salt water, though, basically died. The leaves dried up and the flowers died.

Conclusion

Rugosa roses can live with salt water but begonias cannot. My prediction was incorrect; there are plants with flowers that can tolerate salt water.

Answer the following questions.

1 These steps from the section "Procedure" are out of order. Write 1, 2, 3, 4, and 5 to order them from first to last.

	Mix the salt and water.
	Observe the plants each week.
	Put the plants in a sunny spot.
	Make a prediction.
	Water the plants regularly.

Hint Review the steps of the procedure. Remember that the numbers tell you the order to follow.

2 What does the symbol NaCl stand for?

A. soil

B. salt water

C. rugosa roses

D. table salt

Hint Find the symbol NaCl in the section "Procedure" and see what it refers to.

3 Which section of the experiment includes judgments by the writer, rather than just facts or observations?

A. Procedure

B. Data

C. Analysis

D. Conclusions

Hint A fact is something known to be true. Observations are things that you learn about the world through the senses. A judgment is an informed opinion made after carefully studying information.

4 Suppose you tested another plant like the begonia. How would you expect the fourth entry in the data table to read for that plant if you watered it with salt water?

A. green leaves, flowers blooming

B. lighter leaves, flowers wilting

C. white leaves, new flowers

D. shriveled leaves, dead flowers

Hint The plant in the question is like a begonia, so it should react to salt water the same way. Use the table in the section "Data" to read what a begonia under those conditions looks like in week 4. That's what the plant in the question should look like, too.

Use the Reading Guide to help you understand the passage.

Trees and Shrubs That Tolerate Saline Soils and Salt Spray Drift

Reading Guide

Is salt generally good for most plants? Reread paragraph 1 to find out.

Review the bulleted list. Where does the salt that disturbs plants come from?

How exactly does salt affect trees and shrubs?

The following information about salt water and plants is adapted from the Virginia Polytechnic Institute and State University's Cooperative Extension.

Concentrated sodium (Na) is a component of salt. It can damage plants when it contacts the plant parts above or below ground. High salinity (saltiness) can reduce growth and even cause death. Care should be taken to avoid excessive salt buildup on tree and shrub roots, leaves, or stems. Sites with salty soils, and those that are exposed to coastal salt spray or pavement deicing materials, present challenges to landscapers and homeowners.

Saline Soils

Saline soils occur when salts build up in the soil. Significant salt buildup is uncommon where rainfall exceeds twenty inches per year. However, saline soils do occur in specific places.

- Along the coastline and barrier islands where seawater may flood over the land
- Where salt from spray may collect in the soil
- Along brackish tidal rivers and estuaries; flooding during storms and high tides can deposit salt in low-lying areas . . .
- Along sidewalks and roads where salt is used to remove ice and snow; in areas where treated ice and snow are piled; where vehicles cause salt spray . . .
- In cultivated areas when too much fertilizer is applied . . .

How Do Saline Soils Affect Trees and Shrubs?

Plant root cells contain a membrane that allows water to pass through. The membrane prevents salt from entering. As the soil's salt content increases, it becomes more difficult for water to pass through the membrane into the root. In addition, if salt levels get high enough, they may actually <u>dehydrate</u> roots. That causes "salt burn" by drawing water out of root cells.

High levels of soluble salts also cause changes to soil structure. That can result in compacted soils that are problematic for plants . . .

Find the word *halophytic*. What are halophytic plants?

Would a salt concentration in soil of 1,500 ppm be low or medium?

Two plants of the same species receive salt damage. Plant A receives salt spray, but Plant B is in saline soil. Which plant will likely show signs of damage first?

Plants vary in their ability to grow in salty soils. Plants that grow only in saline soils are called "halophytic," or salt loving. Halophytic plants are generally found in coastal areas, saltwater marshes, and brackish wetlands. The presence of some of these plants (such as spartina and sea oats) indicates that there is saline soil . . .

There is a direct relationship between the amount and duration of salt exposure and potential damage to plants. The higher the amount of salt in the soil, the greater the impact on plants. Salt damage is generally more severe during periods of hot, dry weather.

Measuring Soil Salinity

The amount of salt in the soil can be measured with a soil test. The Virginia Cooperative Extension Service Soil Test Laboratory reports salt levels using the measure "parts per million," or "ppm." Salt concentrations of 1–1,000 ppm are considered low. Those from 1,000–2,000 ppm are medium. With the exception of very salt-sensitive plants, most landscape plants can tolerate salt concentrations in the medium range.

Symptoms of Saline Soil Damage

Plant damage due to saline soils becomes evident more slowly than plant damage due to salt spray. . . . General symptoms include stunted growth and reduced yields. All parts of the plant, including leaves, stems, roots, and fruits, may be reduced in size.

Are you trying to diagnose plant damage? Keep in mind that all of the signs and symptoms can also be caused by a variety of other factors. These factors include root damage, drought, diseases, and chemical misuse. Try to eliminate these other possibilities, and use tools such as soil and water analyses to help you arrive at a correct diagnosis.

Summarize one of the bulleted suggestions for reducing salt damage.

Using salt to deice roads can harm plants. What materials can be substituted for salt?

Refer to the table. How are the Japanese cedar and white poplar alike and different?

Reducing Salt Spray or Salt Spray Damage

Numerous options exist for reducing salt damage. They include:

- Carefully designing planting areas to reduce exposure of trees and shrubs to salt spray. Establish windbreaks to prevent "wind tunnels" that can carry salts farther and at higher speeds. Use salt-tolerant shrubs or plant borders as windbreaks to help stop salt drift before it reaches sensitive plants.
- Erecting burlap fencing or other barriers for winter protection of plants next to roads.
- Grouping trees and shrubs to shield them from wind and drift. Put the most tolerant species in higher-exposure areas to shield less tolerant ones.
- Maintaining soil and moisture conditions to reduce stress and fight drying. If possible, rinse salt spray off trees and shrubs after storms and high winds. Rinse again in early spring to remove salt residue from tender buds and leaves.
- Working in the spring when planting trees and shrubs near roads on which deicing salts are used. This allows plants more time to become established prior to salt exposure. Trees and shrubs that are susceptible to salt damage should be located at least fifty to sixty feet from roads.
- When practical, using cinders, fly ash, or sand for deicing instead of salt.
- Selecting and planting salt-tolerant trees and shrubs. Avoid plants, such as azaleas, that are considered especially sensitive to salt spray.

Short List of Salt-Tolerant Trees

Name	Type of Tolerance	Deciduous/Evergreen
Gray birch	salt spray	D
Japanese cedar	salt spray	E
American holly	salt spray	E
White poplar	saline soils, salt spray	D
Red oak	saline soils	D

Answer the following questions.

1 Which sentence from the passage **best** summarizes the author's purpose for writing it?

   A. Care should be taken to avoid excessive salt buildup on tree and shrub roots, leaves, or stems.

   B. Saline soils occur when salts build up in the soil.

   C. Plants vary in their ability to grow in salty soils.

   D. All parts of the plant, including leaves, stems, roots, and fruits, may be reduced in size.

2 Read this sentence from the passage and the directions that follow.

   High salinity (saltiness) can reduce growth and even cause death.

What is the **most** important reason the author includes this explanation at the beginning of the passage?

   A. to define the word *salinity* in a way that a nonscientist can understand

   B. to identify where plants are most affected by salt

   C. to justify why the text focuses on salt damage and its solutions

   D. to explain what causes salinity and where it comes from

3 The following question has two parts. First, answer Part A. Then, answer Part B.

Part A

Which choice **best** describes the overall text structure of the passage?

   A. sequence

   B. whole to part

   C. part to whole

   D. spatial

Part B

Explain your answer from Part A.

Write your answer on the lines below.

_____

_____

4 Review the main idea of the text, and then look at the table at the end. How does the table add new and important information that is not included in the text? How does that information complete the ideas in the text?

Write your answer on the lines below.

_____

_____

5 The following question has two parts. First, answer Part A. Then, answer Part B.

Part A

What does <u>dehydrate</u> mean?

A. to add salt

B. to burn

C. to dry out

D. to pass through

Part B

Circle the sentence from the passage below that provides context clues to identify the meaning of <u>dehydrate</u>.

> **Plant root cells contain a membrane that allows water to pass through. The membrane prevents salt from entering. As the soil's salt content increases, it becomes more difficult for water to pass through the membrane into the root. In addition, if salt levels get high enough, they may actually <u>dehydrate</u> roots. That causes "salt burn" by drawing water out of root cells.**

6 How is the information in "Which Plants Can Tolerate Salt?" and "Trees and Shrubs That Tolerate Saline Soils and Salt Spray Drift" alike and different? Compare and contrast what you learned from reading the experiment with what you learned from the informational text. Think about how the information is presented in both passages. Cite specific examples and evidence from each passage as needed to support your answer.

Write your response on the lines below.

_____

_____

_____

_____

_____

_____

_____

_____

_____

_____

_____

_____

_____

_____

_____

_____

RI.7.2, RI.7.3, RI.7.9, L.7.6, RH.6–8.2, RST.6–8.1, RST.6–8.2

Analyze Informational Texts

1 GETTING THE IDEA

At times, you will read two or more nonfiction texts on the same topic. This is especially true in science and history classes, when you may read multiple texts to answer a question or to speak and write about a topic knowledgably. When you read multiple texts, it's important to be able to evaluate the texts, compare and contrast their content, and then synthesize, or combine, the information you read.

Evaluate

When reading multiple texts, a good strategy is to examine each text separately before you compare them. Different authors may write about the same topic, but text type, structure, and point of view may be very different. Here are some questions you might ask as you examine a text critically.

Text Considerations	Questions to Ask
text type	What kind of text is it?
structure	How is the information organized?
author's purpose	What is the author's purpose?
point of view	Does the author remain objective and neutral? Does the author show any bias?
style	What tone does the author convey through the use of words? Does the author include examples, comparisons, categories, analogies, or allusions?
main idea or claim	What is the central idea or ideas? What message does the author want to convey?
supporting reasons and details	How does the author support the central idea or claim? Are the details and reasons clear, relevant, and supported by evidence?
evidence	What textual evidence does the author include? Is it based on fact, reasoned judgment, or speculation? Is there sufficient relevant evidence to support the claim?
text and graphic features	Does the text have subheadings, sidebars, or other text features that help readers locate information? Do the graphic features add to the understanding of the text?

Summarize

After you evaluate each text, **summarize** each one. Identify the central idea and the supporting details, reasons, and evidence. Look for key words and phrases that will help you discuss the topic. Keep your summary free of personal opinions or judgments. Even when a text is biased, your summary should be neutral.

Compare and Contrast

Once you have evaluated and summarized each text, you are ready to compare and contrast the texts. Use the answers to the questions you asked about the texts individually to guide you in your comparison.

Read these paragraphs from different sources. Underline the main idea in each. Then think about the text type and the structure of each paragraph. How does this help you identify the author's purpose and point of view?

The Plight of the Mountain Gorilla

Nearly half of the approximately seven hundred mountain gorillas remaining on Earth live on the forested mountain slopes of Rwanda, Uganda, and the Democratic Republic of Congo. These docile creatures are larger than their lowland cousins, with males standing as tall as six feet. They live in communities of around thirty led by a dominant male, who is often called a silverback for the frost of silver hair along its back. The troop feeds on roots, shoots, wild fruit, and trees from their forest home. War and human interference greatly reduced the mountain gorilla's numbers, making them a critically endangered species. Conservation groups have helped prevent extinction of the species. Since their intervention, the population has remained steady and slightly increased.

Saving Mountain Gorillas

It's time to take action before another species becomes extinct. The mountain gorillas of Rwanda, Uganda, and the Democratic Republic of Congo are on the critically endangered list. Mountain gorillas face extinction from habitat loss, poaching, and disease, all at the hands of humans. War and civil unrest have contributed to their decreasing numbers as displaced people moved into their habitats and cut down trees for fuel and lumber products. Other animals were also affected. Conservation groups and individuals work to protect mountain gorilla habitats by encouraging ecotourism, raising environmental awareness, and assisting in the management of natural resources. You can help by making a symbolic zoo gorilla "adoption" to help fund a conservation group.

Both texts deal with the same topic—mountain gorillas. Yet they have different text types, points of view, main ideas and details, and evidence. How does the text type affect the point of view from which the author writes?

Make additional comparisons between the texts. Think about the structure, style, and language of each and how these factors help you evaluate the reasons and evidence presented.

- Is the reasoning sound and backed with sufficient evidence?

- Are all the details relevant? Why or why not?

- Do the paragraphs present similar facts? Is there any conflicting information?

As you compare and contrast texts, your knowledge about a topic increases. You are better able to recognize sound reasoning and relevant evidence. You notice when irrelevant evidence is introduced or when evidence is missing. In the persuasive text, for example, the sentence "Other animals were also affected" is irrelevant. It doesn't relate to the topic of the paragraph, which is the mountain gorilla.

At other times, you may find conflicting information. These differences may depend on the source of the facts. For example, an older source may have outdated information. The difference could also be because of how an author interprets or presents the facts. For example, in the persuasive text, the sentence beginning "War and civil unrest have contributed to their decreasing numbers . . ." implies that the gorillas' numbers are still decreasing. Yet the academic article mentions that conservation efforts have stabilized their numbers and increased them slightly. When you encounter conflicting information, the more recent and academic sources are usually the most reliable.

When you compare and contrast texts, you may find the same information presented in different ways. For example, the academic text states that "nearly half" of the gorillas live in a particular region, while another source might say "50 percent." This is the same fact presented in different ways.

Language Spotlight • Academic Language

Nonfiction texts often contain domain-specific vocabulary that is used specifically when discussing a certain topic. They also include general academic vocabulary. These **academic vocabulary** words are terms that appear in many subjects and even in daily language. They include words such as *analyze*, *summarize*, *evidence*, and *theme*. Sometimes, you can use context to figure out the meaning of academic vocabulary. Read the sentences below. The underlined words are examples of academic vocabulary.

When you <u>conduct</u> a scientific <u>investigation</u>, it is important to follow the steps in the <u>process</u> in the precise <u>order</u>. If you don't, the <u>results</u> may not be what you expected.

How could you use the academic vocabulary when talking about other topics?

Read the passage.

Invaders among Us

It sounds like a scene from a science fiction thriller—plants consuming buildings, mussels blocking water supplies, fish attacking boaters—yet these plant and animal invaders are real. They are nonnative species that enter the United States, either intentionally or by accident, and become harmful to an ecosystem, damage property, and harm people. They can also cost millions of dollars in repair and management costs. While some nonnative species are harmless, these are not.

Kudzu

In 1876, an ornamental plant from Japan was displayed at the Philadelphia Centennial Exposition. The climbing vine had broad green leaves and fragrant purple flowers that hung in clusters. At first, the plant seemed to be harmless. In the mid-1930s to early 1950s, southern farmers were even encouraged to plant it for erosion control.

Once in a warm, humid climate, however, kudzu spread rapidly. A single vine can grow up to a hundred feet in length. Its thick tap root can measure seven inches in diameter, grow up to six feet long, and weigh as much as four hundred pounds. An established plant grows a foot a day and covers anything in its path. It kills the plants it covers by blocking out sunlight. In addition, it has been known to break branches, uproot trees and shrubs, and collapse buildings.

Asian Carp

In the 1970s, catfish farmers in the southern United States imported two species of Asian carp, the bighead carp and the silver carp, to keep their ponds algae free. Unfortunately, flooding caused the ponds to overflow and released the carp into the Mississippi River. Ever since, the fish have been moving north into other rivers and toward the Great Lakes.

Asian carp eat between 5 and 20 percent of their body weight each day. The average adult carp weighs around thirty pounds, but some grow to over a hundred pounds. They have no natural predators and are killing native marine life that depends on plankton for food.

The Asian carp population exploded in the 1990s. Between 1994 and 1997, the commercial catch of the bighead carp increased from 5.5 tons to 55 tons. However, the increase doesn't help the fishing industry because the value of carp is low compared to other fish. The carp also pose a threat to boats and boaters. Silver carp are startled by the sound of boat motors and leap as high as ten feet out of the water. The "flying" fish land in boats, damage property, and injure people.

Burmese Pythons

Over a dozen years ago, Burmese pythons began taking up residence in Florida's wetlands. Pythons are popular pets, but pet owners fail to realize that the nonvenomous snakes are among the largest in the world, reaching lengths of twenty-six feet. Whether the pythons escaped or were intentionally released by pet owners when they got too large, the pythons are now one of the top predators in Florida's Everglades National Park.

Today it is estimated that tens of thousands of pythons live in the Everglades, where they are disrupting an already delicate ecosystem. Sightings of birds and mammals are down by as much as 99 percent in some areas. Pythons have even been known to prey on alligators.

Kudzu, Asian carp, and Burmese pythons are just three examples of how successful invasive species harm ecosystems in multiple ways. While managing the spread of these invaders is important, making sure new invasive species aren't introduced is equally as important.

Answer the following questions.

1 Read all parts of the question before responding.

Part A

Read this sentence from the passage.

> Its thick tap **root** can measure seven inches in diameter, grow up to six feet long, and weigh as much as four hundred pounds.

Which definition **best** defines the academic vocabulary word root as it is used in the sentence?

A. the condition of being settled in a certain place or society

B. a feature that offers support and draws minerals and water from the soil

C. the main component of a word from which it derives its meaning

D. a number multiplied by itself a certain number of times to produce another number

Part B

Think about each definition given for the word root. In which subject area would you be likely to use each definition?

_____

_____

Hint Think about how the word is used in the sentence. What context clues help you choose the correct definition? For Part B, consider each subject you study in school and how you might use the word *root* in that subject.

2 Read all parts of the question before responding.

Part A

What are the **two** central ideas of the passage?

A. Plant and animal invaders may sound like science fiction, but they are real.

B. Invasive species can enter the United States intentionally or by accident.

C. Nonnative species can harm an ecosystem, damage property, and harm people.

D. Invasive species can cost millions of dollars in repair and management costs.

Part B

Summarize how the author develops the first main idea you chose in Part A.

_____

_____

_____

_____

Part C

Summarize how the author develops the second main idea you chose in Part A.

_____

_____

_____

_____

Hint Consider each idea separately before choosing the two central ideas. Ask if each idea is supported by textual evidence in the passage.

3 In the passage, which event reflects the spread of kudzu in the South?

A. In 1876, an ornamental plant from Japan was displayed at the Philadelphia Centennial Exposition.

B. The climbing vine had broad green leaves and fragrant purple flowers.

C. At first, the plant seemed to be harmless.

D. In the mid-1930s to early 1950s, southern farmers were even encouraged to plant it for erosion control.

Hint Ask yourself how and why kudzu was introduced in the South to connect key ideas in the text.

4 The following question has two parts. First, answer Part A. Then, answer Part B.

Part A

Which of the author's claims lacks evidence?

A. Plant and animal invaders may sound like science fiction, but they are real.

B. Invasive species can enter the United States intentionally or by accident.

C. Nonnative species can harm an ecosystem, damage property, and harm people.

D. Invasive species can cost millions of dollars in repair and management costs.

Part B

Which of the claims in Part A has sufficient evidence to support it? Cite textual evidence to support your answer.

_____

_____

_____

_____

Use the Reading Guide to help you understand the passage.

Invader Alert

Reading Guide

What have you learned about ecosystems that would explain the effects of losing one species in an ecosystem? How does this help you understand what might happen if a nonnative species is introduced?

Based on the introductory paragraphs, what are the two central ideas the author will develop?

In paragraph 4, which central idea is being supported?

You have probably learned that the loss of even one species can have devastating effects on an ecosystem. Have you ever wondered, though, what happens if a species is introduced to an ecosystem? Fortunately, most nonnative species have little or no impact. If a nonnative species lacks competitors or predators, however, it becomes invasive and spreads quickly. It can crowd out native species and cause environmental problems. It can also cost millions of dollars a year to keep the invasive species in check and even more to help a damaged ecosystem recover.

So what is being done about invasive species, and how should you help? The U.S. government works with state governments, agencies, and environmental groups to stem the spread of invaders. Here are a few examples of invasive species and how you can help.

In the Water

Southern catfish farmers brought Asian carp to the United States to help keep their ponds clear of algae. The carp weren't a problem until they escaped into the Mississippi River during floods. Ever since, the carp have been swimming north, entering other river systems and devouring algae that native fish and water creatures rely on. The invasive carp can grow to four feet in length and weigh as much as a hundred pounds. Without a natural predator, the carp population continues to grow. In addition, the destructive fish harm property and boaters when they leap out of the water and land in their boats.

To keep the carp from reaching the Great Lakes, a system of electric barriers was built in 2002. So far, $200 million have been spent trying to contain the fish. Today, the barriers are being reinforced, and a mobile system is being designed to assist in emergency situations. Other controls, such as netting, hydrologic solutions, and chemical controls are also being explored.

Which invasive species was introduced to the United States by accident? Which was introduced intentionally?

How does the author organize the text in each section? How does this reinforce the central ideas?

What is the author's point of view concerning invasive species?

These controls won't make a difference if you don't help. When fishing or boating, don't transfer species from one body of water to another. This includes cleaning boats and dumping water that might be left in boat wells and bait buckets. Eggs and larvae of invasive species that you can't see may be in the water. In fact, recreational boats are responsible for the spread of another invasive species, zebra mussels. Zebra mussels cling to the hulls of recreational boats that visit the Great Lakes. When the boats go to another lake without being cleaned, the species is introduced to the new lake.

On the Land

Kudzu is a Japanese vine brought to the United States for the centennial in 1876. The plant wasn't a problem until southern farmers were encouraged to plant it in the 1930s as forage for grazing livestock. The weather and soil conditions suited kudzu. Soon the plant was growing up to a foot a day, covering plants and buildings in its path. The vines destroy crops and timber resources and topple trees and buildings with their weight. Vines grow to be a hundred feet long with some roots reaching an amazing twelve feet into the ground. To make matters worse, new roots can sprout along a vine to start a new plant.

In 1953, kudzu was removed from the list of permissible plants by the U.S. government. In spite of this, kudzu continues to spread. It is estimated that kudzu covers seven million acres of land and costs utility companies $1.5 million a year just to remove it from power lines. To rid an area of kudzu, the vine is cut at the base, and all parts of the plant are destroyed. Areas must be continually mowed to prevent growth. Chemical herbicides and burning help destroy roots, but it can still take several years to reclaim land from kudzu.

You can help by planting only native species in your yard. If you do find and remove an invasive species, destroy all plant parts or bag the plant and dispose of it properly. Some plants, such as kudzu, have been transported hundreds of miles in fill dirt that contained plant roots or seeds. Wherever you go, make sure you don't take an invader with you or bring one home. Clean the soles of your shoes and wash your clothing to ensure that seeds and plant parts don't travel with you.

Reading Guide

Was the introduction of the python to the Everglades intentional or accidental? Explain your reasoning.

What is the purpose of Python Patrol?

How does the law invoked by the Florida Legislature attempt to stem the spread of invasive species?

At Home

Today, the Florida Everglades has a new predator that threatens its delicate balance of nature. This predator is the Burmese python, a snake that grows to an astonishing twenty-six feet. Originally purchased as pets, the snakes either escaped from pet owners or were intentionally released when they got too big. The pythons eat birds and mammals that are prey for other Everglades species. Some pythons even attack and eat alligators.

To fight the problem, The Nature Conservancy in Florida started Python Patrol. Python Patrol has two hundred responders throughout the state who will come to the aid of citizens who spot a python. In addition, the Florida Legislature banned the ownership of eight reptiles in 2010, including the Burmese python. These reptiles are classified as conditional species. This means people owning these reptiles before the 2010 law went into effect can keep the animals if they microchip and cage the reptiles properly.

You can help by being a responsible pet owner. If you can no longer care for an exotic pet, contact a pet store or veterinarian to learn how to find a new owner for the pet. This includes tropical fish, snakes, lizards, spiders, and other animal species.

The solution to invasive species begins with you. Read the latest news about invaders in your state. Become knowledgeable about the problems they pose and how you can help. Find out what plants, insects, or animals you should watch for and what to do if you spot an invasive species. Remember, you may be the first line of defense in stopping an invader.

Answer the following questions.

1 Read all parts of the question before responding.

Part A

Read this sentence from the passage.

> **Have you ever wondered, though, what happens if a species is <u>introduced</u> to an ecosystem?**

Which definition **best** defines the academic vocabulary word <u>introduced</u> as it is used in the sentence?

A. brought into practice or use

B. caused to become acquainted

C. led or brought into a place

D. brought in knowledge of something

Part B

Which sentence most closely matches the definition for <u>introduced</u> you chose in Part A?

A. Although they were introduced to miners during the Gold Rush, Levi Strauss didn't patent his "blue jeans" until 1873.

B. Many flu viruses have been introduced to the United States by international travelers.

C. The new teacher walked into the classroom and introduced himself to each of the students.

D. The coach introduced a series of drills to help us improve our passing game.

2 Which **two** central ideas are developed in the passage?

A. What happens when an ecosystem loses a species?

B. What is being done to stop invasive species?

C. How are invasive species introduced to an ecosystem?

D. How can you help stop invasive species?

3 Read the following sentences from the passage and the questions that follow.

> In addition, the Florida Legislature banned the ownership of eight reptiles in 2010, including the Burmese python. These reptiles are classified as conditional species. This means people owning these reptiles before the 2010 law went into effect can keep the animals if they microchip and cage the reptiles properly.

Part A

Which central idea from the passage is supported by the sentences?

_____

_____

Part B

Using details from the text, what can you infer about the requirements for pet owners allowed to keep reptiles purchased before the 2010 law was enacted?

_____

_____

_____

Answer the following questions about both passages in this lesson.

4 For both passages, consider each author's point of view. Explain how the authors convey their points of view to readers. Cite textual evidence to support your answer.

_____

_____

_____

_____

5 Read all parts of the question before responding.

Part A

Write a brief summary of "Invaders among Us."

_____

_____

_____

_____

_____

_____

_____

_____

Part B

What information would you add from "Invader Alert" to create a summary that would suffice for both passages?

_____

_____

_____

_____

_____

_____

6 You have read two passages about invasive species. Compare and contrast the passages to explain how emphasizing different evidence or presenting different interpretations of the facts advances the presentation of key information.

Cite evidence from each passage to support your reasoning.

Write your response on the lines below.

_____

_____

_____

_____

_____

_____

_____

_____

_____

_____

_____

_____

_____

_____

_____

_____

_____

_____

RL.7.1, RL.7.3, RL.7.9, RI.7.2, RI.7.9, L.7.5.b

Analyze Texts Across Genres

① GETTING THE IDEA

Authors may present information about a single topic in many different ways. Think about the topic of ice skating. One author may write a how-to instruction guide with strategies for learning how to ice skate. Another author may write a realistic fiction story about a girl who is trying out for an Olympic figure skating team.

Fiction vs. Nonfiction

You already know that fiction can be completely made up, while nonfiction presents facts about the world. But fiction and nonfiction also have certain features in common.

Fiction	Both	Nonfiction
• tells a story that is completely or partly made up by the author • includes characters, setting, and plot events • uses dialogue, description, and pacing to enhance the text	• may present information in the form of a story • are told from a particular point of view • can include scientific or historical facts	• gives facts about a topic • may be broken into sections separated by headings • includes graphic features such as diagrams, charts, and graphs

Sometimes, authors use facts about historical events and scientific concepts in fiction stories. But then they also include additional details, characters, and events that are made up. Writers of fiction may also embellish, or exaggerate, details about real events or concepts to make a story more interesting.

The following types of texts include elements of both fiction and nonfiction.

- **Nonfiction narratives** may seem more like fiction stories than informational text, but they are nonfiction because they give facts about real people and events. Authors use dialogue and plot devices like suspense and conflict to make the information read like a story.

- **Science fiction** may include real-life details about science and technology, but it also portrays situations that are not real. Many science fiction stories take place in the future or in space and include monsterlike characters or characters with special powers, such as the ability to fly or travel through time.

- **Historical fiction** tells a story based on a real event from the past, or set in a real time or place from the past. It may include real events or real people like you would read about in a historical text. The made-up details and the embellishments authors add to the facts are what separate it from a historical text. For example, an author may portray factual details about a real event from a made-up character's point of view. Or an author may create an imagined conversation between two real people who were involved in a historical event.

Organization

Nonfiction and fiction texts may be organized, or structured, differently.

In fiction texts, authors use organization to develop the plot.

- Fiction stories often include exposition, rising action, a climax, falling action, and a resolution.

- Stories and plays are generally broken into sections, or chapters, acts, and scenes, with each one building on earlier sections to move the plot toward a conclusion.

- Fiction is often told in chronological, or time, order. But sometimes, authors employ techniques like **flashback**, in which characters remember earlier events.

In nonfiction texts, authors use organization to develop a main idea.

- Nonfiction texts often include a main idea, or several main ideas, that are backed up by supporting details, reasons, and evidence.

- Authors may use different structures, such as chronological order, compare and contrast, cause and effect, or whole to part, to present ideas and explain how they relate.

- Shorter nonfiction texts may be broken up into sections with subtitles or headings, and longer nonfiction texts may be broken up into chapters.

Analyze Texts

When you compare two related texts, pay close attention to the details of each text. Notice how the author of a fictional story may add to or change the facts presented in an informational text.

Now, read each passage below. One is historical fiction and the other is nonfiction. Compare and contrast the topics, writing style, points of view, and people involved in both. Underline any elements that are similar.

A Near Disaster

We continue to face new obstacles each day along this never-ending journey. Mother Nature tests our spirits and our courage every chance she gets. Tonight, she drew in her breath and released it so fiercely that our boat nearly sunk under its might. As usual, my water-fearing husband sunk into a delirious state of panic. I watched in embarrassment as he sunk to his knees and cried out to the heavens. On the shore, the two Americans were waving frantically and rapidly firing off gunshots. *Those two are no better*, I thought. *Did the squall carry these men's senses away with it?* One looked like he was about to jump in the frigid water and swim to us. Before he could take such drastic measures, I reached over the edge of the boat and gathered up their supplies and tools. Once again, I saved their mission.

Sacagawea Saves the Day

Over the course of their expedition, Lewis and Clark encountered challenges such as rough terrain, wild animals, and harsh weather conditions. Their fortitude was consistently put to the test. May 14, 1805 was no exception. On that day, their boats were hit by a sudden storm, and many of their most important supplies fell into the water. They watched in horror from the shore as their equipment bobbed along the rough waves. Lewis considered jumping into the water, but the boat was at least three hundred yards away and the water was freezing and rough from the storm. Even the crew of the boat was in a panic. Charbonneau, the French-Canadian man in charge of steering the boat, didn't even know how to swim. Thankfully for Lewis and Clark, Charbonneau's wife, Sacagawea, remained calm through the ordeal. Two days later, Lewis wrote in his journal that "The Indian woman, to whom I ascribe equal fortitude and resolution with any person on board at the time of the accident, caught and preserved most of the light articles which were washed overboard." It if wasn't for Sacagawea's calm resolve and quick thinking, Lewis and Clark would have watched their efforts sink before their eyes.

Now let's compare and contrast the two passages.

	"A Near Disaster"	"Sacagawea Saves the Day"
Topic	an incident that occurred during the Lewis and Clark expedition	
Type of Text	historical fiction	nonfiction
Point of View	first person	third person
Facts/Details Included	• made-up details that show how Sacagawea felt about the actions of her husband and Lewis and Clark • made-up details to claim that Sacagawea thought she saved Lewis and Clark's mission	• facts about the events of May 14, 1805 • an actual quote from Lewis's journal

The two passages both address a real historical event from May 14, 1805. However, one includes only facts, while the other includes made-up details and character thoughts that were created by the author. "A Near Disaster" is a fictional portrayal of the same events in "Sacagawea Saves the Day." The author embellishes the details and includes thoughts from Sacagawea that were made up to enhance the story. No one can know for sure what Sacagawea was thinking that day.

Language Spotlight • Synonyms and Antonyms

Remember that synonyms and antonyms can help you understand the meaning of words. **Synonyms** are words with almost the same meaning, and **antonyms** are words with opposite meanings.

Read the paragraph below. Underline two synonyms and circle two antonyms for the word in italics.

Their *fortitude* was consistently put to the test. But only the weak would give up without a courageous fight. They were determined not to be remembered as feeble quitters who cowered under the pressure, but rather as the brave explorers they saw themselves to be.

How do the words you circled and underlined help you understand the meaning of *fortitude*?

Read the passage.

The Mysterious Mind of Filippo

The locals in Rome surround me and Pippo as we work at the sites of the ancient ruins. They speak in <u>hushed</u> tones, wondering about our mysterious presence. Many suspect us of practicing geomancy,[1] while others call us treasure hunters. They watch as our crews cart away piles of rubble and create fantastical stories about what we plan to do with it.

Most other visitors to Rome avoid the ruins. With their heads buried deep in *Mirabilia Urbis Romae* (The Wonders of Rome), they tour all the recommended holy sites and stay far from those considered less sacred. So, it's no wonder that Pippo and I have drawn attention to ourselves.

The locals would likely be surprised to know that I am just as unaware of our intentions as they are. My friend, the master goldsmith Filippo Brunelleschi, is not a man to be questioned. If Pippo says, "Let's go to the Pantheon this morning," then we go to the Pantheon. He scribbles frantically on his parchment, but it looks like nonsense to me—secret codes and forbidden Arabic numerals all amounting to a bunch of gibberish. Never have I met a more <u>paranoid</u> fellow. Certainly, I have my own faults, and perhaps that is why our friendship is successful. Most Florentines refuse to deal with either one of us. Part of our incentive to travel to Rome was to get away from Florence and the mistreatment we received there. The magistrates wrongly pointed their fingers in my direction for an offense I did not commit, and Filippo was just as severely wronged by the judges who chose Lorenzo over him. Sure, both he and Lorenzo are brilliant sculptors, but it was Lorenzo's camaraderie with the judges that unfairly bestowed him the commission for the doors. Not surprisingly, Pippo refused to <u>fraternize</u> with the judges and was shunned because of his stubbornness.

But Rome has allowed us to live like kings. No one orders us around or insults our talents, and we can eat, drink, and dress however we please.

Unfortunately, these carefree conditions cannot last forever. Pippo travels back and forth to Florence, and I can see that the allure of home is pulling him away from Rome. Proving his mettle in Rome is worthless to him. He would much rather demonstrate his worth to his own townspeople. Despite his stubborn arrogance, it is obvious that he seeks their approval.

[1] **geomancy**: the practice of trying to predict the future by interpreting patterns of rocks or pieces of earth that are thrown to the ground

Before Pippo sets off for a long stay in Florence, I have to address my curiosity.

"I can see the cogs spinning in your head, Pippo. What is it you plan to do at home? Are you going to convince the city to hold another competition; that you should be the one to finish the Baptistery doors?"

"No, Donatello. Don't be so presumptuous as to assume that I still care about that fixed contest. I can see beyond bronze doors to something much larger and grander, indeed. "

"Which is. . . ?"

"The city has announced a new competition and placed a call for models and designs for the cathedral's dome. Imagine how the Pantheon dome must have looked in all its glory. That same glory will be awarded to me when I prove I can design the most extraordinary dome for the Santa Maria del Fiore. I finally figured it out, my friend, and I am sure even you won't believe me. An egg can sit on its broken shell, without centering. Besides, there's not enough lumber to create the necessary centering, anyway."

I confusedly shake my head and look at him with puzzlement. "You're right; I cannot believe you because I do not understand you. It is as if you speak in a foreign tongue."

"Don't worry, my friend, you will be a believer soon and so will everyone else. Once I demonstrate my model, it will make absolute sense. And then no one will question who should win this competition. One day my dome will rise up into the sky above Florence and the name Brunelleschi will be synonymous with genius.

Answer the following questions.

1 Explain how the point of view in the passage affects what readers learn about Filippo's personality. Use details from the passage to support your response.

Hint Pay attention to details in the passage that show the thoughts and feelings of the narrator. What does the narrator say about Filippo that gives information about his personality? Is this information necessarily true, or is it merely the opinion of the narrator?

2 How can you tell that this passage is historical fiction? Choose **all** that apply.

    A. It includes real people from history.

    B. The passage is told from first-person point of view.

    C. The events are set in the future.

    D. The author included made-up details.

    E. The passage does not have subheadings.

Hint Look back at the characteristics of historical fiction. What elements of historical fiction does this passage include?

3 Read the sentence in each choice. Then, match the underlined word in the sentence to its closest synonym on the right.

A. They speak in <u>hushed</u> tones, wondering about our mysterious presence.	**1.** socialize
B. Never have I met a more <u>paranoid</u> fellow.	**2.** strange
C. Not surprisingly, Pippo refused to <u>fraternize</u> with the judges and was shunned because of his stubbornness.	**3.** quiet
	4. rude
D. "Don't be so <u>presumptuous</u> as to assume that I still care about that fixed contest."	**5.** suspicious
	6. outrageous

Hint Read each choice carefully and use context clues to help you identify the underlined word's meaning. Then, look for the word on the right that has a similar meaning.

4 The following question has two parts. First, answer Part A. Then, answer Part B.

Part A

What does Filippo intend to do back at home in Florence?

A. ask the city to reconsider the competition for the Baptistery doors

B. tell the townspeople about his time studying the ruins in Rome

C. design a model for the cathedral's dome

D. build a new cathedral

Part B

Which sentence from the passage best reveals Filippo's motivations in relation to your choice in Part A?

A. My friend, the master goldsmith Filippo Brunelleschi, is not a man to be questioned.

B. Pippo travels back and forth to Florence, and I can see that the allure of home is pulling him away from Rome.

C. "Don't be so presumptuous as to assume that I still care about that fixed contest."

D. "That same glory will be awarded to me when I prove I can design the most extraordinary dome for the Santa Maria del Fiore."

> **Hint** For Part A, look back at the section of the passage in which Donatello questions Filippo about his return to Florence. After you find what Filippo plans to do in Florence, continue rereading the conversation to discover the reason why he has this goal. This will help you make the correct choice in Part B.

Use the Reading Guide to help you understand the passage.

The First Engineer

Reading Guide

What kind of text is this passage? How can you tell?

Why do some people suggest that Brunelleschi's reaction to the competition resulted in a career change?

Notice how the author clarifies information in paragraph 4 by saying "according to some accounts." Why might the author include this clarification?

For centuries, visitors to Florence, Italy, have marveled at the dome atop the Cathedral of Santa Maria del Fiore. The magnificent egg-shaped dome was the largest in the world at the time it was built, and it was created without any scaffolding. The man who designed the dome, Filippo Brunelleschi, is often considered the first modern engineer. Many people admire him as an artist and problem solver who made tremendous contributions to the fields of art and architecture.

Brunelleschi was born in Florence in 1377, as the second son of a wealthy Florentine notary. Even though his father wanted him to also become a notary, Brunelleschi had other goals. From an early age, he showed an innate ability to solve mechanical problems. His father allowed him to apprentice under a goldsmith named Benincasa Lotti. At the time, goldsmiths were well-respected artists with a wide array of skills, such as setting stones, engraving silver, decorating with goldleaf, and sculpting. Many great artists from Florence began their careers learning from goldsmiths. Two other great artisans, Lorenzo Ghiberti and Donatello, also studied with Benincasa Lotti.

Under Lotti's tutelage, Brunelleschi became skilled at mounting gems, engraving silver, and embossing metals. By the age of twenty-one, Brunelleschi was considered to be a master goldsmith. Then, in 1401, he entered a competition to work on the bronze doors for the Florence Baptistery. His competitors included Lorenzo Ghiberti and five other sculptors. Ultimately, Lorenzo won the assignment.

According to some accounts from the time, Brunelleschi was so angered over how the competition was handled that he left the city of Florence because of it. Some people even point to the lost competition as the reason for Brunelleschi's career changes. It was around this time that Brunelleschi transitioned from sculpting to focus more on architecture.

In the years after the competition, Brunelleschi spent time in Rome studying the ancient ruins. He began his travels with his friend Donatello, and the two became known as "treasure hunters" because of how they explored and excavated the ruins. Yet even Donatello was not fully aware of Brunelleschi's intentions. Brunelleschi surveyed the ancient architecture and made encrypted notes.

What is linear perspective? Why was Brunelleschi's discovery of it called a rediscovery?

The author describes the experiment Brunelleschi conducted. Try to picture his actions in your mind to better understand his demonstration.

Why might artists want their paintings to appear more lifelike?

How was Brunelleschi's model for the dome different than other competitors'?

Some historians theorize that it was Brunelleschi's attempts at drawing the ancient ruins that led him to his greatest discovery. That discovery was actually the rediscovery of linear perspective. Although the concept was used by the Greeks and Romans, the mathematical laws behind it had been lost. Brunelleschi was the one to figure them out again and demonstrate them in an experiment.

With linear perspective, an image on paper can represent a three-dimensional object in a way that looks real. The image can appear to have the same proportions, size, and distance as an actual object. Brunelleschi demonstrated this concept by painting a picture of the Baptistery using linear perspective. He put a hole in the picture and then held the painting up, facing away from his face. In front of him, he also held up a mirror. He looked through the hole in the picture and into the mirror. As he stood facing the Baptistery, the picture he saw in the mirror looked the same as the building in front of him. The experiment showed that linear perspective could create a realistic three-dimensional image.

For future artists, this was a monumental discovery. Painters could use the principles to create buildings and human figures that looked more lifelike. The technique would become even more widespread after another Florentine, Leon Battista Alberti, published detailed instructions about it years later.

Despite the success of Brunelleschi's experiment, he was intent on larger goals. In August 1418, the city of Florence announced another competition. Work on the Cathedral of Santa Maria del Fiore had begun a century before, but the building still remained uncompleted. The city sought models and designs for the cathedral's dome, and Brunelleschi was determined to create the winning model.

Reading Guide

Why was the hoist Brunelleschi invented considered an important discovery?

Pay attention to the details the author provides about the creation of the dome. What do these details reveal about the dome's size?

What honor did Brunelleschi receive after his death?

What is the significance of the inscription on Brunelleschi's tombstone? How does this inscription relate to other details from this passage about Brunelleschi's contributions as an artist and architect?

To demonstrate his plans for the dome, Brunelleschi created a model that was the size of a small building. All the other competitors designed elaborate support framework for the dome. But Brunelleschi's plans were revolutionary. He planned to create an inner dome and then place an egg-shaped dome on top of it. Some people viewed his ideas as impossible and even dismissed him as crazy. But, over time, he proved his plan had merit, and he was eventually awarded the assignment.

More than three hundred men worked on the dome, in some capacity. One of the greatest challenges of the dome's construction was how to transport large building materials hundreds of feet off the ground. To solve this problem, Brunelleschi invented a hoist, which was unlike any machine already in existence. Powered by oxen, the hoist was responsible for lifting over 70 million pounds of materials used to build the dome.

In 1436, the dome was finally completed. And ten years later, Brunelleschi was buried within the cathedral after his death, an honor normally reserved for dignitaries. The inscription on his tomb reads: "Here lies the body of the great ingenious man Filippo Brunelleschi of Florence."

Answer the following questions.

1 Read each event from the passage on the left. Then, match it to an event on the right that happened as a result.

A. Brunelleschi was angered over the competition for the Baptistery doors.

1. Brunelleschi created a revolutionary plan for the cathedral's dome.

2. Brunelleschi left Florence.

B. Brunelleschi and Donatello studied the ancient ruins in Rome.

3. Artists credited Brunelleschi with developing a technique for more realistic paintings.

C. Brunelleschi rediscovered linear perspective.

4. Over 70 million pounds of materials were moved.

D. Brunelleschi invented a hoist to lift heavy building materials.

5. Brunelleschi and Donatello were called "treasure hunters."

2 Read the following sentence from the passage.

> **All the other competitors designed <u>elaborate</u> support framework for the dome.**

Which words are antonyms of the word <u>elaborate</u>? Choose **all** that apply.

A. fancy

B. complicated

C. detailed

D. simple

E. expensive

F. basic

Answer the following questions about both passages in this lesson.

3 Compare and contrast how each passage describes the competition for work on the Baptistery doors. How does the author of "The Mysterious Mind of Filippo" add details to the historical facts?

_____

_____

_____

_____

_____

_____

_____

4 What conclusion can you make based on your reading of "The Mysterious Mind of Filippo" and "The First Engineer"?

A. Brunelleschi did not have many friends.

B. Brunelleschi's ideas were not always understood by others.

C. The city of Florence chose Brunelleschi's design for the cathedral.

D. Linear perspective is still used in art today.

5 The following question has two parts. First, answer Part A. Then, answer Part B.

Part A

Read the sentence from "The Mysterious Mind of Filippo."

> **"One day my dome will rise up into the sky above Florence and the name Brunelleschi will be synonymous with genius."**

What sentence from "The First Engineer" **best** supports the idea that Brunelleschi was later considered a genius?

A. Many people admire him as an artist and problem solver who made tremendous contributions to the fields of art and architecture.

B. Under Lotti's tutelage, Brunelleschi became skilled at mounting gems, engraving silver, and embossing metals.

C. Despite the success of Brunelleschi's experiment, he was intent on larger goals.

D. But, over time, he proved his plan had merit, and he was eventually awarded the assignment.

Part B

Write two supporting details from the "The First Engineer" that explain why Brunelleschi was labeled a genius by future artists and architects.

_____

_____

_____

_____

_____

6 Compare and contrast how information about Brunelleschi's life and work was presented in "The Mysterious Mind of Filippo" and "The First Engineer." How does the author of the fiction passage include details that use or alter history? Be sure to address details about characters, setting, and events. Use textual evidence from each passage to support your response.

Write your response on the lines below.

Read the passage.

The Strange Abilities of Water

Can water remember the chemicals that have been dissolved in it? Can it store and pass along this information? The answer may surprise you. Scientists have been studying water for many years. They have noticed that water may have the ability to do some amazing things.

An Amazing (But Not-So-New) Discovery

In 1988, scientist Jacques Benveniste published a controversial article in the science journal *Nature*. Benveniste observed that blood cells seemed to be able to detect molecules no longer present in a solution. He diluted a liquid containing a chemical. The liquid was so watered down that there was no way any of the original chemical was left in the liquid. Yet when exposed to the dilute liquid, the blood cells behaved as though the chemical was still present. Clearly, something amazing had taken place. The liquid seemed to remember what was once dissolved in it.

Today, some people accept Benveniste's research, while others don't. Many scientists doubt there is a rational explanation for his results. However, nonscientists are more open-minded. For example, practitioners of a form of alternative medicine called homeopathy have believed for a long time that water has memory. In 1796, Samuel Hahnemann, the founder of homeopathy, recognized that large doses of medicines could be harmful. Instead of giving these medicines to patients, he diluted them first, adding more and more water until only an infinitesimal amount of medicine remained. He then tested it on patients and saw that over time, their symptoms disappeared.

Homeopathic medicine is based on the idea that "like cures like." In other words, a chemical that causes symptoms similar to a disease can cure that disease if tiny quantities are used. Adding extremely large amounts of water dilutes the chemical greatly. Dilute it enough and the solution will no longer contain the chemical that made it active. This makes the medicine as safe as water, but patients find the new medicine to be as effective as traditional treatments. Of course, because the medicine is not present, it cannot cause side effects. And because a small amount of medicine can be greatly diluted, homeopathic medicines are much less expensive than medicines prescribed by traditional physicians.

Serial Dilution: Watering Down the Memory-Maker

The method Hahnemann used to reduce the amount of medicine dissolved in water is known as serial dilution. The process is quite straightforward, as shown in the steps below.

Step 1: A series of containers are set up and labeled. Ninety-nine milliliters of water are placed into each container.

Step 2: One milliliter of the medicine is added to the first container. It now contains one part medicine and ninety-nine parts water.

Step 3: The contents of the container are mixed vigorously. Homeopaths think that this violent shaking causes the medicine to affect the structure of the water molecules around them.

Step 4: One milliliter of this well-mixed solution is added to the second container, which contains 99 milliliters of pure water. Mixed together, the resulting solution is much weaker than the first. For every 10,000 molecules in the container, only one is likely to be the medicine. However, according to homeopaths, the medicine is still effective. They think that the shaking causes the water molecules to share information about the shape of the original medicine. That information is passed from water molecule to water molecule.

Step 5: Now 1 milliliter of the weak solution made in step 4 is added to a new container containing 99 milliliters of water. Again, it is mixed vigorously. Now 999,999 out of a million of the molecules in the container are water, and only one in a million are medicine.

Step 6: This dilution continues. After the next container in the series is mixed, only one molecule in one hundred million will be the original medicine.

By the end of the process, the chances of finding any medicine are tiny. In fact, mathematically speaking, there is no chance that any of the original medicine will be in the last, most dilute container.

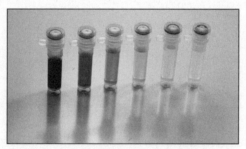

A serial dilution of dye. Notice how the darkness of the liquid in the containers changes dramatically during the series of dilutions.

The Watery Road Ahead

Benveniste and other scientists have found that the structure of water is much more complicated than previously thought. It is not surprising then, that we are continuing to learn more about water's ability to remember chemicals that are no longer present. A recent video clip from a university in Germany shows that water seems to remember information about flowers that have been placed in it. The structure of water droplets viewed under a microscope differs depending on which flower has been placed in the water.

This same video shows that photographs of the structure of water droplets differ, too. The structure differs, depending on which student takes the photo. This is more evidence that data is being stored by the water. Perhaps each of us is passing information along to the water close to us. If so, think of all the information water contains. It could be that the medicines we need have been with us all along.

Answer the questions.

1 This question has two parts. First, answer Part A. Then, answer Part B.

Part A

Which **two** statements are central ideas of the passage?

A. Water has been found to store information about the molecules dissolved in it.

B. Scientists are unwilling to accept results they do not yet understand.

C. Serial dilution is a key technique used in testing and applying water's ability to remember information.

D. Hahnemann's medical preparations would benefit the health of the public.

E. Benveniste's research was controversial.

F. Water has been shown to remember information about flowers.

Part B

Choose one of the central ideas you identified in Part A. Cite two pieces of text evidence that support the idea.

_____

_____

_____

2 The following question has two parts. First, answer Part A. Then, answer Part B.

Part A

Which sentence from the passage states a generalization?

A. Clearly, something amazing had taken place.

B. The liquid seemed to remember what was once dissolved in it.

C. However, nonscientists are more open-minded.

D Today, some people accept Benveniste's research, while others don't.

Part B

What does the generalization you chose in Part A indicate?

A. The author supports the idea that water can remember information.

B. The author rejects the idea that water can remember information.

C. The author thinks more testing needs to be done.

D. The author believes that scientists are difficult to work with.

3 Which excerpt from the passage does the photograph on page 149 **best** illustrate?

A. Adding extremely large amounts of water dilutes the chemical greatly.

B This is more evidence that data is being stored by the water.

C. The liquid seemed to remember what was once dissolved in it.

D. In fact, mathematically speaking, there is no chance that any of the original medicine will be in the last, most dilute container.

4 This question has two parts. First, answer Part A. Then, answer Part B.

Part A

Circle **two** text structures the author uses to organize the passage.

Text Structures	sequence
	part-to-whole
	compare and contrast
	whole-to-part
	spatial

Part B

Choose one structure you circled in Part A and describe how the author organized the text to reflect that structure. How does the structure help the reader better understand the text? Cite textual evidence to support your answer.

_____

_____

_____

_____

_____

_____

_____

_____

5 Some of the steps in creating a serial dilution are shown in the box.

> **Add one milliliter of medicine to a new container of water.**
>
> **Set up and label containers.**
>
> **Dilution series is complete.**
>
> **Add one milliliter of dilute medicine to the container of water.**
>
> **Test solution: Is it weak enough?**

Complete the flowchart by writing each step in the appropriate shape in the chart.

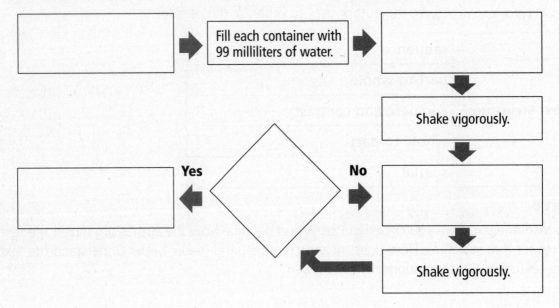

Fill each container with 99 milliliters of water.

Shake vigorously.

Yes   No

Shake vigorously.

Does Water Have Memory?

What does a magician have in common with a chemist and a magazine editor? In the case of magician James Randi and scientists analyzing a controversial scientific paper, the answer is <u>skepticism</u>.

The paper in question was a 1988 article published by a popular and well-regarded scientist in the prestigious journal *Nature*. The author, Jacques Benveniste, observed that extremely weak solutions of an antibody molecule were recognized by white blood cells. However, the solutions were so <u>diluted</u>, or watered down, that no antibodies were present. According to Benveniste, this observation suggested that the water was remembering the molecules that had been dissolved in it. Furthermore, the observation gave support to the idea of homeopathy, an alternative medicine that uses extremely dilute substances to treat illness.

Confirming the Results

Repeating an experiment is not unusual in the sciences. In fact, it is a key part of the scientific method. If a result is real, another scientist should be able to do the same experiment and get the same results. If the results differ, something is wrong.

With this in mind, scientists in Benveniste's lab repeated his procedure several times before publishing. Each time the scientists observed the same thing. Extremely dilute solutions—so dilute that they no longer contained the molecule being studied—were detected by white blood cells. Repeating the experiment seemed to show that Benveniste's results were accurate. It was time to publish. As this was an important result, they chose to share their news in an important journal.

Putting Science to the Test

But where does the magician come into this story? Illusionist James Randi is well known for revealing the tricks behind both magic acts and real-life scams. Like most scientists, Randi is a skeptic, someone who doubts conclusions until he has examined the evidence for himself. Randi, chemist Walter Stewart, and *Nature* editor John Maddox got together to analyze Benveniste's results for themselves.

The men knew it was possible that the scientists in Benveniste's laboratory had somehow influenced the results. There was an easy way to rule out this possibility. Randi and his team would run a blind experiment. The scientists from the first tests were replaced. The containers containing the solutions were covered and hidden in a different location. Then the tubes were identified with a code. They were brought into the lab at the start of the experiment and were covered in paper so that their contents could not be seen. The new scientists would use the exact same procedure as before. However, this time, they would not know which container was which.

Interestingly, the results differed this time. When the scientists could not tell the containers apart, there was no difference in the way the white blood cells behaved. This time, the very dilute solution seemed to "forget" what was once dissolved. It indicated that the water never had memories in the first place.

Controlling Bias

The results seen in this case are not unusual. If a scientist can distinguish between the samples in an experiment, the results may be biased. This is not the same thing as cheating, because this influence can happen without the scientist realizing it. For this reason, when new medications are being tested, neither the researchers doing the testing nor the patients receiving the drugs know exactly what they are getting. Some patients will get the drug being tested. Others will receive a placebo, a pill that looks the same as the drug, but which has no effect. If the patient and researcher are aware which pill is which, the results may be affected.

For instance, if the patient knew he was receiving a drug, he might decide he was feeling better, even if the drug was useless. However, if the patient thought he was receiving the drug, but was actually taking the placebo, he also might decide he was feeling better, even though the placebo is not a medicine. Likewise, if the researcher testing the drug knows which is which, he or she might accidentally say something to the patient to affect the results, or might skew the results based on the intended result. In each case, it would be difficult to figure out whether or not the drug being tested really works. Keeping an experiment blind prevents these biases from contaminating the results.

Can Water Remember?

Because Benveniste's results were discredited, scientists cannot say that water has memory. From what scientists currently understand about water, it does not seem possible that water could remember what was once dissolved in it. The fact that water travels from Earth's atmosphere to Earth and back again helps refute this idea. If water did have memories of chemicals no longer present, it might remember *everything* it contacted on its many journeys through the water cycle. This would include pleasant and not-so-pleasant things, from foods and fragrances to sewage and poisons. How would our bodies tell these many memories apart? That answer is even less clear.

Despite the scientific community's rejection of his ideas about water, Benveniste was undeterred. Until his death, he continued to promote the idea that water has memory. He started a business, claiming he had developed a way to convert the characteristics of water's memory into an electronic signal. That signal could be sent by e-mail and introduced into a new container of water. The water could be used as a homeopathic treatment. The software claiming to accomplish these tasks is available commercially, but has not been tested by scientists outside the company. Scientists may have more analyzing to do.

Answer the questions.

6 Which are logical purposes for why the author might have written "Does Water Have Memory?" Choose **all** that apply.

A. to explain why Benveniste's research might have been flawed

B. to inform about the similarities between illusionism and science

C. to persuade readers that it is important for scientists to follow the scientific method

D. to entertain readers with the idea that water has a memory

E. to inform readers about a new product based on Benveniste's research

F. to explain the difference between credible and invalid research

7 Match the words from the passage in the first column with their antonyms in the second column. Each word has only one antonym.

A. diluted	**1.** weak
	2. pure
B. skepticism	**3.** substitute
	4. medicine
C. placebo	**5.** trust

8 Which statement **best** describes why James Randi and his team analyzed Benveniste's research?

A. They wanted to test their own method of research.

B. They wanted to disprove Benveniste's results.

C. They wanted to make sure Benveniste's results had not been influenced in some way.

D. They wanted to have an article published in the science journal *Nature*.

9 The following question has two parts. First, answer Part A. Then, answer Part B.

Part A

Which is the **most** likely inference a reader might make about the authors of the two passages?

A. The authors are scientists who have experimented with water.

B. The authors disagree on the validity of homeopathic medicine.

C. The authors hold different points of view on the properties of water.

D. The authors have written for science journals.

Part B

Complete the chart with two details from each passage that support your answer to Part A.

"The Strange Abilities of Water"	
"Does Water Have Memory?"	

PERFORMANCE TASK

Both "The Strange Abilities of Water " and "Does Water Have Memory?" discuss Jacques Benveniste's research into the ability of water to remember. Write an essay that compares and contrasts how the two passages approach the topic. Consider the following when writing your response:

- How does the point of view of each passage affect the type of information presented?

- What discrepancies are evident within the information each passage presents? Are these discrepancies differences in facts or interpretation?

- Which passage do you consider more reliable? Explain your reasoning.

Remember to cite text evidence from each passage in your response.

Write your answer on the lines below.

STRAND

3

Writing

W.7.1.a–e, W.7.2.a–e, W.7.3.a, W.7.3.c, W.7.3.e, W.7.4, W.7.5, L.7.1.a

Writing Foundations

① GETTING THE IDEA --

You are often asked to produce different kinds of writing—narratives, reports, and arguments. Whatever the task, using the **writing process** will help you produce a complete, polished piece. The steps in the writing process include prewriting, drafting, revising, editing, and publishing.

Prewriting

Prewriting is the first step in the writing process. It starts with deciding on a topic. Try to choose a topic that isn't too broad or too narrow. For example, the topic "Winter Sports" is too broad because there are too many winter sports. "How to Carry a Snowboard" is too narrow because it could be covered in just a few sentences. However, the topic "Snowboarding" is neither too broad nor too narrow.

After selecting your topic, brainstorm subtopics related to it. A graphic organizer or an outline is a good way to organize your thoughts.

Snowboarding			
Clothing		**Equipment**	
jacket	helmet	board	boots
gloves	goggles	bindings	leash

Prewriting also includes deciding on your audience and purpose. In a test situation, your **audience** will probably be your teacher and your purpose will be to respond to a prompt. Here are some types of writing you might be asked to write.

Text Type	Definition	Language
narrative	describes an event or series of events, which may be true or made up	may be formal or informal
argument	used to influence readers to agree with a claim or to take action; often called persuasive writing	formal
informative/ explanatory	provides facts about real-life people and/or events, or explains how to do something	formal

Your audience and purpose help determine your style, language, and **word choice**. For example, a dialogue in a narrative may use **informal language**, but an argument or informational article requires **formal language**.

Organizing for a Narrative—The beginning of a narrative, sometimes called the **exposition**, introduces the story's **characters**, **setting**, and **conflict**. The bulk of the story is devoted to the **plot**, which includes rising action, climax, falling action, and resolution. The events work together to bring the story to a satisfactory conclusion.

- **rising action:** all the events that lead to the climax

- **climax:** the turning point of the story

- **falling action:** the result of the climax

- **resolution:** the point when the conflict is resolved or the goal is achieved

In writing a narrative, you need to decide from whose **point of view** to tell the story. Below are some narrative points of view from which to tell your story.

- **First-person narrators** use pronouns such as *I, me, my,* and *our*. Only story events that the narrator sees, is part of, or learns about can be included.

- **Third-person limited narrators** use pronouns such as *he, she,* and *they* for story characters. The events in the story, however, revolve around only one character whose actions and thoughts are revealed.

- **Third-person omniscient narrators** also use pronouns such as *he, she,* and *they* for story characters. The events, however, are described from a broader perspective that includes the actions and thoughts of all the story characters.

Organizing for an Argument and Informational Writing—Both arguments and informative writing need a strong introduction that clearly states the claim or main idea and previews what is to come. This is then supported by related reasons or topics, each in its own paragraph. Each paragraph should have its own topic sentence and supporting details. Try to anticipate objections to your claim and address them in a separate paragraph or as they occur.

Using index cards is one way to organize ideas. Write each topic or reason, and then list related details or evidence and counterclaims below it.

Topic 1: Clothing	Reason 1: Snowboarding is fun.
Jacket: not too loose, free arm movement	Good way to get outdoors and exercise in winter
Helmet: snug fit	Objection: too expensive
Gloves: sturdy with wide wrists	Counterclaim: can rent or borrow equipment
Snow pants or bib overalls: warmth	first time out
Goggles: cut glare, protect eyes	

Drafting

In the **drafting** step, you get your ideas down on paper. No one creates a polished piece of writing in the first draft. It's more important to get your ideas down on paper than it is to worry about mistakes.

Revising

Revising is the process of polishing, or improving, your writing. Look for more facts or details to add and places where transitions can help you connect ideas. Also look for repeated or unrelated information to delete. Check the order of your details or evidence to be sure they are arranged from most to least important.

Editing

Editing refers to correcting mistakes in spelling, grammar, usage, and mechanics. When time is short, you may need to combine the revising and editing processes. Use the following checklist to guide your revision.

☐ Does my response answer all parts of the prompt?

☐ Is my claim or main idea clear?

☐ Do I use enough relevant details to support my claim or main idea?

☐ Are my ideas presented in a logical order?

☐ Is my writing style appropriate for my task, purpose, and audience?

☐ Is my writing free of grammar, spelling, usage, and mechanics errors?

Publishing

Publishing is making a clean copy of your paper that incorporates the changes made while revising and editing. When you don't have time to rewrite your draft, be careful to follow your writing plan closely and to make your revisions clearly.

Language Spotlight • Clauses and Phrases

A **clause** is a group of words with a subject and verb. A **phrase** is a group of related words that does not contain both a subject and a verb. Using phrases and clauses will help you connect ideas and make your writing smoother.

	Function	Example
independent clause	tells a complete thought; can stand alone as a sentence	*The girls built a snowman.*
dependent clause	does not tell a complete thought; cannot stand alone as a sentence	*Although it was snowing,* everyone wanted to go.
phrase	shows a relationship between a noun or pronoun and another word in a sentence	The boys went *to the ice rink*.

On a separate piece of paper, write three sentences that include clauses and phrases. Then, discuss your sentences with a partner.

Read the passage.

On the Slopes—or Not?

"Are you ready to hit the slopes to snowboard for the first time, Jose?" Lola asked her friend.

Jose gave her a wry smile and asked, "Do I look ready?"

"Let's take a look at you," said Matt, "to be sure you have everything you need." Matt checked Jose's snow pants to be sure the elastic covered the top of his boots; Lola checked to see if his ski jacket was loose enough; and Jenna adjusted the strap on his helmet to be sure it fit snugly and wouldn't slide around.

Once outside, Matt showed Jose how to put one boot into the binding on the front of the snowboard and to use the other foot to push off, resulting in a skating motion. Jose practiced this movement for several minutes until he got the hang of it.

"I think I have, the idea," said Jose.

"Are you sure?" asked Matt, looking at Jose skeptically.

"Sure, I'm fine; you go ahead," said Jose brightly. "When I start tearing up those gnarly expert slopes with my amazing moves, I'll come find you."

"OK, see you later," said Lola.

Jose watched his friends board the chairlift, and his stomach churned and knotted up. "Now what?" Jose asked himself. He hadn't wanted to show his friends how nervous he was, but now that he was alone, he was starting to panic.

Jose looked around to see if there was anyone who could help. He decided to follow a group of little kids, figuring that they were beginners, and he could copy what they were doing. Unfortunately, they took off like cannonballs, looking just as professional as Jose's friends.

Looking around again, Jose spotted an area that seemed to have a gentle slope to it. Jose "skated" as well as he could to the spot and practiced gliding by lifting his free foot onto the tail of the snowboard, but it was useless; the board just stopped dead.

"You have to put pressure on your front foot as if you are stomping on a bug," called a man with two children in tow. The man demonstrated the motion as he moved his board smoothly across the snow to where Jose was standing awkwardly. After introducing himself as Herb Trotter, the man said he was taking his kids out on their snowboards for the first time to teach them the sport. Mr. Trotter then invited Jose to join them and learn how to snowboard, too. Grinning broadly, Jose enthusiastically accepted the invitation. After practicing skating and gliding on the gentle slope, Mr. Trotter said his students were ready for the chairlift and a slightly more challenging slope.

After successfully negotiating the chairlift, Jose felt ready to conquer the world—that is, until he stood at the top of the slope for his first descent. It looked like he was going down Mount Everest! Mr. Trotter smiled at the expression on Jose's face and reassured him that everyone felt that way on his first descent. Mr. Trotter helped Jose and his kids secure their bindings.

"Follow me," instructed Mr. Trotter, "and imitate my body movements exactly." The three of them did precisely what Mr. Trotter demonstrated; before Jose knew it, he was traversing the slope and he reached the bottom of the mountain without incident! Jose looked back at the slope he had just snowboarded and was amazed to see what he had accomplished. After making a few more runs with Mr. Trotter, Jose practiced by himself.

When Jose was too exhausted to make another run, he spotted Matt, Lola, and Jenna watching him snowboard from the bottom of the chairlift. They all high-fived, congratulating Jose on his progress.

Answer the following questions.

1 This question has two parts. First, answer Part A. Then, answer Part B.

Part A

What is the setting of "On the Slopes—or Not?"

A. Jose's backyard

C. a snowy playground

B. Trotter Mountain

D. a ski resort

Part B

Circle words in the passage that help identify the setting.

Hint Think about the surroundings and the objects in them that indicate where the story takes place.

2 The following question has two parts. First, answer Part A. Then, answer Part B.

Part A

From whose point of view is the story narrated?

A. in the first person from Jose's point of view

B. in the first person from Mr. Trotter's point of view

C. in the third-person limited from Jose's point of view

D. in the third-person omniscient from an outside observer's point of view

Part B

Explain why you chose your answer to Part A.

Write your answer on the lines below.

_____

_____

_____

_____

Hint What kinds of pronouns are used? Whose actions and thoughts are revealed? Which character do you get to know best?

3 The author wants to replace the underlined word in the following sentence with a more precise word or phrase.

> **Mr. Trotter smiled at the expression on Jose's face.**

Which precise word or phrase **best** replaces the underlined word?

A. frowned   C. laughed uncontrollably

B. giggled uproariously   D. chuckled

Hint Think about how an involved father might react in this situation. Which word or phrase has a meaning that shows this more clearly than the word *smiled*?

4 Write each of the following sentences under the story element to which it belongs.

A. They all high-fived, congratulating Jose on his progress.

B. He hadn't wanted to show his friends how nervous he was, but now that he was alone, he was starting to panic.

C. The three of them did precisely what Mr. Trotter demonstrated; before Jose knew it, he was traversing the slope and he reached the bottom of the mountain without incident!

D. He decided to follow a group of little kids, figuring that they were beginners and he could copy what they were doing.

Conflict:

_____

_____

Rising Action:

_____

_____

Climax:

_____

_____

Resolution:

_____

_____

Hint Think about the order of events. How does each one contribute to the satisfactory conclusion of the story?

Use the Reading Guide to help you understand the passage.

Snowboarding 101

Reading Guide

How is the information in this passage organized?

The author uses subheadings to divide the passage into smaller sections. What do the headings help you understand about the passage?

Snowboarding is a great activity for people of all ages, giving them a chance to get outdoors and get some exercise during those cold winter months. Having the right clothing and equipment, however, is critical to making the experience a dream come true instead of a nightmare.

In the Beginning . . .

Believe it or not, the first commercial snowboard started out as a kids' toy. In 1965, an innovative Michigan father bolted two kids' skis together in an effort to get his children outdoors in the winter. The father, Sherman Poppen, later added a rope to the front of the board for balance; his wife, Nancy, called the invention a Snurfer, combining the words *snow* and *surfer*. The new "toy" became an instant hit with kids in the neighborhood. Six months later, Poppen applied for and received a patent, and mass production of Snurfers began.

In 1972, Dimitrije Milovich began producing snowboards for adults, which were the first modern-day snowboards. Later, Milovich was instrumental in getting snowboarders accepted at ski resorts, which had previously banned them for insurance reasons.

Clothing

To really enjoy snowboarding, you need to be able to stay comfortable, warm, and dry for the entire day. Choose a jacket that isn't too loose, but make sure it allows for free arm movement. Elastic around the bottom of the jacket and knit cuffs on the sleeves will help prevent snow from getting inside your jacket. Snow pants or bib overalls will keep the bottom half of your body warm and dry.

There are specially designed snowboarding gloves, but any sturdy glove with a long, loose wrist will be adequate for beginning snowboarders. When choosing a crash helmet, be sure to pick one that can be adjusted to fit your head snugly; don't let it cover your eyes or slide around. Goggles cut down on glare and help protect your eyes from snow, wind, and airborne debris.

How are the details organized in the sections "Equipment" and "Starting Out"?

Why is it important to organize the details in this way?

How would a different organization make the comprehension more difficult?

Equipment

It is highly recommended that you visit a sports equipment store to get your snowboarding gear fitted by a trained, professional fitter. He or she will know how to identify your "lead," or controlling, foot—the one that goes into the binding at the front of the snowboard. The fitter can also identify a board that's the right length and width for you, depending on your height and weight. Consider getting a stomp pad, which is similar to a friction plate. Located above the back binding, it gives you a secure place to rest your foot while gliding.

Choose your boots before selecting your bindings; the boots should fit snugly without pinching or rubbing. Check to be sure that your foot doesn't slide around inside the boot; because if you can't control your foot inside the boot, you won't be able to control the snowboard. There are two kinds of bindings that you can choose to fit your boots: strap bindings and speed-entry bindings. Speed-entry bindings are, of course, more convenient, but they are also more expensive, so weigh your options when choosing your equipment.

Last but not least, you will need a leash, which is simply a strap that keeps the snowboard attached to your body so that it doesn't go flying away. The humble leash is inexpensive and important because most ski resorts won't let you snowboard without one.

Starting Out

For your first excursion in snowboarding, find a flat area or one with a gentle slope. Strap in your lead foot, leaving the other foot free. Keeping your knees bent, balance on your lead foot and kick off with your other foot, as you would if you were skateboarding. Keep propelling yourself forward with this skating motion until you feel comfortable and balanced. With that step mastered, you're reading to try gliding, which is just putting the loose foot on the snowboard (or stomp pad) instead of the ground.

Reading Guide

What details do you learn in this section?

How does the section heading help you anticipate what you will learn?

How does the conclusion reinforce the main idea of the passage?

Up and Down the Hill

To get onto the chairlift, skate up to the line and wait for the attendant to signal when it's safe to move into position. Looking over your outside shoulder, get ready to sit down when the lift gets to the back of your legs. To get off the lift, put your lead foot down and push off with the free foot, moving far enough away from the chair so that you don't interfere with other people getting off the lift.

Now you're ready for your first descent, which will be the scariest. Skate or glide to the top of the slope and plant the downhill edge of your board perpendicular to the mountain to prevent it from sliding out from under you. Strap in your back boot securely and check your leash. Stand up straight, bend your knees, put pressure on your lead foot, and let gravity take over. You can control your speed by traversing across the mountain by shifting your weight from one edge to the other. Stopping, one of the most critical snowboarding skills, is accomplished by turning your snowboard so that you are perpendicular to the mountain and then leaning into the hill.

Despite its humble beginnings as a kids' toy, snowboards and snowboarding have become a major force in winter sports. In 1998, snowboarding was recognized as an Olympic sport. Snowboarding's popularity has grown so much that the number of snowboarders is expected to overtake the number of skiers within the next few years.

Answer the following questions.

1 Which statement **best** describes the unstated main idea of the passage?

A. Snowboarding is a popular winter sport that requires special equipment and dedication to master.

B. To get onto the chairlift, skate up to the line and wait for the attendant to signal when it's safe to move into position.

C. Despite its humble beginnings as a kids' toy, snowboards and snowboarding have become a major force in winter sports.

D. For your first excursion in snowboarding, find a flat area or one with a gentle slope.

2 Which two skills should you master before getting on a chairlift and snowboarding downhill?

A. staying dry and warm

B. skating and gliding

C. traversing and stopping

D. edging with the board downhill

3 Underline the dependent clause in the following sentence. Then, explain how the dependent clause connects the ideas.

Wearing goggles cuts down on glare from the snow, which, in turn, helps you see better.

Write your answer on the lines below.

_____

_____

4 Match each of the following statements to the category under which it could be organized.

A. **Clothing**

B. **Equipment**

C. **Starting Out**

1. You can carry your snowboard under your arm like a book or behind your back with both arms securing the board.

2. When choosing your jacket and pants, look for fabrics that repel moisture.

3. Most goggles have interchangeable lenses, enabling you to choose the best color for the conditions.

5 The author wants to add a transition sentence between the sections "Clothing" and "Equipment." Which of these sentences provides the **best** transition?

A. The most important thing to do when carrying your snowboard is to be aware of your surroundings so that your snowboard doesn't bang into anyone.

B. After learning how to skate on your snowboard, you will need to learn how to glide.

C. Learning how to stop is one of the most valuable skills you will need as a snowboarder.

D. Once you know that you can stay warm and dry, you are ready to look at the gear you will need.

6 In "On the Slopes—or Not?" you read about a boy who was trying snowboarding for the first time. In "Snowboarding 101," you read about the history of snowboarding and how to start out in the sport. Imagine that you have moved to an area with a nearby ski resort. Write a letter to a former friend, persuading him or her to visit you and to try snowboarding. Be sure your argument includes a strong claim about the benefits of snowboarding as well as counterclaims to any objections that your friend might raise. Usually, when writing an argument, you should use a formal style, but when writing a letter to a friend to persuade him or her to do something, you may use an informal style.

Use the writing process to plan, write, revise, and edit your persuasive letter. Be sure to include an introduction, body, and conclusion.

You may plan your argument in the space below. Write your argument on the following pages.

Plan

Write your argument on the lines below.

_____

_____

_____

_____

_____

_____

_____

_____

_____

_____

_____

_____

_____

_____

_____

Write a Response to Literature

❶ GETTING THE IDEA

When you write a **response to literature**, you make a claim about one or more literary texts, such as fiction, poems, or plays. You base your claim on an analysis of and reflection on the texts, using textual evidence to support your ideas.

Understanding a Prompt

You will often be asked to respond to a writing prompt about a text or texts you've read. This response may ask you to focus on one or more elements of a text or texts. For example, you might be asked to analyze character, plot, setting, or author's style. Or you might be asked to explain how one or more of these elements contributes to the text's theme, or central meaning.

Read the example below and circle the titles of the two texts. Then, underline the verbs in the prompt that identify what it is asking you to do with these texts.

> Compare and contrast the ways in which racism affects Cassie, the narrator of Mildred Taylor's novel *Roll of Thunder, Hear My Cry*, and the first-person narrator of Langston Hughes's poem "I, Too, Sing America."

Stating a Claim

Because the prompt above asks you to *compare* and *contrast* the ways in which racism affects the narrators in the two texts, you'll have to make a claim about how their challenges in the face of racism are alike and different. To state a claim that satisfies all parts of a prompt, it can be helpful to turn the prompt into questions that guide your writing.

- How does racism affect Cassie in *Roll of Thunder, Hear My Cry*?

- How does racism affect the first-person narrator of "I, Too, Sing America"?

- How are the characters' situations alike and different?

To make a claim, think about what you believe about the texts and the characters. To find supporting evidence for your claim, think about what details from the text led you to make it. Look over notes you took as you read, or reread the texts with the writing prompt in mind.

Organizing Your Ideas

Using a graphic organizer is a good way to plan and organize your ideas.

Claim	Cassie from *Roll of Thunder, Hear My Cry* and the narrator in "I, Too, Sing America" are similar in that they are both African Americans in a racist society who nonetheless find ways to survive and succeed. However, the ways in which racism challenges them are different.
Reason	Both Cassie and the poem's narrator are victims of racism.
Supporting facts and details	• Townspeople treat Cassie badly because she is African American. • The narrator of the poem is made to eat in the kitchen instead of joining company at the dining table.

Developing Your Response

When you write an **introduction** to a response to literature, introduce the texts you're discussing and state your claim in an opening statement. For example:

> The characters in both *Roll of Thunder, Hear My Cry* and "I, Too, Sing America" experience racism in their everyday lives. However, in *Roll of Thunder, Hear My Cry*, the author presents the dangers of this racism in greater detail.

Once you've stated your claim, provide reasons and evidence to make a case for why readers should agree with it. To support the claim above, you'd look for moments in which the characters from the two texts confront racism. You would also look for ways in which the two texts handle this topic differently.

To make the comparisons between two texts clear, use transition and connecting words to discuss similarities and differences. Look at how the words *both*, *however*, and *while* are used below to compare the two texts.

> <u>Both</u> Cassie and the poem's narrator experience racism in their everyday lives. Cassie endures unfair treatment from the townspeople, and the narrator of "I, Too, Sing America" is unfairly made to eat separately from company. <u>However</u>, *Roll of Thunder, Hear My Cry* goes into great detail about how the characters' physical safety is threatened, <u>while</u> the poem's narrator does not mention his physical safety.

The last paragraph of your writing is the **conclusion**. It restates your position and summarizes the most important ideas. For example:

> *Even in the face of tremendous struggle, both Cassie's family and the narrator of the poem find strength and continue to fight against racism.*

Finishing up

Be sure you reread your writing to check that your opinion is clear and your reasons are logically organized. Proofread your work for errors in grammar, mechanics, and spelling.

Use the following checklist to guide your revision.

- ☐ Does my response answer all parts of the prompt?
- ☐ Is my position clearly stated?
- ☐ Do I use enough textual evidence to support my claim?
- ☐ Is the response well organized and focused?
- ☐ Is my writing free of errors?

Language Spotlight • Misplaced and Dangling Modifiers

Modifiers are words or phrases that tell about who is doing the action in a sentence or what action is being done. If a modifier is misplaced or dangling, it can cause confusion about what is happening in a sentence or who is doing the action.

Suppose you wanted to say that John won an art award but no other awards Look at how the placement of the word *only* changes the sentence below.

Misplaced Modifier: Only John won the art award.
Corrected Use of Modifier: John won only the art award.

The first sentence below includes a dangling modifier (underlined).

Dangling Modifier: <u>By keeping the farm</u>, injustice was fought by Cassie's family.
Corrected Use of Modifier: By keeping the farm, Cassie's family fought injustice.

In the first sentence, the phrase "by keeping the farm" is a dangling modifier because it is not clear from the rest of the sentence who is doing this action. In the second sentence, it is clear that Cassie's family is keeping the farm.

Suppose you wanted to say that you were about to fall down the stairs but did not. Underline the sentence that correctly places the modifier to express this meaning.

I almost fell all the way down the stairs. I fell almost all the way down the stairs.

Rewrite the sentence below to fix the dangling modifier.

Looking into the distance, the hills looked small to me.

Read the poems.

A Linnet[1] in a Gilded Cage

by Christina G. Rosetti

A linnet in a gilded cage,
A linnet on a bough,[2]
In frosty winter one might doubt
Which bird is luckier now.

But let the trees burst out in leaf,
And nests be on the bough,
Which linnet is the luckier bird,
Oh who could doubt it now?

A Song of Flight

by Christina G. Rosetti

While we slumber and sleep,
The sun leaps up from the deep,
Daylight born at the leap,
Rapid, dominant, free,
5   Athirst to bathe in the uttermost sea.

While we linger at play
If the year would stand at May!
Winds are up and away,
Over land, over sea,
10   To their goal, wherever their goal may be.

It is time to arise,
To race for the promised prize;
The sun flies, the wind flies,
We are strong, we are free,
15   And home lies beyond the stars and the sea.

[1] **linnet**: a type of bird
[2] **bough**: a branch

Answer the following questions.

1 Which of these is true of how both poems use literary devices to express their common theme?

A. Both use allusions to classical texts to express a theme related to freedom.

B. Both use the metaphor of flying to express a theme related to freedom.

C. Both use personification of the sun and the wind to express a theme related to freedom.

D. Both use similes about nature to express a theme related to freedom.

> **Hint** Look for examples of each type of literary device in each poem. Remember that the literary device must appear in both poems, not just one.

2 The following question has two parts. First, answer Part A. Then, answer Part B.

Part A

Which of these is true of how the tone of the two poems is different?

A. "A Linnet in a Gilded Cage" is reflective, and "A Song of Flight" is triumphant.

B. "A Linnet in a Gilded Cage" is playful, and "A Song of Flight" is somber.

C. "A Linnet in a Gilded Cage" is celebratory, and "A Song of Flight" is angry.

D. "A Linnet in a Gilded Cage" is mournful, and "A Song of Flight" is happy.

Part B

Using a line from each poem as evidence, explain how the poet establishes the tone you selected for each poem in Part A.

_____

_____

_____

_____

> **Hint** How do you feel as you read each poem? What kind of statements does each poem make: are they forceful, light, curious? All of these things contribute to the poem's tone.

3 An author of a poem often uses repetition of words or phrases to get a message, or theme, across. Reread the lines from the poem below, both of which use the word <u>now</u> and talk about being lucky.

In frosty winter one might doubt **Which bird is luckier <u>now</u>.**	**Which linnet is the luckier bird,** **Oh who could doubt it <u>now</u>?**

Which of these **best** describes how the author uses repetition to express a theme?

A. The author uses repetition to make a point that a bird that has a warm home in winter is the luckier bird.

B. The author uses repetition to pose a question about which bird is luckier and then answers the question by saying the bird that is free is luckier.

C. The author uses repetition to pose a question about which bird is luckier and then concludes that the question cannot be answered.

D. The author uses repetition to repeat the same statement: that a free bird is luckier.

Hint Reread each set of lines in the context of the poem. Does anything change in the poem between these two lines? Think about how the second set of lines relates to the first set of lines. Do the lines express the same idea or different ideas?

4 A student made the following claim about the poem "A Song of Flight."

In "A Song of Flight," the poet gives the sun and wind human characteristics in order to show that humans can be free like the sun and wind.

Underline **two** lines in the poem that the student could use to support this claim.

Hint The student is making a claim about personification, so you will need to look for examples of personification in this poem. You will also need to look for evidence that the poem is using this literary device to make a statement about humans.

Use the Reading Guide to help you understand the passage.

The Story of an Hour

by Kate Chopin

Reading Guide

Pay close attention to how the author describes Mrs. Mallard.

How does Mrs. Mallard react to her husband's death in this section?

What does the author reveal about Mrs. Mallard's character?

Knowing that Mrs. Mallard was afflicted with a heart trouble, great care was taken to break to her as gently as possible the news of her husband's death.

It was her sister Josephine who told her, in broken sentences; veiled hints that revealed in half concealing. Her husband's friend Richards was there, too, near her. It was he who had been in the newspaper office when intelligence of the railroad disaster was received, with Brently Mallard's name leading the list of "killed." He had only taken the time to assure himself of its truth by a second telegram, and had hastened to forestall any less careful, less tender friend in bearing the sad message. . . .

She wept at once, with sudden, wild abandonment, in her sister's arms. When the storm of grief had spent itself she went away to her room alone. She would have no one follow her.

There stood, facing the open window, a comfortable, roomy armchair. Into this she sank, pressed down by a physical exhaustion that haunted her body and seemed to reach into her soul. . . .

She was young, with a fair, calm face, whose lines bespoke repression and even a certain strength. But now there was a dull stare in her eyes, whose gaze was fixed away off yonder on one of those patches of blue sky. It was not a glance of reflection, but rather indicated a suspension of intelligent thought.

There was something coming to her and she was waiting for it, fearfully. What was it? She did not know; it was too subtle and elusive to name. But she felt it, creeping out of the sky, reaching toward her through the sounds, the scents, the color that filled the air.

How does the author show that Mrs. Mallard is wrestling with her emotions in this section?

What does the author mean by the line "she would live for herself"? Consider how this line relates to Mrs. Mallard's visions for her future life.

Now her bosom rose and fell tumultuously. She was beginning to recognize this thing that was approaching to possess her, and she was striving to beat it back with her will— as powerless as her two white slender hands would have been. When she abandoned herself a little whispered word escaped her slightly parted lips. She said it over and over under the breath: "free, free, free!" The vacant stare and the look of terror that had followed it went from her eyes. They stayed keen and bright. Her pulses beat fast, and the coursing blood warmed and relaxed every inch of her body.

She did not stop to ask if it were or were not a monstrous joy that held her. A clear and exalted perception enabled her to dismiss the suggestion as trivial. She knew that she would weep again when she saw the kind, tender hands folded in death; the face that had never looked save with love upon her, fixed and gray and dead. But she saw beyond that bitter moment a long procession of years to come that would belong to her absolutely. And she opened and spread her arms out to them in welcome.

There would be no one to live for during those coming years; she would live for herself. There would be no powerful will bending hers in that blind persistence with which men and women believe they have a right to impose a private will upon a fellow-creature. A kind intention or a cruel intention made the act seem no less a crime as she looked upon it in that brief moment of illumination.

And yet she had loved him—sometimes. Often she had not. What did it matter! What could love, the unsolved mystery, count for in the face of this possession of self-assertion which she suddenly recognized as the strongest impulse of her being!

"Free! Body and soul free!" she kept whispering.

Why does Mrs. Mallard now wish that her life will be long?

How does the author show how Mrs. Mallard reacts when she sees that her husband is still alive?

What do the doctors say about Mrs. Mallard's death? What do the doctors think happened? How does this relate to Mrs. Mallard's true feelings?

Josephine was kneeling before the closed door with her lips to the keyhole, imploring for admission. "Louise, open the door! I beg; open the door—you will make yourself ill. What are you doing, Louise? For heaven's sake open the door."

"Go away. I am not making myself ill." No; she was drinking in a very elixir of life through that open window.

Her fancy was running riot along those days ahead of her. Spring days, and summer days, and all sorts of days that would be her own. She breathed a quick prayer that life might be long. It was only yesterday she had thought with a shudder that life might be long.

She arose at length and opened the door to her sister's importunities. There was a feverish triumph in her eyes, and she carried herself unwittingly like a goddess of Victory. She clasped her sister's waist, and together they descended the stairs. Richards stood waiting for them at the bottom.

Someone was opening the front door with a latchkey. It was Brently Mallard who entered, a little travel-stained, composedly carrying his gripsack and umbrella. He had been far from the scene of the accident, and did not even know there had been one. He stood amazed at Josephine's piercing cry; at Richards' quick motion to screen him from the view of his wife.

When the doctors came they said she had died of heart disease—of the joy that kills.

Answer the following questions.

1 Explain how the author uses an event from the story's plot to shape the reader's understanding of Mrs. Mallard's character. Be sure to mention what the event allows the reader to understand about Mrs. Mallard.

_____

_____

_____

_____

_____

2 The following question has two parts. First, answer Part A. Then, answer Part B.

Part A

Match each section of the passage with the word that **best** describes Mrs. Mallard's state of mind in that section.

A. before learning of her husband's death		**1.** rejuvenated
B. soon after learning of her husband's death		**2.** fragile
C. right before learning her husband is still alive		**3.** triumphant

Part B

Write a sentence from the passage that provides evidence for each description in Part A.

_____

_____

_____

_____

_____

3 Reread the sentences from the passage below.

> **But she felt it, creeping out of the sky, reaching toward her through the sounds, the scents, the color that filled the air. . . . She was beginning to recognize this thing that was approaching to possess her, and she was striving to beat it back with her will—as powerless as her two white slender hands would have been.**

Which of these **best** describes how the author uses language in this excerpt?

A. The author uses precise description to show that Mrs. Mallard immediately feels clear and decisive after the announcement of her husband's death.

B. The author uses metaphors and similes to describe a feeling of relief that is beginning to come over Mrs. Mallard.

C. The author uses sentences that are clear and to the point in order to explain how Mrs. Mallard feels after her husband's death.

D. The author uses descriptions of Mrs. Mallard's actions in order to subtly hint at what she is feeling about her husband.

4 The following question has two parts. First, answer Part A. Then, answer Part B.

Part A

Underline the claim that is **best** supported by evidence in the passage.

Claims	Mrs. Mallard experiences an immediate feeling of joy and freedom when she learns of her husband's death.
	Mrs. Mallard has some sadness about her husband's death, but she ultimately finds her new independence incredibly freeing.
	Mrs. Mallard is devastated by her husband's death and dreads the idea of living the rest of her life without him.

Part B

Write two sentences from the passage that you could use as evidence to support the answer you chose in Part A.

_____

_____

_____

_____

5 Reread the last sentence from the passage.

When the doctors came they said she had died of heart disease—of the joy that kills.

By including this sentence, do you think the narrator meant to show that the doctors' point of view on Mrs. Mallard's death was correct, or that this point of view was mistaken? Use examples from the text to support your claim.

_____

_____

_____

_____

_____

_____

_____

_____

_____

_____

_____

_____

_____

_____

_____

6 Write an essay that compares and contrasts how the author of "The Story of an Hour" and the author of the two poems use different literary devices to explore the theme of freedom. These literary devices may include character development, description, plot, and figurative language, among other possibilities. Be sure to include specific details from each text to support your ideas.

You may plan your essay in the space below. Write your essay on the following pages.

Plan

Write your essay on the lines below.

W.7.3.a–e, L.7.2.a

Write a Narrative

① GETTING THE IDEA

Narrative writing is writing that develops real or imagined experiences to entertain a reader. Some narratives are fictional, while other tell true stories, but all narratives have characters, a setting, a plot, and a point of view. To plan your narrative, think about these elements first.

Choose a Setting, Characters, and a Point of View

The **setting** provides a context, or backdrop, for the events that will occur in the narrative. The setting should match the kind of story you're telling. For example, a science fiction story might be set on a distant planet in the future.

The **characters** will carry out the action in your narrative. You can develop your characters through what they say, do, and think. Their actions and words both reveal what they're like and help to build the narrative's plot.

The **point of view** of your story, or who tells it, affects how much the reader will know about different characters and events. You might write in the first person if you want to explore the thoughts, feelings, and unique voice of a single character. If you'd like to present the points of view of many characters, third-person omniscient might be a better choice.

Plan Out the Plot with a Story Map

To plan the **plot**, or the events in your story, it can help to make an outline of what will happen in the beginning, middle, and end of the story. The beginning of the story is where a writer introduces the plot conflict. The author can then use the events of the story to have the characters work through the conflict. The conclusion, or end of your story, will show how the conflict is resolved. The following story outline shows one way to organize plot details.

Conflict: Alicia finds a beautiful bracelet and wants to keep it.
Event 1: Alicia finds a bracelet on the sidewalk and picks it up. She looks around, but there's nobody there. She puts the bracelet on her wrist and continues home.
Event 2: Alicia's mother notices the bracelet and is concerned because it looks expensive. When Alicia admits that she found it, they return it at the police station.
Conclusion: The police locate the owner, who gives Alicia a reward for returning it. Alicia buys herself a bracelet with the reward money.

Write Your Narrative Draft

The goal when writing your narrative is to orient your readers at the beginning and then keep them engaged until the end. You can use the following techniques to keep your writing clear and interesting.

Establish a Context and Point of View When you establish a **context**, you pull your readers into the world of your story, which includes a setting and characters. You introduce a narrator with a clear point of view to act as a guide for your readers. The reader must understand these narrative elements right away so the story events that follow will make sense.

To get your readers' attention, you might start in the middle of the action. Or you could start with a gripping description of the setting or characters. Introducing the conflict early keeps your readers engaged to find out how it's resolved.

Organize a Well-Structured Event Sequence Once you've gotten your readers' attention, you need to be sure the event sequence that follows unfolds in a logical way, so they can follow what happens.

- **Transitional words** and phrases help you convey sequence, show time passing, or change the setting. Here are some examples: *then* (sequence), *arriving at school* (changes setting), *the following week* (time passing).

- Pay attention to **pacing**, or how quickly the story moves. Long sentences full of description tend to move slowly, while short, action-packed sentences move quickly. As the writer, you can slow down or speed up the pacing to reflect story events. For example, a character description might move more slowly than a tense, suspenseful part.

- The sequence of events should lead your characters to a **resolution** of the story's conflict. If an event doesn't drive the plot forward, you may not need it.

- Your **conclusion** should resolve the story's conflict and end the story in a satisfying way that makes sense with events that have already occurred. It may also serve as a time to reflect on, or hint at, the story's themes.

Add Description and Dialogue **Description** gives the details of your story and creates a clear picture for your reader. **Precise language** captures the action, while **sensory details** describe how things look, feel, taste, smell, and sound. However, make sure you don't get lost in the details; your descriptions should be relevant to the story. For example, a description of someone baking makes sense in a story about cooking, while a description of a football game makes sense in a story about football.

Let some of your story come out in the **dialogue**. Good dialogue gives each of your characters a unique voice and helps readers get to know them better.

Extend an Existing Narrative

Sometimes, you will be asked to continue or finish an existing narrative. You will add your own original details, but you'll also need to make sure your writing is consistent with the first part of the story. To do this, review how the author presents the characters, setting, plot, and theme, and make sure the new parts you write make sense with these elements. For example, the dialogue you write should reflect how the characters speak, and the new events you write should follow from what has already happened in the story.

Revise and Edit Your Narrative

Once your draft is complete, revise your work using the following checklist.

- ☐ Do I orient and engage my reader at the beginning?

- ☐ Does my sequence of events unfold in a logical way, with careful pacing?

- ☐ Do I introduce and develop characters in an interesting way?

- ☐ Is there a clear, consistent point of view or multiple points of view?

- ☐ Do I use engaging dialogue, relevant descriptive details, and reflection?

- ☐ Does my ending make sense with the events and resolve the story's conflict?

The editing process is also the time to double-check your grammar and think about grammatical tricks that can make your sentences more clear or interesting.

Language Spotlight • Commas and Coordinate Adjectives

It's important to use a comma between coordinate adjectives, or adjectives that appear next to each other and describe the same noun. For example: *It was a cool, cloudy day*.

You can tell that adjectives are coordinate adjectives if they still sound right when you reverse them or put the word *and* between them. If this doesn't work with a pair of adjectives, you don't need a comma between them. For example: *I saw a dark brown dog*.

Look at the two sentences below. Add a comma to the sentence that needs one.

I saw a fascinating enjoyable movie.

Raul had a tough school day.

Read the passage.

Julie's Decision

It was the most momentous decision I had made in all my eighteen years, and the first ultra-important decision I made as an adult without consulting my parents, so it was with more than a little sense of dread that I left the recruiter's office after what felt like signing away my childhood. I reminded myself: I'm legally an adult, I'm a senior in high school, and I can do this! And I did, but I didn't anticipate feeling so terrified of telling my parents.

I might've been the first person in my family to enlist in the Air Force, but I wasn't the first to join the military; both my parents had been soldiers, and in fact, that's how they had met. But despite their own history, my parents were always urging me to consider other careers.

"Be a teacher," my mother said constantly.

"Or a flight attendant," my father suggested. "You could fly for free when you're not working and see the world that way."

But I didn't want to be a teacher or a flight attendant, although my dad was closer to the truth: I did want to fly, but as the pilot. Unfortunately, becoming a pilot is expensive if you go to flight school, so the best plan, in my mind, was to get flight training from the Air Force, and then go to college without plunging my family into an abyss of debt.

I knew my reasons were sound, but I also knew my parents would react emotionally and get really upset about my decision. Dad still calls me his "little girl," even though I'm an inch taller than Mom, and Mom still gives me a glass of milk and oatmeal-raisin cookies for my after-school snack.

I felt absolutely, positively terrified, like terror times ten trillion, when I thought about the conversation I would have to have with them very soon, so I did what anyone would do when there's something unpleasant on the horizon: I procrastinated. Instead of rushing home to share my less-than-welcome news, I sat on the steps of the public library and called my best friend, Lila.

"I did it!" I said. "I enlisted, and I start basic training in Texas in August."

I heard Lila say, "Wow," followed by a long, profound silence.

"Are you there?" I asked, thinking maybe we just got disconnected.

"Yeah," Lila said. "I'm just stunned. I can't believe my best friend is going to be in the military. Are you scared?"

"Yes," I answered truthfully. "Right now, I'm totally petrified . . . of telling my parents."

Lila laughed and then tried to encourage me, "Be brave and get it over with quickly so we can go to the movies later with Duncan and Sonali."

After we hung up, I decided to rehearse what I would say when I got home. "Mom, Dad," I'd begin. "I have something important to tell you—"

But I didn't get a chance to rehearse much more than that: just then, out of nowhere, my parents appeared on the sidewalk in front of me.

"There you are!" I heard Mom's distinctive, lilting voice. "Your father and I were worried you were so late, so we thought we'd go for a walk and see if we could run into you, and we did!"

She sounded so cheerful, so happy to see me; this wasn't how I pictured it. I thought we'd be sitting solemnly in the living room when I sprang this on them, all of us aware that something important was about to happen. I wondered, should I just blurt my news out now, here, in the street?

Answer the following questions.

1 How does the author's choice of point of view in "Julie's Decision" contribute to what readers know about the characters and events of this narrative? Be sure to identify the point of view in your answer.

_____

_____

_____

_____

_____

_____

_____

_____

> **Hint** When an author chooses a point of view, he or she makes a choice about what he or she can include in the story. To identify the point of view, pay attention to pronoun use. To identify its effects, notice what you know and don't know about the characters and events.

2 The following question has two parts. First, answer Part A. Then, answer Part B.

Part A

Which of these sentences includes a transitional word or phrase?

A. "Be a teacher," my mother said constantly.

B. I knew my reasons were sound, but I also knew my parents would react emotionally and get really upset about my decision."

C. "Yeah," Lila said. "I'm just stunned."

D. After we hung up, I decided to rehearse what I would say when I got home.

Part B

Underline the transitional word or phrase in the response you selected in Part A and explain how it is used in the sentence.

_____

_____

> **Hint** Remember that authors use transitional words or phrases to "get somewhere" in the story. They usually refer to location, time, or order of events—an author may use them to show time passing, to shift the setting, or to make the sequence of events clear.

3 Which of these **best** describes how the author uses Julie's action of enlisting in the Air Force, and then being afraid to tell her parents about it, to develop her character?

A. The author uses these actions to develop the idea that Julie is trying to get over a lifelong fear of her parents.

B. The author uses these actions to develop the idea that Julie makes impulsive decisions without always thinking them through.

C. The author uses these actions to develop the idea that Julie is in a transitional phase between childhood and adulthood.

D. The author uses these actions to develop the idea that Julie is influenced by her parents' opinions more than her friends' opinions.

> **Hint** Reread the parts of the story where Julie describes her reasons for enlisting and her reluctance to tell her parents. What does her thought process suggest about her character? Which of the choices above is supported by evidence in the story?

4 "Julie's Decision" needs an ending. Think about how the author has developed the characters and the story's conflict. Use what you have learned about these elements to write three paragraphs to finish the story. Provide a logical conclusion, and make sure to use narrative techniques such as dialogue and sensory language in your writing.

_____

_____

_____

_____

_____

_____

_____

_____

_____

_____

_____

_____

_____

_____

_____

_____

_____

_____

> **Hint** Look back at how the author orients the reader by establishing a context and a point of view. Pay attention to how the author develops the conflict and engages the reader in the story. Use these elements to help you write a conclusion to the story.

Use the Reading Guide to help you understand the passage.

Finding the Words

Reading Guide

What does the author do to establish a context in paragraph 1?

How does the author present information about Joel and Jake in this section?

Look for how the author uses transitional words and phrases to connect ideas.

Jake Washington and Joel Mitchell grew up next door to each other in a high-rise apartment building in New York City. They had a lot in common. They were the same age and had been classmates since pre-kindergarten. They played the same school sports and liked the same music. Sometimes, the two boys even finished each other's sentences as if they were reading each other's mind. They were more like brothers, or maybe close cousins, than just neighbors and classmates. So, when Joel asked Jake if he could borrow twenty dollars, Jake didn't think twice about opening his wallet and giving his friend his last two ten-dollar bills. Joel thanked Jake before taking the money, shoving it into the back pocket of his jeans, and promising to pay it back the following day.

That was two weeks ago. Jake suspected that Joel had forgotten all about the debt. The problem was, Jake needed that twenty dollars today to pay his share of an expensive gift he and his older sister, Vanessa, had picked out for their parents' twentieth wedding anniversary. The antique brass candlesticks they had selected at a fancy store would be held for them only until this afternoon at five o'clock.

Jake knew he shouldn't have left this to the last minute. He had just kept hoping that Joel would miraculously remember the borrowed twenty dollars and pay it back without needing a reminder. Now, Jake realized that wishful thinking was not a very reliable method of getting your best friend to repay a loan. In addition, so much time had already elapsed that Jake felt uncomfortable about bringing up the subject of the borrowed twenty dollars.

"Just ask him," Vanessa said in a matter-of-fact voice. The two siblings were sitting together eating breakfast. "It's not such a huge deal, you know. Just tell him you need the money to buy a present for Mom and Dad, and you need it now, not tomorrow or next week. He'll understand. He's, like, your best friend."

How much time passes in paragraph 1? How do you know?

How does the author show Jake's difficulty making a decision in this section?

Pay attention to how the author uses description and dialogue to reveal information about Jake.

What words might you use to describe Jake?

One part of Jake knew that his sister was right. It didn't need to be a big deal, and Joel would understand. But another part of Jake felt paralyzed, like in one of those dreams where you want to run away from something scary, but your legs just won't move.

Jake finished his cereal and said good-bye to his sister. Then he grabbed a jacket and his school backpack as he left the apartment to walk to school.

Even though it felt incredibly awkward, Jake had to figure out some way to ask Joel to pay back the money. He knew he had to do it today, and he hoped Joel had the money handy.

As he walked, Jake tried to come up with a strategy, a way to remind Joel about the loan without seeming too pushy. Jake remembered participating in role-playing exercises at school where students pretended to be someone else to better see another person's point of view. While Jake waited for the traffic light to turn red, he thought about how he might start a conversation with Joel about the borrowed money, and how Joel might respond.

"Hey, Joel," he might begin, "can I have that twenty you owe me?" *No*, Jake thought, *that seems too abrupt. Maybe it would be better to bring the topic up in a more roundabout way.* "Hey, Joel, how's it going? Do you want to play basketball later, and could you bring that twenty you owe me?" Jake thought that was a bit more casual, but it still felt and sounded clumsy. The light turned green, and Jake hurried the rest of the way to school so he wouldn't be late.

Joel and Jake had a different block of classes that morning, so Jake didn't run into Joel until lunch, and Joel seemed to be in a rush. "Got to eat and run," he told Jake with his mouth full.

"But I needed to talk to you about—" Jake wanted to articulate at least some of what he had planned to say out loud to Joel, to at least open the topic, but Joel interrupted him.

"I know you need to talk to me about basketball, but we can do that tomorrow," Joel said over his shoulder as he was busing his tray. Jake followed him, even though he hadn't even touched his lunch. Jake had to tell Joel he didn't want to talk about basketball and that he needed the twenty dollars back today or he wouldn't be able to pay his share of his parents' anniversary gift and his sister would be furious with him.

If only he could find the words.

Answer the following questions.

1 How does the relationship between Joel and Jake that the author describes in the beginning paragraphs provide a context for the events that occur in this passage? Select **all** answers that are supported by evidence in the passage.

   A. Knowing about Joel and Jake's relationship helps readers understand why Joel seems to be avoiding hanging out with Jake.

   B. Knowing about Joel and Jake's relationship helps readers understand why Jake is able to lend Joel money so easily.

   C. Knowing about Joel and Jake's relationship helps readers understand why Jake feels awkward about asking Joel to repay him.

   D. Knowing about Joel and Jake's relationship helps readers understand why Joel doesn't pay back the money right away.

2 Reread the following sentences from the passage.

   So, when Joel asked Jake if he could borrow twenty dollars, Jake didn't think twice about opening his wallet and giving his friend his last two ten-dollar bills. Joel thanked Jake before taking the money, shoving it into the back pocket of his jeans, and promising to pay it back the following day.

   Rewrite this section using dialogue instead of description.

   _____

   _____

   _____

   _____

3 The following question has two parts. First, answer Part A. Then, answer Part B.

Part A

What point of view does the author use in this passage?

A. third-person limited from Vanessa's point of view

B. third-person limited from Jake's point of view

C. third-person omniscient

D. first person from Jake's point of view

Part B

Why do you think the author chose this point of view, and how does it contribute to the reader's experience of the story?

_____

_____

_____

_____

_____

_____

_____

_____

4 Reread these sentences from the passage.

> One part of Jake knew that his sister was right. It didn't need to be a big deal, and Joel would understand. <u>But another part of Jake felt paralyzed, like in one of those dreams where you want to run away from something scary, but your legs just won't move.</u>

How does the author's use of description in the underlined sentence contribute to the reader's understanding of Jake's state of mind?

_____

_____

_____

_____

5 Reread these sentences from the passage.

> As he walked, Jake tried to come up with a strategy, a way to remind Joel about the loan without seeming too pushy. Jake remembered participating in role-playing exercises at school where students pretended to be someone else to better see another person's point of view. While Jake waited for the traffic light to turn red, he thought about how he might start a conversation with Joel about the borrowed money, and how Joel might respond.

Underline **two** transitional phrases in this section.

6 Use details from the passage to write an original continuation of "Finding the Words" that tells what happens when Jake is finally able to talk to Joel. Make sure you use narrative elements such as sensory language, pacing, transitional words, and dialogue to convey the events of your conclusion in a logical and interesting way. Also, make sure the characters and point of view are consistent with the rest of the passage.

You may plan your narrative in the space below. Write your narrative on the following pages.

Plan

Write your narrative on the lines below.

Research Skills

❶ GETTING THE IDEA

For certain types of writing, you need to use facts and information that you find through the research process. There are specific research skills related to this process, including:

- identifying, generating, and refining research questions.

- performing search techniques related to your question.

- choosing appropriate print and digital sources.

- taking relevant notes on those sources.

Step one is developing a research question that is relevant to the topic. It is also important to choose a question that interests you.

Brainstorm Ideas

Begin by thinking of ideas that are relevant to the assigned topic. Record those ideas using a graphic organizer, such as an idea web or a chart, or listing them on a piece of paper. It is important to get your ideas down so you don't forget them.

Generate and Refine Research Questions

Use those ideas to form a few questions that you will need to do research to answer. As you begin your research, you can refine your questions to make sure they are not too general or too specific for your topic. Also, consider how interested you are in them. Try to pick something that you are excited to learn about.

When doing research, one question usually leads to another. Remember to explore your topic in a variety of ways. You may need to generate additional research questions in order to focus on an idea that interests you most.

Step two includes performing searches at the library or through an online search engine.

- The library offers a wealth of information in the form of books, magazines, journals, newspapers, encyclopedias, almanacs, CD-ROMs, and many other print and media formats. It is an ideal place to start your research.

- The Internet is an ever-growing collection of information. When performing Web searches, select information carefully. Always look for education and government Web sites first. Avoid sites created by individuals who are not experts in the subject area.

Also, be sure to use descriptive search terms when searching for information in a computerized card catalog at the library or online. Include keywords that are very specific to your topic to narrow the results as much as possible. For example, if you are researching the nesting habits of leatherback sea turtles, you might use the terms *nesting*, *leatherback*, and *turtle* together. Searching for just one of those terms alone would be too broad and get you too many results.

Step three includes choosing appropriate print and digital sources during the course of your library and Internet search. Relevant sources should be:

- accurate, providing correct facts and details.

- **credible**, which means trustworthy and believable.

Suppose you are doing research for a project on leatherback sea turtles. Let's take a look at some possible sources to see if they are both accurate and credible.

A blog describing a personal experience with a leatherback	A news article about the local nesting sites of leatherbacks	An educational site that gives information about leatherback nesting habits
This blog is not necessarily accurate because the writer may not correctly remember the details, and there is no other observer to support the information. It may be credible, however, if you are looking for a first-person account.	Newspapers typically have fact-checkers that make sure the information given is accurate. As a result, a news article is likely a credible source that can be trusted.	Web sites ending in *.gov*, *.edu*, and *.org* are usually run by experts in their field. The content of an educational site can be relied upon as accurate and credible.

Step four includes taking relevant notes on your sources.

Gathering Relevant Information

When taking notes, choose textual evidence that directly supports your main ideas and conclusions. Any other information is unnecessary and does not belong in your report. Look at another marine life example. Suppose you were researching the migration of humpback whales between the Caribbean and Iceland. Underline information that is relevant to the topic. Cross out any information that is irrelevant.

- Humpbacks move north to colder waters in the spring.

- Humpbacks can be seen in Bermuda and New England as they make their journey.

- Humpbacks are known for their beautiful whale songs.

- Humpbacks travel 3,100 miles from the Caribbean to Iceland.

Quoting and Paraphrasing Sources

When taking notes, it is important that you do not **plagiarize** the data, or copy it word for word, without giving credit to the original source. Instead, you can **quote** the source by including quotation marks around exact words from the text, or you can **paraphrase** source information by putting it into your own words. Here's an example of how you would quote and paraphrase the following text.

Many marine experts believe that sound is an important part of a humpback's life. It plays a role in a whale's development and emotional stability. So, soothing sounds could possibly put a whale in a good mood.

Quote: According to marine experts, sound may have the ability to put a humpback whale "in a good mood."

Paraphrase: Sound plays an important role in a humpback's development and emotional state. It might even affect a whale's mood.

Citing Sources

Finally, when using notes from sources, always remember to **cite**, or list, the source as a bibliographical reference. There are different citation styles that you can use.

Type of Text	Example Citation
book	Cary, Sam. *Whales Everywhere*. Miami: Pundit Books, 2010.
magazine article	Oros, Miguel. "The Secret Life of Humpbacks." *Our Planet*. February 2010: 12–18.
encyclopedia article	"Humpback Whale." *World Book Encyclopedia*. 2012.
Web site	"Family Bonds in Humpbacks." *WhaleWorld* 4 Oct. 2012. Regensville Research Centre. 14 Jul. 2011. http://whaleworld.com/humpbacks/family.html.

Language Spotlight • Quotation Marks to Cite Research

When citing research, you can:

- use an introductory phrase and a comma.

According to Eleanor Roosevelt, "It is not fair to ask of others what you are unwilling to do yourself."

- make the quote part of your own sentence.

Although Helen Keller believed "the world is full of suffering," she felt "it is full also of the overcoming of it."

Read the passage.

New Coral Reef Research Center Offers Hope for Future

The local businesses in South Florida are breathing a collective sigh of relief. The future of their economy, based almost entirely on the coral living just off the coast, has been given a boost of support. That support comes in the form of the Center of Excellence for Coral Reef Ecosystems Research, a fancy name for a facility that is basically devoted to protecting coral reefs.

Opened in September 2012, the research center is located in Hollywood, Florida, on the southeast coast of the state. Its purpose is to sustain the environment for the surrounding reefs. But it also aims to protect the economy of the region.

Coral is a living creature that grows larger over time and clusters together into colonies. As these colonies multiply, they form reef ecosystems where many types of marine life find food and shelter. About 25 percent of fish species in the ocean rely on coral reefs in some way. In addition, the reefs act as a barrier against wave surges that occur during hurricanes and other large storms.

All of this is a big responsibility for one small living thing—especially when the world seems to be against it! Every day, ocean temperatures are rising and people are overfishing. Careless tourists are damaging the reefs. Ocean pollution is also causing a decline in coral. These factors upset the balance of the reefs. Soon, more coral will be dying than being born. It is estimated that 25–30 percent of the world's reefs have already been damaged or destroyed as a result.

If this destruction continues, it will not only affect the surrounding coastal environment. It will also have a huge impact on the local economy. Businesses in the area rely on the reefs. Dive shops, hotels, restaurants, and tour companies all count on tourists to spend their money. After all, the reefs in Florida are the most-visited reefs in the world. They contribute to more than $6 billion a year of South Florida's economy.

In an attempt to help both the environment *and* the economy, the new research center has gotten down to business. It is currently studying the overall health of coral reefs to determine if and how they can recover. In relation to this, it is looking at climate change and pollution to figure out the best way to solve these problems. Researchers are carefully monitoring the water flow around the reefs and even studying the coral within the reefs to determine how old they are.

The facility itself is more than sufficiently equipped to carry out its research goals. There are plenty of labs, state-of-the-art equipment, and even a marine science library and auditorium. There is also a land-based coral nursery, where researchers are busy raising baby coral. They collect coral larvae in the reefs and bring them into the nurseries where they are protected. When the time is right, researchers transplant the healthy coral back to the reefs to help strengthen the ecosystem.

The center's goals are just as impressive on a global scale. The center is recording changes to coral reefs around the world and studying the percentage of decline to see how much that decline rate is increasing as each year goes by. This information should help researchers answer their most urgent questions about coral reefs so that they may learn how to save these rain forests of the sea. The people of South Florida are keeping their fingers crossed that the facility will be able to achieve its goals. The rest of the world should be, too.

Answer the following questions.

1 A student is writing a report on how researchers are able to raise coral babies at the facility in Hollywood, Florida. Reread paragraph 7 from the passage and the directions that follow.

The student read an additional source and made a list of information based on her research. Circle **two** pieces of information from this new source that are **most** relevant to the research topic.

> The algae that live inside the coral skeleton give coral its color.
>
> Coral larvae grow a hard skeleton that protects them if they are moved.
>
> Salt water is pumped through a filtration system when it comes into the research facility.
>
> There are coral nurseries off the Fort Lauderdale coast, as well.
>
> Many coral species release sperm and eggs into the ocean based on the moon cycle in the month of August.

Hint Underline the topic of the student's research report. Find two pieces of information that directly support that topic.

2 The following question has two parts. First, answer Part A. Then, answer Part B.

Part A

Renee is writing a research paper about the global effects of reef destruction. She is using the passage for her research. Which conclusion can Renee make based on the evidence in the text?

A. It is too late to stop the destruction of most of the world's coral reefs.

B. Coral reefs will eventually disappear if nothing is done to preserve them.

C. The main effect of reef destruction will be the damage it does to the global economy.

D. All coral reefs have been equally damaged by careless human actions.

Hint Find the part of the passage that discusses global reef destruction. What point does the author make about preserving coral reefs around the world?

Part B

Which sentences provide textual evidence for your answer to Part A? Circle **all** that apply.

A. In an attempt to help both the environment *and* the economy, the new research center has gotten down to business.

B. In relation to this, it is looking at climate change and pollution to figure out the best way to solve these problems.

C. Researchers are carefully monitoring the water flow around the reefs and even studying the coral within the reefs to determine how old they are.

D. The center is recording changes to coral reefs around the world and studying the percentage of decline to see how much that decline rate is increasing as each year goes by.

E. This information should help researchers answer their most urgent questions about coral reefs so that they may learn how to save these rain forests of the sea.

Hint Which sentences directly support the answer you chose in Part A? Remember that Part B has more than one correct answer.

3 A student is writing a research report about coral reefs in Florida. He has read the passage and gathered information from an additional source.

Read the paragraphs from each source and the directions that follow.

New Coral Reef Research Center Offers Hope for Future

If this destruction continues, it will not only affect the surrounding coastal environment. It will also have a huge impact on the local economy. Businesses in the area rely on the reefs. Dive shops, hotels, restaurants, and tour companies all count on tourists to spend their money. After all, the reefs in Florida are the most-visited reefs in the world. They contribute to more than $6 billion a year of South Florida's economy.

Additional Source

The Center of Excellence for Coral Reef Ecosystems Research in South Florida has created new jobs in the academic field and in construction. It will hire fifty graduate students for research purposes with the aim of preserving coral reefs on a local and global scale. The federal government backed this initiative, providing a $15 million grant to help with funding the research facility.

Which point could the student include in his report based on evidence in both sources?

A. Communities should look to their local governments for support in improving their economies.

B. The federal government has indirectly supported the economy of South Florida.

C. The research center solved South Florida's economic problems before it addressed the problem of coral reef destruction.

D. Research projects are the best solutions available for improving local and global economies.

Hint Combine information from the two sources to develop a new understanding. What does the passage say about South Florida's businesses? How does this information relate to government involvement in the new research center?

---

4 Jacob is writing a report about the destruction of coral reefs. Read the paragraph from the passage. Then, read the directions that follow.

> **All of this is a big responsibility for one small living thing—especially when the world seems to be against it! Every day, ocean temperatures are rising and people are overfishing. Careless tourists are damaging the reefs. Ocean pollution is also causing a decline in coral. These factors upset the balance of the reefs. Soon, more coral will be dying than being born. It is estimated that 25–30 percent of the world's reefs have already been damaged or destroyed as a result.**

Part A

Underline the details from the paragraph that explain the challenges that coral reefs face.

> **Hint** Look for descriptions of stressors to the coral reef ecosystem. Only underline text that specifically explains a challenge that coral reefs face.

Part B

Paraphrase this information so that it could be included in Jacob's report.

_____

_____

> **Hint** Restate this information in your own words, as if you were describing something you learned to someone else.

Use the Reading Guide to help you understand the passage.

U.S. Coral Reefs

Reading Guide

Note the organizational structure of the Web page. What is its primary purpose—to entertain or provide information?

How do the facts on the page relate to facts you read in the previous passage? Synthesize, or combine, what you know to develop new conclusions.

The United States has coral reefs in the Atlantic, Caribbean, Gulf of Mexico, and Pacific regions.

Atlantic

A main U.S. shallow-water reef resource is the Florida Keys off the coast of South Florida. This is the third-largest reef in the world. It covers more than 2,800 square nautical miles and is home to more than 5,500 marine species. About 84 percent of U.S. reefs are found in Florida. The reefs help to generate billions of dollars in income and thousands of jobs.

There is also a deep-water reef off the Oculina Banks near the southern Atlantic coast.

Caribbean

Coral reefs are found in Puerto Rico and the U.S. Virgin Islands. These reefs are popular tourist spots because they are quite diverse. The variety of colorful fish species and other marine life are responsible for much of the income generated in this region.

Gulf of Mexico

Coral reefs exist on salt domes off the Texas coastline. Salt domes are exactly what they sound like. They are dome-shaped structures made out of salt that has been forced up from the ground. This area is identified as having the northernmost reef in North America.

Pacific

The Hawaiian Islands have an enormous collection of beautiful coral reefs that extend more than ten thousand square miles. These reefs generate significant income for the state of Hawaii.

How Coral Reefs Help U.S. Coasts
- They reduce wave energy during large storms.
- They are a source of food and shelter for marine life.
- They are a source of medicines and health products.
- They are an educational and recreational resource.
- They generate billions in tourism-related income.
- They support local fishing industries.

Coral Reefs

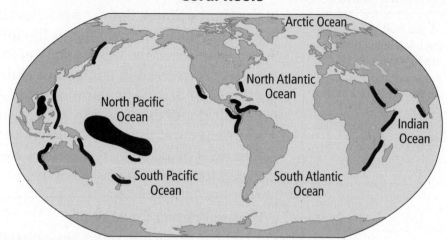

Shallow-water coral reefs are found near the equator in tropical or subtropical waters.

The Future of U.S. Coral Reefs

Coral reefs play a vital role in maintaining a marine ecosystem and supporting its region's economy. But U.S. reefs are suffering the effects of natural and human-based stresses. Runoff from farms and factories has contaminated the reef waters. Every day, fertilizer, pesticides, and other chemicals enter the environment and damage the living things that exist there. Pollution and rising water temperatures have also had a devastating effect on coral reefs, which rely on clear water at a specific temperature range to survive. Illegal fishing and overfishing have reduced the health of the reef ecosystem, and marine debris has blocked the sunlight and clouded the waters.

A Symbiotic Relationship

Coral polyps and algae have a *symbiotic* relationship. That means they help each other. Coral polyps are tiny animals that do not move. They stay in one place and use their tentacles to catch food. A type of algae lives inside the coral polyps for protection. It uses photosynthesis to make its own food. The coral polyps eat the food that the algae make. This mutually beneficial relationship helps coral polyps and the algae survive.

Reading Guide

As you read, think about the information that you would want to include in a research report about coral reefs. How would you paraphrase this information? What details could be quoted?

Unfortunately, coral reefs have been declining for decades in the United States. Some researchers believe that they could completely disappear within our lifetime. In 1996, the United States announced the U.S. Coral Reef Initiative to support coral reef conservation efforts on a global scale, but reefs have continued to decline at alarming rates. About 25 percent of all ocean life depends on coral reefs as a source of food and shelter. These reefs cover less than 2 percent of the ocean floor. More action must be taken by researchers and the general public for the reefs to have a chance to survive.

How to Protect Coral Reefs

- Manage boats and other vessels so that they do not hit the reefs.
- Reduce pollution and runoff through legislation and enforcement.
- Carefully monitor tourist activities.
- Ensure a healthy fish community in the reef and clean water surrounding the reef.
- Introduce healthy coral polyps to damaged reef ecosystems.

Answer the following questions.

1 A student is writing a research report about the relationship between coral polyps and algae. He would like to find additional informational online. Which terms should he enter into an Internet search engine to give him the **best** chance of finding this information?

   A. how coral and algae eat

   B. coral polyp specifics

   C. algae and coral polyps

   D. how algae grow in water

2 A teacher has asked Katarina to write an opinion article about the importance of Florida's coral reefs. Read the following paragraphs from the two texts that you have already reviewed. Then, read the directions that follow.

New Coral Reef Research Center Offers Hope for Future

The local businesses in South Florida are breathing a collective sigh of relief. The future of their economy, based almost entirely on the coral living just off the coast, has been given a boost of support. That support comes in the form of the Center of Excellence for Coral Reef Ecosystems Research, a fancy name for a facility that is basically devoted to protecting coral reefs.

U.S. Coral Reefs

A main U.S. shallow-water reef resource is the Florida Keys off the coast of South Florida. This is the third-largest reef in the world. It covers more than 2,800 square nautical miles and is home to more than 5,500 marine species. About 84 percent of U.S. reefs are found in Florida. The reefs help to generate billions of dollars in income and thousands of jobs.

Part A

How do **both** texts support the opinion that Florida's coral reefs are important in multiple ways?

_____

_____

Part B

Underline the evidence in **both** texts that supports your answer.

3 A student is using the Web page "U.S. Coral Reefs" as a source for her research report.

What is the correct way for the student to restate the information about the U.S. Coral Reef Initiative?

A. In 1996, the United States announced the U.S. Coral Reef Initiative to support coral reef conservation efforts on a global scale, but reefs have continued to decline at alarming rates.

B. The "U.S. Coral Reef Initiative" helps to support coral reef conservation efforts on a global scale, but reefs continue to decline.

C. The U.S. Coral Reef Initiative, created in 1996, was created "to support coral reef conservation efforts on a global scale," but coral reefs are still declining.

D. Reefs have continued to decline at alarming rates despite that, in 1996, the United States announced the U.S. "Coral Reef" Initiative to support coral reef conservation efforts on a global scale.

4 A student is using the passage "New Coral Reef Research Center Offers Hope for Future" and the Web page "U.S. Coral Reefs" to learn more about why coral reefs are so important to the marine environment.

Which sentence from the Web page disagrees with details in the passage?

A. Coral reefs play a vital role in maintaining a marine ecosystem and supporting its region's economy.

B. Pollution and rising water temperatures have also had a devastating effect on coral reefs, which rely on clear water at a specific temperature range to survive.

C. Unfortunately, coral reefs have been declining for decades in the United States.

D. About 25 percent of all ocean life depends on coral reefs as a source of food and shelter.

5 Stephen is writing a report on coral reefs and has narrowed the focus to "Garbage and Coral Reef Destruction." He must use trustworthy and appropriate sources for this topic.

Circle the **best** source for Stephen to use in his report.

A. www.factsaboutgarbage.com
Garbage is a real problem across the United States and even the world. People are throwing too many things away, and landfills are getting higher and higher. Soon there will be no room left. . . .

B. www.mydailyobservationalblog.com/garbage/oceans
So today I went down to the beach to catch a little sun and found that it was littered with the remains of a picnic from yesterday. Disgusting! I felt so bad for the fish that would have to deal with all that garbage. It can't be good for their health. . . .

C. www.oceanstressors/garbage.thu.edu
One of the biggest stressors to ocean life is garbage that people carelessly throw away. Marine debris floats on the surface of the water and blocks sunlight for important plants in the shallow waters below. . . .

D. www.garbagecleanupASAP.net
Welcome! Come join a group that cares about the environment. We organize garbage cleanups in parks, on beaches, even in the middle of the ocean. Stop turning our planet to garbage and start cleaning it up! . . .

E. www.TakingOutTheGarbage.com
Let's talk garbage for a moment. Did you realize that you probably throw away much more than you should? Many items can be recycled and used in another way. Take a look at some of the examples below. . . .

6 You have read two texts that include facts and details about coral reefs and the need for reef conservation, "New Coral Reef Research Center Offers Hope for Future" and "U.S. Coral Reefs."

Consider the information each author provides about protecting coral reefs.

Write a report about conserving and protecting coral reefs. Include information about the threats coral reefs face, why they need to be protected, and what is being done to protect them. Remember to use evidence from both texts to support your ideas.

You may plan your report in the space below. Write your report on the following pages.

Plan

Write your report on the lines below.

W.7.2.a–f, L.7.1

Write an Informative or Explanatory Text

① GETTING THE IDEA

Informative or explanatory text provides information or explains something. These forms of writing require you to answer a specific question about a text using textual evidence or to complete research to write a longer report about a topic.

Your informative writing should have a clearly defined topic supported by organized, well-chosen facts and evidence.

Define Your Topic
If you are responding to a question or prompt, your topic is defined for you. Pay close attention to the focus of the prompt.

Read the prompt below. Underline the specific topic you should focus on when writing your informative essay.

> Based on the information in the text "Guide to American Football," write a report to explain why the quarterback is so essential to a team's success.

Form a Thesis Statement
A **thesis statement** is a sentence in which you state your central idea, or the main point of your writing. All other ideas in your supporting paragraphs should relate to the thesis statement. Here's an example of a well-written thesis statement.

> The quarterback is essential to a football team's success because his completed passes allow the team to move down the field and eventually score.

Notice how this thesis clearly addresses the prompt by answering why the quarterback is essential. It also tells readers what the text will be about.

Organize Your Ideas
Once you have written your thesis statement, it's time to start planning your response. If you are writing a short informative paragraph, your response should include your thesis statement and supporting details. For a longer informative text, you should have a strong introduction, supporting body paragraphs, and a conclusion.

A graphic organizer, such as a chart, can help you organize your ideas. Here is how one student organized her ideas in response to the prompt above.

Introduction	Body Paragraphs	Conclusion
• thesis statement • preview of ideas that will be discussed in essay	Main Ideas: • the most successful teams in history have had quarterbacks with impressive records; much of a team's success is due to the quarterback • when quarterback plays well, the entire team does well; completed passes move ball down the field • when quarterback does not play well (throws interceptions), the entire team suffers; other team gets the ball and scores more	• concluding statement about how history demonstrates importance of quarterback • final thought about pressures placed on quarterback

Choose Information to Support Your Ideas

An informative essay should include well-chosen facts, examples, definitions, or other information. They should be **relevant**, which means they relate to the topic. They should also be **credible**, which means they are accurate and from reliable sources.

Look at the three pieces of information below. Which is the most relevant to address why a quarterback is essential to a team's success?

- As of 2013, there are thirty-two teams in the National Football League (NFL).

- Millions of Americans watch football every Sunday during the NFL football season.

- During a game, the quarterback often tells his teammates what play, or course of action, to follow.

Paraphrase or Quote Your Sources

When you use information from a source, you should **paraphrase**, or rewrite the information in your own words. Taking sentences right from a source without giving the author credit is called **plagiarism** and is stealing.

Sometimes, you may need to include the exact words from a source. In this case, quote the source exactly and **cite**, or identify, it. Look at the following example.

> According to a Forbes business writer, "The NFL is a quarterbacks' league. Elite QBs [quarterbacks] control the action more than ever . . ."

Write Your Draft

Style When you write, use a **style** that fits your audience and purpose. For an informative or explanatory text, use a formal style. Your writing should sound academic, not conversational. Avoid the use of contractions, slang, and shorthand.

Precise Language Be sure to define and elaborate on domain-specific words because your audience may be unfamiliar with your topic. Also, use **precise language** to clearly explain the information you present. Exact nouns, verbs, adjectives, and adverbs will make your meaning clear.

Transitions Include **transitions** to connect ideas and the body paragraphs. Some examples are *in addition*, *therefore*, *however*, or *on the other hand*. These words show how concepts are related and can help your writing flow better.

Provide a Conclusion

An informative or explanatory text should end with a conclusion that sums up the topic and leaves readers with a final thought. For an informative paragraph or short essay, you need to write only a concluding statement. For a longer text, such as a lengthy report, compose a concluding paragraph or section.

Review Your Work

After you have finished writing, reread your work to make sure it is clear and well organized. Use this checklist to guide you as you make changes to your work.

- [ ] Is my thesis statement clear?
- [ ] Are all the facts and details relevant and credible?
- [ ] Do I use precise language and a formal style?
- [ ] Do I paraphrase or quote sources correctly?
- [ ] Does my conclusion sum up the topic for readers?
- [ ] Is my writing free of grammar and spelling errors?

Language Spotlight • Subject-Verb Agreement

In your writing, the subject and verb of each sentence must match. Singular subjects require singular verbs, while plural subjects require plural verbs.

Singular subject and verb: Kim is writing an essay about field hockey.

Plural subject and verb: Kim and her friends are doing homework.

Revise the following sentences so the subject and verb agree.

1. The team captain and her teammates was nervous before the big game.

2. To warm up for practice, Sasha run a mile around the track.

Read the passage.

Setting Goals

A basketball player wants to help her team get to the state championships. By the end of the season, the team reaches the championship game and wins the title. A sophomore who runs track decides to increase his speed. In four months, he runs faster than he ever has before. A tennis player thinks she needs to improve her serve. Within a year, she scores more points from a much stronger serve. What do these three people have in common? They are all teenage athletes who set goals and accomplished them. Setting goals can help athletes both young and old face challenges and achieve success.

There are three types of goals athletes set for themselves. Outcome goals relate to winning competitions or gaining awards. Performance goals relate to improving abilities. Process goals relate to the ways an athlete works to reach an outcome goal or performance goal. For example, a swimmer can set a performance goal of swimming a lap in less than a minute. He can then set a process goal of swimming an extra hour a week to help improve his performance.

Setting goals is not easy. Sometimes, athletes make goals that require a lot of practice or are hard to achieve. Following the three guidelines below can help you achieve success.

Tip 1: Set Specific, Realistic Goals

The best goals are specific and realistic. For example, it is not very helpful for a softball player to say, "I am going to become a better player." Instead, a specific goal such as "I am going to improve my batting average[1] by fifty points" makes more sense. In addition, goals should be realistic. If a goal is almost impossible to achieve, it will only result in feelings of disappointment and regret. Breaking goals into smaller steps can make them more realistic. For example, a runner new to marathon training shouldn't set a goal of running twenty-six miles on the first day of training. She may start the first week of training by running four miles a day, and then increase her goal to six miles a day, and so on, until she reaches twenty-six miles in one day.

Tip 2: Take Time to Achieve a Goal

Most goals can't be reached overnight. So, it is important to remember to work toward slow, steady progress. Pay attention to the small improvements and give yourself credit for each minor accomplishment you make toward your goal.

[1] **batting average:** a measure of a baseball or softball player's performance at bat

Tip 3: Don't Allow Roadblocks to Stop Your Progress

It is unrealistic to expect everything to go smoothly. Many athletes often experience obstacles on the road to success. These roadblocks do not always mean an athlete has failed to reach a goal. Often, they are a sign it might be best to examine the problem in a new way or to vary your approach. For instance, imagine a basketball player wanted to score more points in a game. So he focused on improving his jump shot, which helped only a little. He then realized he needed to find better ways to communicate with his teammates in the middle of games. Once he did that, they passed the ball to him more often, he had more opportunities to score, and he gained more points per game.

Following these three tips can not only help athletes reach their dreams, but it can also help anyone—from a member of the debate team to a student preparing an important report—achieve success. In fact, setting goals and working toward them is a major part of life. It is the best way to accomplish anything you want to do.

Answer the following questions.

1 A student is writing guidelines for setting goals. Which of the following sentences would make the **best** thesis for the student's guidelines?

    A. Athletes can set different kinds of goals to achieve success.

    B. Setting unrealistic goals can lead to failure.

    C. One example of a goal is to run a mile in under eight minutes.

    D. Do not let anyone set goals for you.

> **Hint** Remember that a thesis statement introduces the central idea of an informative text. It should clearly explain the topic and make it obvious to readers.

2 Summarize the information the author provides to show how people can set and accomplish goals.

Write your answer on the lines provided.

_____

_____

_____

_____

> **Hint** When you summarize, you should include all the main points the writer makes. What is the main information the author includes to develop the topic of setting and accomplishing goals? The subheads in this passage can help you identify the writer's main points.

3 Circle **three** transition words or phrases in paragraph 4 of the passage.

> **Hint** Remember, writers include transitions to connect ideas in a text.

4 The following sentences could be included in the passage. Which one is the **best** example of precise language?

A. Setting goals can help people in many, many ways.

B. A golfer may set a goal of hitting under ninety strokes.

C. It helps to follow different things when you set goals.

D. Everybody should think about goals.

> **Hint** Precise language uses specific nouns, verbs, adjectives, and adverbs to convey the writer's meaning clearly. Choose the sentence that uses the most exact words.

Use the Reading Guide to help you understand the passage.

One Amazing Athlete

Reading Guide

What is the central idea of this passage?

How did Betty Robinson begin her racing career?

The author includes a quote from Betty. What does this quote show about the time period in which Betty first began to race?

The year was 1928, and the place was Amsterdam. A sixteen-year-old athlete from the United States was preparing to run the 100-meter dash. It was the first time women athletes were allowed to compete in track-and-field events at the Olympics, and this was the first race of the 1928 Games. At the sound of the starting gun, the athletes raced down the track. The 100-meter race is very fast, and it came down to a photo finish between the American and a racer from Canada. In the end, the American athlete won, and she became the first woman to ever win an Olympic gold medal in track and field. Her name was Betty Robinson, and her story is an example of setting goals to achieve success.

Nicknamed "Betty," Elizabeth Robinson was born in Illinois in 1911. When she was in high school, an assistant track coach happened to spot her running to catch a train. Realizing she could be a track-and-field athlete, the coach asked her to run fifty yards down a school hallway as an informal tryout to gain a spot on the team. Betty later told the *Los Angeles Times*, "I had no idea that women even ran then. That is when I found out that they actually had track meets for women."

Betty began to practice and prepare for races. Each race presented a new goal, and once she achieved it, she moved on to the next. Three weeks after joining her high school team, she made her debut at a regional race where she came in second. In her next race, she equaled the world record at that time, which was 12.0 seconds in the 100-meter dash. In her third race, Betty finished second and qualified for the 1928 Olympic team. Before then, racing was not considered to be "ladylike" or "genteel" enough for women. However, Betty and her teammates were determined to prove any naysayers wrong.

After gaining a spot on the team, Betty Robinson sailed to Europe with the Olympic team. Along the way, she worked out on a quarter-mile track made of linoleum that was placed along the deck of the ship. Regular practice helped her prepare for the next goal, winning a gold medal at the Olympics. But first, she had to run qualifying races in Amsterdam. She finished second in her trial race and first in her semifinal.

Circle an example of precise language in the passage. Notice how the author's use of precise language helps you understand the specifics of the events.

How does the writer connect ideas within the text?

What challenges did Betty face in her life?

The author says Betty inspired future female runners. What details in the text show how Betty was inspiring?

In fact, she became the only American to reach the finals in the 100-meter dash, and, in the end, she brought home the gold. Although the finish was too close to call at first, the judges quickly declared Betty the winner. She beat Fanny Rosenfeld of Canada—who had been favored to win—with a final time of 12.2 seconds. Betty later said, "When the flag went up after the race, I started crying like a baby."

Three years later, Betty faced an even greater challenge. In 1931, she was riding in a small plane with her cousin near Chicago. The plane crashed, and at first the two were presumed to be dead. Although they both survived, Betty suffered severe head injuries, along with a broken arm and leg. She spent a long recovery in a hospital, and for four months she was in a wheelchair or on crutches. Also, a silver rod and pin were inserted into her broken leg to stabilize it and support the bone, and her leg became half an inch shorter than the other one.

It seemed like Betty might never race again, but she was determined not to give up. So she set another important goal for herself. She intended to make the Olympic team again. It took several long, difficult years of rehabilitation and recovery. But Betty made a comeback in 1936 when she qualified for the Olympic relay team. However, her injured leg was still stiff, and she could not bend her knee. So unlike the other racers, she had to make a standing start, rather than a crouching start. However, she was still fast enough to race and win. Her team captured the gold medal in the 100-meter relay dash at the 1936 Games in Berlin.

Betty Robinson later married Richard Schwartz and they started a family. After she stopped racing, she became a coach and a public speaker. She also was inducted into the National Track and Field Hall of Fame and the United States Track and Field Hall of Fame.

As the first female Olympic gold medal winner in a track-and-field event, Betty Robinson Schwartz inspired future female runners, including Florence Griffith Joyner, who broke the world record for women in the 100-meter dash in 1988. Betty proved she was one amazing athlete who would not let adversity stand in her way.

Answer the following questions.

1 What is the author's main point?

   A. Betty Robinson was only a teenager when she began racing and won her first gold medal.

   B. Betty Robinson set goals and overcame adversity to achieve great success in her sport.

   C. Betty Robinson's world-record time in the 100-meter dash was one and a half seconds slower than the current record.

   D. Betty Robinson was in a horrible plane crash that nearly ended her athletic career.

2 Write two paragraphs to explain how Betty Robinson recovered from the plane crash in 1931 and reestablished her racing career.

3 A student is writing an essay about Betty Robinson and has included the following sentences. Which one does **not** include correct subject-verb agreement?

A. Betty was discovered by her coach while running to catch a train.

B. The teammates practiced on a special track as the ship sailed to Europe.

C. Betty and her teammates was able to capture gold at the 1936 Olympics.

D. I think Betty's story is all about triumph over adversity and difficult odds.

4 The following sentences could be included in the passage. Which one is the **best** example of formal style?

A. Wow, Betty Robinson must have been incredibly fast!

B. Betty won the gold medal just four months after she started racing.

C. People must have been stupid to think that women should not race.

D. Betty was the coolest racer who ever lived, and other people look up to her.

5 The following question has two parts. First, answer Part A. Then, answer Part B.

Part A

Read the following statement from the passage.

> **So unlike the other racers, she had to make a standing start, rather than a crouching start.**

What is the meaning of the domain-specific phrase crouching start?

A. a start behind a designated line

B. when a runner starts running after the buzzer sounds

C. when a race starts off with a hurdle

D. a starting position in which a runner bends down to prepare for running

Part B

Which sentence from the text **best** explains the meaning of crouching start?

A. In her third race, Betty finished second and qualified for the 1928 Olympic team.

B. Although the finish was too close to call at first, the judges quickly declared Betty the winner.

C. But Betty made a comeback in 1936 when she qualified for the Olympic relay team.

D. However, her injured leg was still stiff, and she could not bend her knee.

6 In your own words, write an informative essay about how setting goals can help students achieve success. Explain what goals are and how to set them. Draw on evidence from "Setting Goals" and "One Amazing Athlete" to support your ideas.

You may plan your informative essay in the space below. Write your essay on the following pages.

+---+
| **Plan** |
| |
| |
| |
| |
| |
| |
| |
| |
| |
| |
| |
| |
| |
| |
| |
| |
| |
| |
| |
| |
| |
| |
+---+

Write your essay on the lines below.

Write an Argument

An **argument** is an attempt to convince others to think or act in a certain way. Its main purpose is to persuade its audience, or readers. When you write an argument, you need to organize your ideas and present them clearly in order to support your position or claim.

If you are responding to a prompt, be sure to address all parts of the directions. If you do not have a strong opinion about an issue, you need to look at both sides to figure out which side of an issue you will support. It may help to brainstorm some ideas using a chart or another graphic organizer. In the example below, a student is brainstorming about whether the United States should continue making pennies.

Issue	
Should the U.S. continue producing and using pennies?	
Reasons For	**Reasons Against**
• We have always used pennies. We need them to make exact change. • If we don't have pennies, the prices of many products might go up as much as four cents.	• Pennies are not worth much. • Making change is more cumbersome because of pennies.

Once you have decided on the focus of your argument, it is time to state a **claim**, or position, and write a thesis statement. A **thesis statement** is a sentence in which you state your claim, or the **main point** you will make in your essay. All other ideas in the essay should relate to the thesis statement. Here's an example of a well-written thesis statement.

> Professional athletes need a salary cap to put an end to their excessively high salaries.

This thesis statement reveals that the argument will be about the salary caps of professional athletes. The student's position is that salary caps should exist.

Evidence

You will need to find appropriate evidence from sources to use in your argument. Look for evidence (such as facts, examples, and data) that supports your claims. Also, be sure that your evidence is accurate, relevant, and up-to-date. Any errors will cause your readers to doubt the validity of your argument.

Structure

Once you know what you are writing about, create an **outline** to plan the main ideas of your argument. An outline should include all of the main parts of your argument: the introduction, body, and conclusion.

- The **introduction** is the first part of your argument. The purpose of the introduction is to preview what is to come in your written argument and to capture your audience's attention. In an essay, the introduction should be at least one paragraph long and must include your thesis statement.

- The **body** of your argument will develop the position you have presented in your thesis statement. It consists of several **supporting paragraphs**. Each supporting paragraph has its own **topic sentence** and should develop a single **supporting reason** with facts, examples, and other relevant details. Be sure to explain how each supporting reason connects with your thesis statement. This is where you will use relevant sources that include your facts.

- The **conclusion** is the end of the composition. A good conclusion restates the thesis, summarizes the main points, and gives readers something to consider.

To make sure your writing follows a logical argument structure, it helps to create an outline. Look at the sample outline below.

I. Introduction (thesis): Professional athletes need a salary cap to put an end to their excessively high salaries.

II. Body

    A. The high salaries of professional athletes result in higher ticket prices.

    B. Athletes' exorbitant salaries send the wrong message to young people.

    C. Playing sports is not a job that justifies such high salaries.

III. Conclusion: It's time for a change; athletes do not merit high salaries.

Good arguments acknowledge **opposing claims** and **refute** them, or prove them wrong. If you don't refute an opposing claim, you are arguing against yourself. Read the example of an opposing claim and its refutation below.

> Opposing Claim: Athletes claim that team owners make so much money that their salaries represent a fair share of the owners' profits.
>
> Refutation: There is nothing fair about the profit that either owners or players make at the fans' expense.

Style

Everyone has a unique style of writing. However, there are a few techniques you can use to convey your message in a polished way. Make sure you use transitions in your argument. **Transitions** are words and phrases that clarify the relationships among your ideas, such as *for example, in contrast, in addition,* and *however.*

Your writing style should also be **formal**. Use standard English. Do not be too casual or use slang. Remember that your audience for school assignments is your teacher and sometimes your fellow students. It should not sound like an e-mail or a text message that you write to a friend.

Review Your Work

After you have finished writing, it is important to read your work and make any necessary revisions and edits. Keep this checklist in mind as you review your argument.

- ☐ Do I address all parts of the prompt?
- ☐ Do I develop the claim using clear and convincing reasoning?
- ☐ Do I use enough relevant evidence from the texts?
- ☐ Is my response appropriate to the task, purpose, and audience?
- ☐ Do I include a strong introduction and conclusion?
- ☐ Does my response follow a logical order?
- ☐ Is my language formal, precise, and descriptive?
- ☐ Do I use enough transitions to link ideas?
- ☐ Is my writing free of grammar, mechanics, and spelling errors?

Language Spotlight • Vary Sentence Patterns

Whenever you write, aim to vary the types of your sentences. This helps you signal the different relationships among ideas. Read the set of related sentences below. How do the different sentences show relationships between the ideas?

simple	I don't have time for a second sport.
compound	I like soccer, but I like lacrosse better.
complex	Although I like soccer, I like lacrosse better.
compound-complex	Although I like soccer, I like lacrosse better, and I don't have time for a second sport.

On a separate sheet of paper, make up your own set of related sentences. Be sure they show the relationships between ideas. Share you sentences with a partner.

Read the passage.

Why the United Nations Is Still Necessary

On October 24, 1945, the United Nations (UN) came into existence. Its creation was spurred on by the trauma and chaos of World War II. The purpose of the UN is to govern international behavior in order to keep peace among all nations. Since its inception, the United Nations has played a vital role in peace keeping, literacy, humanitarian aid, and human rights. Many opponents of the UN are blind to the benefits of over sixty years of UN programs and policies. However, it is absolutely necessary that the UN remain in existence.

One of the most important roles of the UN is to promote world peace. It is the UN that has been instrumental in bringing an end to conflicts throughout the world just since the 1990s. Sometimes peace was achieved through UN mediation. Other times, third parties brought peace with UN support. Some places where the UN was able to promote peace are Sierra Leone, Liberia, and Burundi. Over the history of the United Nations, sixty-nine peacekeeping and observer missions have restored order. They helped countries once in conflict to recover. To support the continued peace, the International Atomic Energy Agency of the UN has agreements with over 170 countries concerning the safe guarding of nuclear material.

In another role, the UN has been active in more than a hundred countries promoting democracy. Some countries that have benefited from the intervention of the UN are Cambodia, El Salvador, and South Africa. By providing election advice, assistance, and monitoring, the UN has enabled the people in many countries to participate in free and fair elections.

In addition, the UN has developed strong literacy and health programs targeted at developing countries. Thanks in part to the UN, 84 percent of adults in developing countries can read, and 89 percent of the children attend primary schools. UN programs for girls and women have raised female literacy to 79 percent globally. Because of health and nutrition programs implemented by UN agencies, infant death rates in third-world countries have dropped to 1 in 18. Smallpox has been eradicated from the planet, thanks to the UN. Polio is another disease that is on the verge of being eliminated. Because of the UN's Global Polio Eradication Initiative, almost five million children who would have been paralyzed by this disease can walk today.

So, would all these global changes have occurred without a central world agency such as the UN? Given the often-explosive nature of nationalism, it does not seem likely. The UN provides a forum for countries of the world. In this forum they can align their nationalistic goals with those that are in the best interest of all nations.

Answer the following questions.

1 This question has two parts. First, answer Part A. Then, answer Part B.

Part A

Which sentence states the author's claim about the United Nations today?

A. The UN no longer benefits member nations and should be dissolved.

B. The UN is essential and should receive continued support.

C. The UN was established in the aftermath of World War II.

D. The role of the UN should be expanded only in the developing world.

Part B

Underline **one** sentence in the passage that supports your answer to Part A.

Hint Think about the purpose of the argument. What does the author want readers to believe?

2 The following question has two parts. First, answer Part A. Then, answer Part B.

Part A

Circle one clear reason the author gives that is supported by relevant evidence in the passage.

A. The United Nations has focused its attention on human rights around the world.

B. The United Nations promotes industrial development in developing countries.

C. The United Nations has developed strong literacy and health programs targeted at developing countries.

D. The United Nations provides a forum for third-world countries to pursue their interests.

Part B

Find two sentences in the passage that give evidence to support your answer to Part A.

Write the sentences on the lines below.

_____

_____

_____

Hint This question asks you to do two things. First, identify a reason given in the passage that has evidence to back it up. Then, choose two facts that directly support the reason you circled.

3 According to the information from the passage, what effect did UN programs have on health? Cite and summarize specific details from the passage.

Write your answer on the lines provided.

_____

_____

_____

_____

_____

Hint In your answer, write a main idea to state what the UN did for world health in general. Then, support this main idea with what it specifically did.

4 The writer wants to add a sentence to the conclusion to further support the argument.

Which sentence is **best** to add?

A. In conclusion, I think it's a good idea for the UN to be around for lots of years.

B. Therefore, opponents of the UN do offer some legitimate reasons for its abolishment.

C. Thus, every country has a voice, and that dialogue is crucial in this modern world.

D. Nevertheless, if there were more countries taking part in the UN, the world would be a better place.

Hint Think about the following questions to help you decide: What kind of information belongs in the conclusion? Which sentence keeps to the formal style of the argument?

Use the Reading Guide to help you understand the passage.

Is the United Nations Still Necessary?

Reading Guide

Notice how the author introduces the topic. What background information do you learn? How does the background information set up the issues around the topic question?

The United Nations' role in the modern world has been scrutinized again and again. Some people feel that the organization is ineffectual in dealing with today's problems. Others feel the United Nations (UN) is still an important forum for world peace and social and humanitarian issues. To come to a decision about the need for the UN, it is important to learn reasons for both views, as well as to understand the history and purpose of the UN.

The role that the UN came to play in the world was defined at the end of World War II. At that time, people were tired of the agony of war. They felt that such a devastating worldwide tragedy must not happen again. These feelings were similar to those people felt after World War I, when the League of Nations was formed to "promote international cooperation and to achieve peace and security." However, with the onset of World War II, it was obvious that the League of Nations failed to deliver on its promise.

In 1941, at the beginning of World War II, world leaders Franklin D. Roosevelt and Winston Churchill met at what became known as the Atlantic Conference. Both leaders were convinced that another world organization should be formed to replace the League of Nations. At the end of this meeting, the leaders released the Atlantic Charter. It advocated global cooperation to foster democracy, human rights, and economic development; to establish peace; and to protect the sanctity of territorial borders. After the war, this document became the cornerstone for the charter of a new world organization, which Roosevelt named the United Nations. Its charter empowered the UN to conduct peacekeeping operations.

For over seventy years the UN has been the world forum for conflict resolution. But today, not everyone agrees that it is still necessary.

How does the background information help you understand the topic question?

What are some transitions that connect ideas in the paragraphs and sentences?

What style is this passage written in: formal or informal? How can you tell?

Think about who the most likely audience of this passage is.

Since there have been so many conflicts since the establishment of the UN, opponents do not feel the UN is a success. They point to these conflicts as a sign of its failure. Some call for the abolishment of the UN entirely. Besides the UN's inability to ensure peace, opponents point out that the United Nations is powerless to make countries follow international law. Some powerful countries feel free to act aggressively. Smaller nations with powerful allies may believe that they, too, can flout international law.

Critics also contend that the UN has become a bloated, ineffective bureaucracy with a lot of redundancy in responsibilities. For example, the UN has three different commissions that study the very same issues in standards for foods: the UN Economic Commission for Europe, the World Health Organization, and the Food and Agriculture Organization. These UN commissions also do the same work as the U.S. Food and Drug Administration and the European Food Safety Authority.

In fact, in a recent *New York Times* article, Jean-Pierre Lehmann, a professor of international political economy in Lausanne, Switzerland, commented, "Generally, the UN has been a terrible disappointment compared to the ideals with which it was established. It serves as a gravy train for a very bloated employment system, and, yes, there is huge overlap between the agencies."

A final reason to abolish the UN is the huge expense to the United States. The United States contributes money that totals over one-fourth of the UN budget. In 2009, the United States paid $6 billion. In 2010, the United States paid almost $7.7 billion. In fact, the United States now pays double the amount it paid just a decade ago. Opponents of the UN ask, if the UN is a global organization, why aren't other countries paying their fair share?

Reading Guide

Notice how the passage is organized. How does this help you understand both sides of the issues?

What words or phrases are particularly effective?

On the other hand, those in favor of the UN want the organization to grow in importance rather than be abolished. They point to a more global society in which countries of the world are less isolated now than in the past. Today's issues, such as climate change and economic policy, are global concerns. These concerns need to be aired in a central place where all countries have an equal voice and can discuss and contribute to solutions.

UN supporters also maintain that the UN's human rights and global relief programs have had a tremendously positive impact in the world. UN world health initiatives have been equally impressive in improving the quality of life in developing countries. To counter inefficiency and corruption, supporters advocate reform, such as adjusting the UN management structure, adding a peacekeeping commission, and allocating additional resources. They say that more support—not abolishing the UN—is the better solution.

So, is the United Nations a bloated bureaucratic nightmare or a shining light of hope? Should the world community end the nightmare or change the lightbulb? People will continue to debate and choose sides because of the lofty goals and responsibilities with which the UN is entrusted. Although people may never totally agree on the UN's fate, the more people learn about the United Nations, the stronger their basis will be for an informed opinion.

Answer the following questions.

1 This question has two parts. First, answer Part A. Then, answer Part B.

Part A

Which of the following **best** summarizes the claim made by the author of this passage?

A. There is definite proof that the UN is necessary for developing countries.

B. The United States could replace the UN because it pays for most of its costs anyway.

C. It is important to learn about the UN in order to form a sensible opinion about its necessity.

D. The United Nations was started because of the chaos in the world that resulted from World War II.

Part B

Which sentences from the passage **best** support your response to Part A? Choose **all** that apply.

A. In fact, the United States now pays double the amount it paid just a decade ago.

B. The role that the UN came to play in the world was defined at the end of World War II.

C. To come to a decision about the need for the UN, it is important to learn reasons for both views, as well as to understand the history and purpose of the UN.

D. Although people may never totally agree on the UN's fate, the more people learn about the United Nations, the stronger their basis will be for an informed opinion.

2 The writer wants to add a sentence to the introduction.

Which sentence **best** fits the content and style of the introduction and uses a transition?

A. Therefore, don't believe everything you read about the United Nations.

B. For example, it is important to read all you can about what the UN is doing.

C. Thus, the availability of reliable information is crucial to the future of the UN.

D. However, using the available information may not result in a strong opinion.

3 Complete the outline to show how this passage is organized.

I. Introduction

_____

_____

_____

_____

II. Body

A. Information about

_____

_____

B. Reasons why

_____

_____

C. Reasons why

_____

_____

III. Conclusion

_____

_____

_____

_____

4 Which sentences from the passage give reasons why the UN is no longer needed? Circle **all** that apply.

A. Its charter empowered the UN to conduct peacekeeping operations.

B. The United States contributes money that totals over one-fourth of the UN budget.

C. Smaller nations with powerful allies may believe that they, too, can flout international law.

D. Critics also contend that the UN has become a bloated, ineffective bureaucracy with a lot of redundancy in responsibilities.

E. They point to a more global society in which countries of the world are less isolated now than in the past.

F. UN world health initiatives have been equally impressive in improving the quality of life in developing countries.

5 Read the sentences from the passage and the directions that follow.

> **The United States contributes money that totals over one-fourth of the UN budget. In 2009, the United States paid $6 billion. In 2010, the United States paid almost $7.7 billion. In fact, the United States now pays double the amount it paid just a decade ago.**

Rewrite the sentences so they are more varied and show the relationships between the reasons and evidence.

_____

_____

_____

_____

_____

6 Imagine that you are part of a Congressional committee that is attempting to convince lawmakers to bring up legislation to end the United States' membership in the United Nations. Write an argument against the United States' involvement in the United Nations based on the passages "Why the United Nations Is Still Necessary" and "Is the United Nations Still Necessary?" Be sure to consider the claims, reasons, and evidence presented in both passages. Include your own insights and observations, and provide supporting evidence from both sources. Be sure to address at least one opposing claim.

You may plan your argument in the space below. Write your argument on the following pages.

Plan

Write your argument on the lines below.

Revise and Edit

Good writers spend a lot of time writing a text. Usually they don't get everything right the first time. They have to revise and edit their drafts to make them better.

Revising

When you **revise**, you read your draft carefully. You look to see if your ideas make sense and if they follow a logical order. You look for words and phrases to convey your ideas precisely. Then you make changes to refine your work. When you revise, think about the following aspects to make your writing the best it can be.

Phrases and Clauses

Sentences are made up of phrases and clauses. Understanding what they are and how they function can help you write better. Including phrases and clauses in your writing can add extra details that make your writing more interesting.

- A **phrase** is a group of related words without a subject and predicate. A phrase is used as a single part of speech.

  phrase: in the park; on Saturday

- A **clause** is a group of words with a subject and a predicate. An **independent clause** expresses a complete thought and can stand on its own. A **dependent clause** expresses an incomplete thought and cannot stand on its own.

  independent clause: I baked chocolate chip cookies.

  dependent clause: that smelled delicious

Sentence Types

Using a variety of sentence types helps you signal different relationships among ideas in your writing.

A **simple sentence** expresses one complete thought; it is an independent clause. It has a subject and a predicate. Underline the subject in this sentence.

　　The beachcombers looked for unusual shells.

A **compound sentence** expresses two or more complete thoughts. It is made up of two independent clauses joined by a comma and a **coordinating conjunction** such as *and, but, or*, or *so*. Underline the independent clauses in this sentence.

　　Anna found a sand dollar, **so** she was very excited.

A **complex sentence** is made up of an independent clause and one or more dependent clauses. The clauses are joined by a **subordinating conjunction** such as *after, where, because, if,* or *since*. The subordinating conjunction shows a relationship between the two clauses. Underline the dependent clause below.

After the others left the beach, Anna found more beautiful shells.

A **compound-complex** sentence has two or more independent clauses and one or more dependent clauses. Underline the independent clauses below.

Anna stayed on the beach; although it was cool, she watched the waves.

Editing
After you revise your draft, **edit** it for errors in grammar.

Phrases and Clauses as Modifiers
Phrases and clauses can act as adjectives or adverbs. An **adjective phrase** or an **adjective clause** usually comes after the noun or pronoun it modifies.

adjective phrase: The students on the committee had a meeting.

adjective clause: This is the phone that is the latest model.

An **adverb phrase** tells when, where, how, why, or to what extent. An **adverb clause** modifies a verb, an adjective, or another adverb.

adverb phrase: My dad is great at video games.

adverb clause: After I programmed my phone, I called you.

Misplaced and Dangling Modifiers
Place the modifier as close as possible to the word it describes.

A **misplaced modifier** is in the wrong place in a sentence. It seems to modify the wrong word and makes the sentence confusing.

misplaced modifier: I looked for the life jacket my father bought in the shed. (This implies that my father bought the jacket in the shed.)
correct modifier: I looked in the shed for the life jacket my father bought.

A **dangling modifier** occurs when the word it modifies is missing from the sentence.

dangling modifier: Kayaking in the lake, a turtle swam by. (This implies that the turtle was kayaking in the lake.)
correct, modifies the pronoun I: Kayaking in the lake, **I saw** a turtle swim by.

Subject-Verb Agreement
Singular subjects require singular verbs. Plural subjects require plural verbs.

singular subject: Carlos **is going** to the park with his friends.

plural subject: Carlos and his friends **are going** to the park.

Proofreading

Proofread to make sure you have used correct capitalization, punctuation, and spelling in your writing. Here are some things to look for.

Commas and Coordinate Adjectives

Coordinate adjectives are adjectives with equal weight in describing a noun. The order of coordinate adjectives can be reversed, and the adjectives will still make sense. Use a comma to separate two coordinate adjectives. Use commas and the word *and* to separate more than two adjectives.

> *coordinate adjectives:* We got ready for some cold, windy weather.
> We got ready for some windy, cold weather.

A **non-coordinate adjective** is usually the last adjective in a series and is often considered part of a noun. It's order *cannot* be reversed with another adjective. A comma does not separate a non-coordinate adjective from another adjective.

> *non-coordinate adjective:* Our yard has a tall pine tree. (NOT *a pine, tall tree*)

Quotation Marks to Cite Research

When citing research, use quotation marks to cite the source. You can use an introductory phrase and a comma or a colon.

According to the National Weather Service, "Weather and climate sensitive industries in the United States account for about one-third of the nation's Gross Domestic Product."

You can also make the quote part of your own sentence.

After analyzing its data, NOAA said that August 2013 tied for "the fourth warmest August since record keeping began in 1880."

Correct Spelling

Think about the spelling patterns and rules you know. Check your writing to see whether you have followed the rules. When you are unsure how to spell a word, use references if you can.

Language Spotlight • Eliminate Wordiness and Redundancy

Use simple words that make your point, and eliminate words that repeat ideas. Read the sentences below. Note which words were deleted in the second sentence.

> *wordy/redundant*: Aaron is an awesome guitarist who plays the guitar well.

> *clear*: Aaron plays the guitar well.

How would you eliminate wordiness and redundancy in this sentence?

> On the occasion of taking a shopping trip to the mall, I may buy two shirts.

This passage contains mistakes. Read the passage.

The Case of the Missing Antique Bracelet

(1) Sitting at the dressing table in her bedroom, Angelica's arm turned every which way and admired her bracelet. (2) Its pearls and miniature gold roses looked so delicate and graceful when she casually moved her arm. (3) The smooth, luminous pearls gleamed, and the gold roses shone while tiny diamonds refracted the sunlight and sparkled from mounts in the center of the roses.

(4) Mom had presented it to Angelica a few months ago when she had turned thirteen.

(5) "You are becoming a young lady," Mom had said. (6) "Your grades are excellent, and you are loving and respectful, so I think you are mature enough to own this family heirloom."

(7) Although the bracelet was an exquisite work of art, Angelica treasured it most because of its history: the bracelet had originally belonged to Angelica's great-grandmother, Cecelia. (8) Cecelia passed it down to Grandmamma, who was her only daughter, when she was thirteen. (9) Grandmamma continued the tradition by giving the bracelet to Mom on her thirteenth birthday, and now Angelica was included in the tradition.

(10) Mom's voice broke into Angela's musings. (11) "Hurry, or you'll miss the bus," Mom said.

(12) Angelica quickly gathered up her books and her lunch, said good-bye to Mom and Grandmamma, and zoomed out the door.

(13) Tuesday was her busiest day at school with her science lab, algebra, and Spanish, giving Angela hardly a moment to breathe all day. (14) At dismissal time, as she collected her things from her locker, she looked at her arm and realized that her bracelet was missing. (15) Her stomach clenched. (16) What had happened to the bracelet, and how could she have been so careless?

(17) Nearly frantic, Angelica turned to see Juanita walking toward her.

(18) Angelica wailed, "I lost my antique bracelet, and I simply can't face my mother and grandmother until I find it."

(19) "Angelica, it's both auspicious and fortunate for you that I arrived," Juanita told her. (20) "In case you forgot, I'll remind you of my alter ego: Juanita Sherlock Fregosa, semiprofessional detective and locator extraordinaire of missing possessions."

(21) "Can you really help me?" Angelica implored.

(22) "Undoubtedly!" Juanita assured her. (23) "I'm engaging my superior sleuthing brain now."

(24) "The things in your backpack is where we should start," Juanita continued. (25) "Then we're going to retrace your steps and inspect every nook and cranny in the school." (26) Juanita dumped Angelica's backpack on the floor and combed through the pile of books, keys, cosmetics, and assorted trinkets. (27) No luck. (28) Next they checked the school's lost-and-found but found nothing there, either. (29) Then the girls carefully examined each classroom, the cafeteria, and the corridors but came up empty-handed.

(30) When the girls finally arrived back at Angelica's locker, Juanita squeezed her eyes shut and stroked her chin. (31) "I believe your bracelet is at home," she said.

(32) "That's impossible," responded Angelica. (33) "I was wearing it at breakfast, and I know I didn't take it off."

(34) "Why don't I go home with you so we can double-check?" asked Juanita.

(35) The girls walked in. (36) Grandmamma waved. (37) Something on her arm sparkled.

(38) "Oh, you have it! I'm so relieved," gasped Angelica when she spied the bracelet dangling on Grandmamma's slender wrist. (39) "I thought I had lost my bracelet for good."

(40) "I found it on the floor under your chair," Grandmamma explained.

(41) Angela turned to Juanita. "You've earned your reputation as an excellent sleuth."

(42) "I'm delighted to be of service," Juanita grinned.

(43) Grandmamma began unclasping the bracelet, but Angelica stopped her. (44) "Maybe I'm not mature enough to take care of the family heirloom just yet. (45) Would you keep it in your jewelry box for me?" Angelica asked. (46) "I'll let you know when I'm ready for it."

(47) Grandmamma hugged her and smiled. (48) "Such a mature, responsible idea," she said.

Answer the following questions.

1 This question has two parts. First, answer Part A. Then, answer Part B.

Part A

Read the sentences from the passage.

(35) The girls walked in. (36) Grandmamma waved. (37) Something on her arm sparkled.

What is the **best** way to improve variety and show the relationship in the ideas in the sentences? Choose **all** that apply.

A. Combine all the sentences into a compound-complex sentence.

B. Combine sentences 35 and 37 into a complex sentence.

C. Use a coordinating conjunction to join sentences 36 and 37.

D. Combine sentences 36 and 37 into a compound sentence.

Part B

Write the revised sentences on the lines below.

_____

_____

> **Hint** What do you know about compound, complex, and compound-complex sentences? Think about what you know about using conjunctions to join parts of sentences and make connections between ideas.

2 The following question has two parts. First, answer Part A. Then, answer Part B.

Part A

Which sentence from the passage is wordy or redundant?

- **A.** Its pearls and miniature gold roses looked so delicate and graceful when she casually moved her arm.

- **B.** Tuesday was her busiest day at school with her science lab, algebra, and Spanish, giving Angela hardly a moment to breathe all day.

- **C.** "Angelica, it's both auspicious and fortunate for you that I arrived," Juanita told her.

- **D.** Then the girls carefully examined each classroom, the cafeteria, and the corridors but came up empty-handed.

Part B

Rewrite the sentence so it is no longer wordy or redundant.

_____

_____

> **Hint** Think about the most important words in the sentence. Eliminate any words that you do not need or that repeat the same idea.

3 The following question has two parts. First, answer Part A. Then, answer Part B.

Part A

Read the following excerpt from the passage. Underline the error in subject-verb agreement.

"The things in your backpack is where we should start," Juanita continued.

Part B

Rewrite the sentence so it is correct.

_____

_____

> **Hint** Find the subject and then decide whether it is singular or plural. Which form of the verb matches the subject?

4 The following question has two parts. First, answer Part A. Then, answer Part B.

Part A

Read the excerpts from the passage. Find the sentence with the dangling modifier.

A. Sitting at the dressing table in her bedroom, Angelica's arm turned every which way and admired her bracelet.

B. Grandmamma continued the tradition by giving the bracelet to Mom on her thirteenth birthday, and now Angelica was included in the tradition.

C. At dismissal time, as she collected her things from her locker, she looked at her arm and realized that her bracelet was missing.

D. Grandmamma began unclasping the bracelet, but Angelica stopped her.

Part B

Rewrite the sentence you found in Part A so it is correct.

_____

_____

Hint Remember that a dangling modifier occurs when the word it modifies is missing from the sentence. Which sentence seems to be missing a word?

This passage contains mistakes. Use the Reading Guide to help you find the mistakes and understand the passage.

Louis Armstrong, the Father of Jazz

Reading Guide

Does the author vary the sentence types?

Does the author order and punctuate serial adjectives correctly?

(1) Have you ever heard the scintillating sounds of jazz music? (2) Today's jazz owes an enormous debt to Louis Armstrong. (3) Considered one of the founders of jazz, Armstrong was one of the most important musicians of the twentieth century.

A Difficult Start

(4) Louis Armstrong was born on August 4, 1901. (5) An African American, he grew up in dire poverty in the segregated southern city of New Orleans, Louisiana. (6) Living in an unstable family, his mother and sister were supported in part by Armstrong, who had to leave school in fifth grade to earn money. (7) He traveled the streets of New Orleans to any job where he could make a few pennies. (8) Just a child, he sang on street corners, cleaned the tops of graves, sold coal, and loaded junk wagons. (9) But rather than being Armstrong's undoing, this was the start of his musical education.

(10) New Orleans was full of music, and wandering the city exposed Armstrong to its musical richness. (11) Neighborhood music clubs sent the sounds of blues and ragtime into the streets. (12) Funerals and holiday parades made liberal use of rollicking spirited brass bands. (13) Even getting arrested at age eleven and going to reform school for eighteen months was a blessing in disguise for Armstrong. (14) There he received his first formal music lessons, joined the school band playing the cornet and bugle, and eventually became its director. (15) Armstrong had found his passion and began planning for a lifetime as a musician.

Reading Guide

Has the author eliminated wordiness and redundancy?

Has the author placed modifiers as close as possible to the words they describe?

From Student to Pro

(16) After Armstrong was released from reform school, he devoted his teen years to music and learning his craft. (17) Thirteen-year-old Armstrong began playing with street musicians and in clubs all over New Orleans. (18) His playing caught the attention of Joe "King" Oliver, a locally famous cornet player and coleader of the Kid Ory Band, the most popular band in New Orleans. (19) Oliver soon became Armstrong's teacher and mentor and taught him more about jazz. (20) Oliver and his band had a new style of playing that combined blues, ragtime, and band music. (21) This innovative music became known as jazz.

(22) At seventeen, Armstrong replaced Oliver in the Kid Ory Band when his mentor moved to Chicago. (23) The following year, Armstrong began playing jazz on Mississippi riverboats, where the riverboat musicians helped him improve his ability to read music. (24) They also taught Armstrong the business side of a musician's life—how to organize and manage professional bookings.

Influences on Jazz

(25) During the 1920s, Armstrong rose from being a local jazzman to an international star. (26) At age twenty-one, he moved to Chicago to rejoin his mentor in Oliver's Creole Jazz Band. (27) A year later, he made his first recordings. (28) He moved to New York City to join the Fletcher Henderson Orchestra in 1924, and a year after that moved back to Chicago. (29) Armstrong traversed the country playing with a variety of musicians and recording songs that became jazz hits for the remainder of his twenties.

(30) Armstrong became an innovator in jazz. (31) When he began playing in New Orleans in his teens, jazz was an ensemble, or group, performance. (32) Armstrong's daring and innovative cornet and trumpet solos changed that. (33) His solos were masterworks of improvisation. (34) Instead of relying on a printed musical score, he made up the music on the spot. (35) He used new rhythms in his playing and coaxed his horn to reach impossibly high notes.

(36) The innovation extended to Armstrong's singing. (37) With his rasping voice, he recorded the hit tune "Heebie Jeebies," which introduced scat singing to the world. (38) Scat is a type of improvised singing that replaces words with nonsense syllables, such as "dip-be-do-de-dip" or "ta-de-da-da-de." (39) The result is a string of sung syllables that sound like a musical instrument.

Reading Guide

Does the author use correct subject-verb agreement?

Is all the punctuation and spelling correct?

(40) Armstrong's musical selections were also groundbreaking. (41) In his recordings, he played and sang not only jazz pieces but also popular songs in a distinctive jazz style. (42) This made jazz enormously popular and paved the way for later mainstream popular singers such as Bing Crosby.

"Satchmo" Is Born

(43) By the 1930s Armstrong had begun appearing in movies and Broadway shows and was hugely popular both in the United States and in Europe. (44) The 1930s heralded a number of firsts for Armstrong. (45) He was the first African American musician to write an autobiography and the first African American to host a radio show and get star billing in a movie.

(46) It was on his first trip to Europe in 1932 that Armstrong acquired his famous nickname—"Satchmo." (47) A British editor mispronounced Armstrong's childhood nickname "Satchelmouth," earned because of his wide grin. (48) Armstrong liked Satchmo and used the new name himself from then on.

(49) During World War II, Armstrong frequently played for soldiers on military bases. (50) After the war and through the late 1960s, Armstrong toured in the United States and the rest of the world, often giving three hundred concerts in a year. (51) In 1964, Armstrong's recording "Hello, Dolly!" reached number one on the pop charts, bumping the Beatles down to number two. (52) At age sixty-three, Armstrong was the oldest musician ever to reach number one.

(53) His world tours spread goodwill for the United States and earned him the nickname "Ambassador Satch." (54) With his broad smile and perpetually optimistic outlook on life, audiences admired him. (55) The sunny outlook that touched so many people is captured in Armstrong's introduction to his hit song "What a Wonderful World." (56) Armstrong said And all I'm saying is, see what a wonderful world it would be if only we would give it a chance. (57) Love, baby, love. (58) That's the secret. (59) Yeah.

Farewell to Satchmo

(60) Louis Armstrong died at home in Queens, New York, on July 6, 1971. (61) More than twenty-five thousand fans came to pay their respects to the jazz great. (62) Millions more around the world mourned his passing.

Answer the following questions.

1 This question has two parts. First, answer Part A. Then, answer Part B.

Part A

Read the following excerpt from the passage. Underline the sentence with a dangling modifier.

(4) Louis Armstrong was born on August 4, 1901. (5) An African American, he grew up in dire poverty in the segregated southern city of New Orleans, Louisiana. (6) Living in an unstable family, his mother and sister were supported in part by Armstrong, who had to leave school in fifth grade to earn money. (7) He traveled the streets of New Orleans to any job where he could make a few pennies. (8) Just a child, he sang on street corners, cleaned the tops of graves, sold coal, and loaded junk wagons. (9) But rather than being Armstrong's undoing, this was the start of his musical education.

Part B

Rewrite your answer to Part A so it is correct.

_____

_____

_____

2 Choose the sentence that shows the correct order of adjectives and use of commas.

   A. Funerals and holiday parades made liberal use of rollicking, spirited brass bands.

   B. Funerals and holiday parades made liberal use of spirited rollicking brass bands.

   C. Funerals and holiday parades made liberal use of rollicking, brass, spirited bands.

   D. Funerals and holiday parades made liberal use of rollicking, spirited, brass bands.

3 Read the excerpt from the passage.

Oliver soon became Armstrong's teacher and mentor and taught him more about jazz.

Rewrite the excerpt to eliminate wordiness and redundancy.

_____

_____

_____

4 Read the excerpt from the passage.

Armstrong traversed the country playing with a variety of musicians and recording songs that became jazz hits for the remainder of his twenties.

Which **best** shows how to rewrite the sentence to correct the misplaced modifier?

A. For the remainder of his twenties, Armstrong traversed the country playing with a variety of musicians and recording songs that became jazz hits.

B. Armstrong traversed the country playing with a variety of musicians for the remainder of his twenties and recording songs that became jazz hits.

C. Playing with a variety of musicians, Armstrong traversed the country recording songs that became jazz hits for the remainder of his twenties.

D. Playing with a variety of musicians and recording songs that became jazz hits for the remainder of his twenties, Armstrong traversed the country.

5 Read the following excerpt from the passage.

(56) Armstrong said And all I'm saying is, see what a wonderful world it would be if only we would give it a chance. (57) Love, baby, love. (58) That's the secret. (59) Yeah.

Rewrite the excerpt so it is punctuated correctly.

_____

_____

_____

_____

_____

6 Reread the passage "Louis Armstrong, the Father of Jazz." Based on information in the text, write an essay that explains and summarizes one aspect of Louis Armstrong's life and contributions that you find most remarkable. Remember to use textual evidence to support your ideas.

When you are finished, check to make sure you have followed the rules of grammar usage, punctuation, capitalization, and spelling.

You may plan your essay in the space below. Write your essay on the following pages.

Plan

Write your essay on the lines below.

Read the passage.

Elizabeth I of England

Queen Elizabeth I ruled over England for nearly half of the sixteenth century. She oversaw a Golden Age during which her country dominated Europe and the globe. So it's all the more surprising to learn that Elizabeth was the queen who almost wasn't!

Elizabeth was born in 1533 to Henry VIII and his second wife, Anne Boleyn. When Anne did not produce a male heir, Henry VIII had her arrested and beheaded. He then sent Elizabeth and her older sister Mary away from his court. Elizabeth spent years being raised by a nanny in a faraway castle until being welcomed back by Henry's sixth wife, Catherine Parr. Catherine made sure that young Elizabeth received the best education available. Elizabeth even became fluent in six languages.

After Henry VIII's death in 1547, his son Edward became king. Edward was rather sickly, though, and was only king for a few years. The intrigue surrounding the monarchy exploded after Edward's death. Edward had chosen his cousin Lady Jane Grey to follow him as monarch. However, many British people favored Mary, Elizabeth's older sister. Lady Jane ruled as queen for only nine days before being overthrown by Mary's supporters. Once Mary was queen, palace spies uncovered a plot to overthrow her. Elizabeth was suspected of trying to overthrow her sister, although no ties linked her to the plot. Mary had her younger sister arrested and held in the Tower of London, a castle that was used as a prison. Elizabeth narrowly escaped being executed for this plot. Mary continued to rule as queen until her death in 1558.

Elizabeth became queen when she was twenty-five years old. Even though England was a powerful country, Elizabeth faced a number of problems both in and out of the country. Internally, England was divided between religious factions who fought against each other. Before Henry VIII's marriage to Anne Boleyn, people in England belonged to the Catholic Church. When Henry wanted to divorce his first wife to marry Anne, he left the Catholic Church to create the Church of England. Freedom of religion did not exist at this time, so Henry's actions made all English citizens members of the Church of England whether they wanted to be or not. Henry's actions also set off a series of religious conflicts between the Puritans and the Catholics that lasted for years to come. To try to find a middle ground, Elizabeth openly supported the Church of England, but did not really care how the English citizens worshipped in private.

England also experienced political tensions throughout Europe when Elizabeth I came to the throne. England, France, and Spain seemed to constantly be embroiled in skirmishes over land. Elizabeth's older sister, Mary, had even married Philip II of Spain in hopes of creating an alliance between the two countries. When Mary died, Philip approached Elizabeth about a marriage between the two of them, but she refused. This rebuff led Philip to launch a group of 130 ships, called the Spanish Armada, in hopes of taking Spanish control of England from Elizabeth. Knowing this marked a crucial point in her rule, Elizabeth mounted a horse to rally the English troops herself. She said, "'I know I have the body of a weak, feeble woman; but I have the heart and stomach of a king—and of a King of England, too." English forces then defeated the Spanish Armada in a stunning military victory.

Elizabeth I knew how to gain favor to get the support of key people. She often rode about the countryside on horseback. This allowed English citizens a chance to see her while also making her seem more like one of them. While Elizabeth relied on advisors, she made most decisions by herself. A detailed spy network existed during Elizabeth's reign. Since Elizabeth was aware of the plots to overthrow the monarchs before her, she was determined to avoid any such issues while she was queen. Elizabeth also expanded England's role around the globe. She sponsored the explorer Sir Francis Drake, giving him permission to raid any Spanish ships or settlements. He later became the first person to sail around the globe.

Elizabeth's independence and reign marked a high point in English history. Some consider her to be one of the strongest monarchs ever to rule England. The fact that Elizabeth ruled alone, despite numerous offers of marriage, set her apart in history. The world at this time was dominated by men; women only ruled if there was no male heir. While queen, Elizabeth not only held her own, but made England a more powerful country than it was when she first became queen.

Answer the questions.

1 The writer of the passage used the graphic organizer below to brainstorm ideas and details related to the topic. Complete the organizer so it reflects the final passage.

Topic	Details

2 This question has two parts. First, answer Part A. Then, answer Part B.

Part A

Carla wrote the following sentences for a report about Henry VIII. Identify the sentence that contains a misplaced modifier.

A. Henry VIII reigned as the king of England from 1491 to 1547.

B. To be king, Henry married six times hoping to gain a male heir.

C. Henry's third wife, Jane Seymour, finally gave birth to a boy who was named Edward VI.

D. As king, Henry's son Edward VI served for only a short time.

Part B

Rewrite the sentence you chose so it is correct.

_____

_____

3 Read all parts of the question before responding.

Part A

A student is writing a report about Elizabeth I's sponsorship of Sir Francis Drake. Underline one detail from the passage that the student might include in the report.

Part B

Complete the chart using the detail you identified in Part A. Quote the detail in the first row. Paraphrase it in the second row.

Quote	
Paraphrase	

Part C

The student is continuing her research online. Which search terms would likely generate the most useful results in an Internet search?

A. Elizabeth I Queen of England Sir Francis Drake

B. Sir Francis Drake privateer

C. Elizabeth I Sir Francis Drake influence

D. Sir Francis Drake Spanish colonies

Read the passage.

Fun and Games in Elizabethan England

Queen Elizabeth I ruled England from 1558 to 1603. During the Elizabethan era, the country enjoyed power among other nations and prosperity at home. Knights reigned supreme, with jousting, hunting, falconry, archery, and theater providing the main sources of entertainment, just the way that sports, movies, and TV do today.

Elizabeth I's status as a young, unmarried queen fostered the era of knights. A code of conduct dictated that knights show great courage in battle while also displaying courtly manners and chivalrous behavior. Even though the feudal system of knights and vassals no longer existed, Elizabeth would confer the title of knight as a matter of prestige and thanks for service. Nobles would host tournaments in which they competed in various games and often vied for the sponsorship of the women in attendance.

Jousting tournaments featured knights charging each other on horseback. While medieval jousts sometimes involved the death of the knights, Elizabethan jousts mainly just served as entertainment and were conducted under strict rules. In an individual joust, two knights on horseback would charge each other from opposite directions. Each knight would carry a shield and a lance. The object would be to strike one's opponent enough to unseat him from his horse. It was considered very poor form to strike a horse. Jousters sometimes also quickly rode toward rings hanging from a horizontal pole. In this game, the knight would try to plunge his lance through a ring and carry it away. Winning knights were often awarded golden rings by the ladies of the royal court in attendance.

Hunting enjoyed great popularity during the Elizabethan Era. Hunts would be all-day affairs in which both men and women participated. Hunting was often considered a sport for nobility, since Forest Laws dictated that all forests were owned by the king or queen. Sixty-nine royal forests existed during Elizabeth's reign. Commoners were banned from hunting in these areas unless given express permission to do so. Both men and women participated in bow and stable hunts. In this type of hunt, nobles on horseback would follow hunting dogs, which would chase a quarry into an enclosed area. The nobles would then shoot the quarry, often deer, with a bow and arrow at close range. Only men usually engaged in at-force hunts. These hunts usually chased wild boar, often considered the most dangerous and unpredictable prey.

Falconry, or hunting with birds of prey, also proved to be a popular sport in Elizabethan England. Queen Elizabeth herself participated in falconry. It was also known as a sport of nobility, since people in lower classes did not usually have the money required to train the birds. Many nobles employed a falconer whose job involved caring for and training the birds to get used to the human contact necessary for the sport. To get a young hawk used to humans, it was taken from a nest at an early age and taught to eat from the falconer's hand while sitting on his arm. Over time, the hawk was taught to grab food from a human hand in mid-flight. Eventually, the hawk would be trained to catch game, or quarry, before returning to its handler for a reward. Bells were often attached to a hawk's legs so its trainer could hear where it was.

Citizens of all social class learned archery. Beginning about age seven, almost all males were taught to shoot a bow and arrow. Doing so provided a means of hunting for food as well as a type of personal protection. Archery contests also provided entertainment and a way for citizens to demonstrate their skills with a bow. Most archers at this time shot with a longbow. Even Elizabeth I was skilled at shooting the weapon and used it herself for sport and to hunt.

Aside from sports, many citizens of Elizabethan England enjoyed attending the theater. The great English playwright William Shakespeare rose to prominence during Elizabeth I's reign. The queen enjoyed performances of Shakespeare's plays and sometimes had his players come to her castles to give private performances for her and her court. The queen enjoyed Shakespeare's plays so much that she became one of his patrons to provide financial support. The playwright even alludes to the queen in some of his plays, notably in *A Midsummer Night's Dream* when he refers to a "fair vestal throned by the west." Average citizens also enjoyed Shakespeare's plays at the Globe Theatre outside London. For a fee, they would crowd together to catch Shakespeare's newest comedy or drama in seating divided by social classes. Just another Saturday night in Elizabethan England!

Answer the questions.

4 Two students are holding a debate focused on the following statement.

> **When it came to enjoying the entertainment of the Elizabethan era, the nobility had an advantage over those in the lower class.**

Tasha supports the statement, while Jerrod opposes it. Complete the chart with one reason and relevant evidence from the passage that supports each student's side.

Tasha's Position	Jerrod's Position
Reason:	Reason:
Evidence:	Evidence:

5 The left-hand column contains additional details the author of "Fun and Games in Elizabethan England" could include in the passage, as well as one irrelevant detail. Match each detail on the left to its best fit on the right.

A. Elizabeth I's successor, James I, also enjoyed Shakespeare's plays.

1. paragraph 7

B. Jousts were held on a tilt-yard.

2. paragraph 4

C. Robert Dudley and William Cecil acted as advisors to Elizabeth I.

3. paragraph 2

D. Hunts provided a way for the nobility to interact socially as well as train for war.

4. paragraph 3

E. Knights promised to uphold the values of honor, faith, courage, and loyalty.

5. does not fit in the passage

6 The following question has two parts. First, answer Part A. Then, answer Part B.

Part A

Ron is writing a report about William Shakespeare. Rewrite these sentences from his report to correct errors in grammar and spelling and to more concisely and clearly convey the ideas.

A. Shakespeare would sometimes perform several, full-length plays in a day while continuing to write with the group.

_____

B. Today, Shakespeare's collection of plays form the bases of much of English literature.

_____

C. Poet, playright, and world-renown literary figure William Shakespeare lived from 1564 to 1616.

_____

D. Hamlet became one of Shakespeare's best-known dramas. Much Ado About Nothing became one of Shakespeare's best-known comedies.

_____

E. Outside London in the late 1500s he joined a theatrical, acting company called the Lord Chamberlain's Men and performed at the Globe Theatre.

_____

Part B

Reorder the sentences so that they form a clear and logical paragraph. Write the letters of the sentences ordered correctly in the boxes below.

☐   ☐   ☐   ☐   ☐

In "Elizabeth I of England" and "Fun and Games in Elizabethan England," you learned about a former queen of England and about forms of entertainment that were popular during her reign. Based on what you have learned, decide what you think was the most significant accomplishment that came out of the reign of Elizabeth I and write an essay supporting your choice. Support your claim with clear reasons and supporting text evidence from both passages.

Use the space below to plan your writing.

Plan

Write your response on the lines provided.

Listening

Listen to Informational Presentations

1 GETTING THE IDEA

A **presentation** is a speech, talk, or multimedia display that can inform or persuade the audience. You will come across a variety of presentations at school and in life. They include lectures, oral reports, online videos, and audio recordings. This lesson covers **informational presentations**. This kind of presentation informs the audience by giving facts and ideas that explain, teach, or tell about a topic.

Listening to Presentations

There are a number of ways to listen to a presentation. A teacher might read the text aloud, or you might be in charge of the equipment that controls the presentation. You may be required to press "play" on audio equipment to listen to recording or use a computer to watch a video presentation. No matter how the information is presented, you must try to be attentive at all times. One challenge of listening to a presentation is to reduce distractions and stay focused. There is no option of going back and rereading parts that you missed the first time. That is why it is so important to pay close attention at every moment.

Listen for Main Idea and Details

Identifying the key ideas as you listen will help you better understand a presentation. Listen carefully for the speaker's main points. What supporting ideas and evidence does the speaker offer to support those points? **Evidence** is facts or information that help prove that an idea is true. Try to identify the following ideas in the presentation:

- main idea and details that support it

- examples that explain why the main idea is important or interesting

- evidence in support of the main idea or an author's claim

Listen for the Speaker's Purpose

The speaker's purpose is the main reason the speaker decides to speak about the topic. In an informational presentation, the purpose is usually to inform the audience about a topic. In other presentations, it could be to entertain or to persuade the audience to think a certain way.

Listen for Structure

Informational presentations can use different structures to organize facts, details, and events. Identifying how a presentation is organized can make it easier to follow the ideas and remember them later. Listen for the following clues in a presentation to identify the structure.

Structure	Format
chronological order (sequence)	The presenter describes a process or series of steps. Dates, numbers, or time-order words such as *first*, *next*, and *finally* signal that order.
cause and effect	The presenter describes an event (cause) and something that happened as a result (effect). Listen for signal words such as *because*, *therefore*, and *as a result*.
problem and solution	The presenter describes a problem and how it was solved. Keywords include *problem*, *challenge*, *resolution*, and *success*.
compare and contrast	The presenter describes how two or more topics, events, or people are alike and different. Listen for words such as *both*, *alike*, *on the other hand*, and *however*.

Pay Attention to Visuals Aids

Presentations can include **visual aids**. These features can clarify what the audience hears or add new information to what the speaker says. They might include print materials like maps, charts, graphs, or photographs. In a multimedia presentation, including one displayed on a computer, there could be video, sound effects, and animation. Live presentations, where the speaker talks directly to the audience, can be enhanced by slides, props, and any of the same features used in a multimedia display. Pay special attention to these visual features because they can help you better understand the presentation (and make it more fun).

Take Notes

Taking notes is a great way to help remember what you hear and create a record that you can refer to later. Sometimes you will take notes on paper, and other times you will type into a pop-up computer notepad. Here are some tips for taking good notes:

- Include only key words and phrases.

- Start on a new line to write new ideas.

- Use abbreviations whenever possible so that you can write ideas faster.

- When writing on paper, draw quick sketches or make arrows to connect related ideas.

- Write quickly but neatly enough for you to understand your writing later.

Listen Twice

You will usually have a chance to listen to a presentation more than once. If someone reads the presentation out loud, he or she will usually read it twice. If you listen to an audio or video recording, you can go back and play it again. Very few listeners can catch every idea and detail the first time. You should expect to listen again in order to hear all of the information. Listen for different things each time you hear the presentation.

First Listen

During the first listen, identify the speaker's main points. Use what you know about the structure of an informational text to help you identify the main ideas and the most important supporting details. An informational text usually states the main idea in an introduction. Then it follows with key supporting details. As you listen, write the main idea and supporting details in your notes. Also, write down any questions that you have for the speaker.

Second Listen

The second time, listen to confirm your notes, and make any corrections if you need to. Also listen for evidence that supports the main idea and add those ideas to your notes. Try to answer any questions you wrote after the first listen.

After the Presentation

Once you have listened to the presentation a second time, summarize it in your own words. Talk with classmates about the presentation and share your ideas and opinions. If you still have questions, talk about them with other students or your teacher. Then, evaluate the presentation. Did the speaker:

- have a clear main idea?

- include supporting details?

- provide enough evidence?

Language Spotlight • Consult Reference Materials to Verify Meaning

When you listen to an informational presentation, you might hear unfamiliar words. If so, write them down, spelling them as best you can. Try to figure out the meaning of the words if you listen to the presentation a second time. The presenter might give context clues to help you figure out the meaning. Later, look up the words in a print or online dictionary to verify the meaning.

One student heard the following sentence in a presentation about history:

The two parties could not settle the case, so they entered into arbitration.

Use a dictionary to verify the meaning of the underlined word.

Listen to the passage your teacher reads aloud and look at the photograph. Take notes in the space below.

A Visit to the Maya Civilization

Notes

Answer the following questions.

1 What is the main idea of the presentation? In your own words, summarize the key concepts that it is **mostly** about.

_____

_____

> **Hint** Check your notes to find the most important idea from the presentation.

2 Match each word on the left with its definition on the right.

A. architecture		**1.**	simple pictures or symbols that represent words
B. hieroglyphics		**2.**	dates when night and day are equal length
C. remnants		**3.**	the art of designing and constructing buildings
D. equinox		**4.**	small remaining pieces of something
E. civilization		**5.**	a social group with advanced development

> **Hint** Listen for context clues in the presentation to define the words. If that does not help, use reference materials to verify the meaning.

3 How do the remains at Chichén Itzá support the idea that the ancient Maya were remarkable builders?

    A. Chichén Itzá includes the tallest pyramid ever built in the ancient world.

    B. The pyramid at Chichén Itzá has a mathematical design that coordinates with the calendar.

    C. Chichén Itzá is still the largest city in the Yucatan.

    D. The buildings at Chichén Itzá show no signs of decay since they were first built over a thousand years ago.

> **Hint** Think about why Chichén Itzá is special. Which statement about Chichén Itzá among the answer choices is true?

4 Identify and explain **two** key details that support the main idea that ancient Maya were excellent builders.

_____

_____

_____

_____

_____

> **Hint** The presentation includes specific information about three ancient Maya sites. Explain how two of them support the main idea.

Use the Listening Guide to help you understand the passage your teacher reads aloud and study the photograph. Take notes in the space below.

What Happened to the Ancient Maya?

Listening Guide

When did the Maya empire flourish? What happened to it?

Identify three theories to explain why the Maya civilization disappeared.

What reason disputes the natural disaster theory?

What evidence supports the plague theory? What evidence disputes it?

What is the most likely explanation for the disappearance of the Maya?

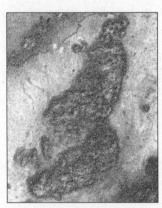

NASA images, like this one of Earth from space, might help pinpoint the location of Maya ruins.

Notes

Answer the following questions.

1 What is this presentation about? In one or two sentences, write a summary in your own words.

_____

_____

_____

_____

2 How could a natural disaster like a flood cause the Maya empire to collapse indirectly, if one did not destroy the civilization directly?

A. by destroying the food supply

B. by creating plagues

C. by triggering other natural disasters like volcanoes and earthquakes

D. by changing the weather

3 How can archaeologists use modern technology to learn about the Maya empire and its downfall? Use the photographs and the information in the presentation to support your answer.

_____

_____

_____

_____

4 Which theories does the presentation suggest could cause the disappearance of the Maya empire? Choose **all** that apply.

    A. natural disaster

    B. fighting with Spanish explorers

    C. food shortage

    D. plague

    E. climate problems

5 What evidence suggests that plagues were **not** the sole cause that wiped out the Maya empire?

_____

_____

6 How is "What Happened to the Ancient Maya?" organized? What is the structure? How does the structure help the listener to better understand the main points of the presentation?

Write your answer on the lines below.

_____

_____

_____

_____

_____

_____

_____

_____

_____

_____

_____

_____

_____

_____

_____

_____

_____

_____

_____

_____

LESSON 19

Listen to Persuasive Presentations

1 GETTING THE IDEA

In a **persuasive presentation**, the main goal of the speaker is to persuade or convince an audience to think, feel, or act in a certain way. The speaker states a claim or an argument and then tries to influence the audience by supporting that claim with reasons and evidence.

Listening to a Presentation

A persuasive presentation may take many forms. Sometimes, the speaker is in front of you in the classroom or at a school assembly. At other times, you may be asked to play an audio recording, watch a video presentation, or listen as your teacher reads aloud. In each case, your responsibility as the listener is to pay attention and listen carefully.

Purpose When you listen to a persuasive presentation, your purpose is to:

- identify the speaker's **claim**, or argument.

- identify the **reasons** and **evidence** the speaker uses to back up the claim.

- decide whether the reasons and evidence are **relevant** and sufficient.

- determine whether the speaker effectively supports the claim.

- be ready to **summarize** what you heard after the presentation.

Taking Notes When you listen to a presentation, taking notes will help you remember what you have heard. To take notes, record the key words and ideas you hear and not every detail. You can also use abbreviations, circle key points, and draw arrows to help you remember connections between ideas. Remember that your notes are just for you. They don't have to be neat, but they should be legible.

Multimedia and Visual Displays Many presentations also include multimedia and visual displays. These may include video or audio clips, soundtracks, posters, charts, graphs, or photos. Think about why the speaker included these features. Do they provide additional information for you to consider? Are they relevant to the presentation, or are they just for show?

Sometimes, you will be able to listen to a presentation twice. Each time you listen, you can understand the presentation better if you listen for different things.

First Listen

On the first listen, identify the speaker's claim. What is the speaker trying to persuade you to think or believe? What action are you being asked to take? Then, listen for the reasons and evidence that support the claim. A good persuasive presentation will have these features:

- an **introduction**, which states the claim

- support of the claim with reasons and evidence

- an **opposing argument** and a **rebuttal** to counter it

- a restatement of the claim and summary of the main points in the **conclusion**

As you listen, take notes to identify the speaker's claim and the reasons and evidence the speaker provides. If you have any questions, jot them down. You can listen for the answers to your questions during a second listen.

Second Listen

Before you listen for a second time, review your notes. If something is unclear, circle it. The second listen is the time to clarify and verify your notes. As you listen, add details to your notes. You might, for example, place a check (✓) or a plus sign (+) by relevant reasons and evidence and a minus sign (–) by irrelevant points. Listen for the answers to your questions.

Listening for Speaker's Purpose or Motive

On the second listen, tune in to the reasons and evidence the speaker uses to support his or her claim or argument.

- Does the argument make sense? Is it logical? Is the reasoning sound?

- What evidence supports the claim? Is it reliable, relevant, and sufficient? Is any evidence irrelevant?

- Do multimedia or visual displays support the claim? Are they relevant?

- What is the author's **motive** for writing the speech?

Motive	Examples
social	The speaker wants to improve a community, encourage volunteerism, or support a worthy cause.
commercial	The speaker wants to promote a business idea, sell a product, or make money.
political	The speaker wants to run for an office, change a law or rule, or bring about a change in school policy or government.

Listening for Persuasive Techniques Remember that reasons are opinion-based statements. Listen for the way in which the speaker presents his or her reasons. Does the speaker use a persuasive technique to sway your opinion? The kind of technique used may give clues to the speaker's motive. For example, if a speaker's motive is commercial, he or she might use a bandwagon appeal to sell a product. If, however, the motive is political, the speaker might use name-calling to discredit an opponent.

After the Presentation

Once you have listened to the presentation a second time, summarize it in your own words. You might expand on your notes or make an outline to highlight the key points and details. This will help you keep the most important parts of the presentation in mind as you answer questions about it or discuss it with your classmates.

Evaluating Presentations Use your notes and your summary or outline to evaluate the presentation. Decide whether or not the speaker:

- stated the claim or argument clearly.

- supported the claim with sound reasons and relevant and reliable evidence.

When you evaluate a presentation, remember that you might not agree with the speaker's claim or argument. Even if you disagree with the speaker, the claim or argument may still be sound. By the same token, agreeing with a speaker's claim or argument doesn't necessarily mean it was well supported. You should try to evaluate the claim objectively without letting your personal feelings or beliefs affect the evaluation.

Language Spotlight • Analogies

Like similes and metaphors, an **analogy** is a type of figurative language that makes a comparison between two things that are seemingly different. In an analogy, the inference is that if two or more things agree with one another in some respects, they will probably agree in others. "Fish is to water as bird is to air" is an example of an analogy. Persuasive presentations often use analogies to appeal to an audience or to make a point. What items are being compared in the following analogies? What inference is being made?

Jeans are to your wardrobe as fingers are to a hand.

Using a calculator is to the present as using an adding machine was to the past.

Sometimes finding a good bargain is like looking for a needle in a haystack.

**Listen to the passage your teacher reads aloud and look at the picture.
Take notes in the space below.**

Buy American? My Answer Is No!

Notes

Answer the following questions.

1 This question has two parts. First, answer Part A. Then, answer Part B.

Part A

What claim or argument is made in the presentation?

A. Americans should buy products made from natural resources.

B. Americans should buy only products made in the United States.

C. Americans should not worry about buying products made in other countries.

D. Americans should buy both American-made products and those made in other countries.

Part B

Write **two** reasons or examples from your notes that support the claim.

_____

_____

> **Hint** A speaker's claim or argument is the main point he or she wants to make. Your answer to Part B should support the claim you chose in Part A.

2 Read this paragraph from the presentation and the directions that follow.

> **"Almost all economists say it's nonsense," seconded another economist. He continued, "We should buy things where they're cheapest. This frees up more of our resources to buy other things, and other Americans get jobs producing those things." Economists study our economy.**

Underline the sentence that is **most** relevant to the claim that cheap imports kill American jobs. Cross out the sentence that is **irrelevant** to the claim.

> **Hint** A reason that is relevant supports a claim or an argument. A reason that does not directly support a claim is irrelevant.

3 Read all parts of the question before responding.

Part A

Which of the following statements is an analogy?

A. Many people equate buying American with patriotism and buying un-American with treason.

B. They believe that buying so many imported goods from China hurts our economy.

C. A cheap, robust imports marketplace helps not only American workers and families but local farmers, manufacturers, and small businesses as well.

D. So blaming our economic woes on buying goods made in China and other countries doesn't really make sense.

Part B

What inference is being made in the answer you chose for Part A?

_____

_____

Hint Remember that an analogy makes a comparison between two items.

4 In **three** sentences, write a summary of the speaker's argument.

_____

_____

_____

_____

_____

Hint A summary includes only the key points and details.

Use the Listening Guide to help you understand the passage your teacher reads aloud and study the photograph. Take notes in the space below.

Why I Buy American and You Should, Too

Listening Guide

What are the most important ideas to write down in your notes?

What ideas did you understand more deeply in the second listen?

How can you summarize the passage in a few sentences?

Notes

Answer the following questions.

1 This question has two parts. First, answer Part A. Then, answer Part B.

Part A

What is the **main** purpose of this presentation?

A. to convince Americans that foreign products are unsafe

B. to convince listeners that American products are worth their cost

C. to convince listeners to buy American-made products

D. to convince listeners to buy foreign-made products

Part B

Write **two** reasons or examples from your notes that support the claim you chose in Part A.

_____

_____

2 Read all parts of the question before responding.

Part A

Which of the following statements is an analogy?

A. Money is important, but so is our environment.

B. Buying foreign products is to our economy as factories are to pollution.

C. Factories in foreign countries don't have the strict environmental standards that factories in the United States have.

D. And foreign goods don't just magically appear in our stores.

Part B

What inference is being made in the answer you chose for Part A?

_____

_____

3 Which sentence from the presentation is an irrelevant piece of evidence to support the claim made by the speaker?

A. In 2007, twenty-four kinds of toys were recalled for safety reasons in the United States.

B. And in that same year, a Chinese-made toothpaste was recalled because of the possibility it contained a poisonous chemical.

C. The Chinese government promised to clean up its act, but problems with imports from China continue today.

D. I'm not willing to risk my health for a few dollars saved at the store.

4 Underline the sentence from the passage that **best** states the claim for buying American-made products.

> **It may feel as though I'm getting a bargain on those jeans or these T-shirts, but only if I don't think too hard about what went into creating these garments. In November 2012, more than one hundred workers died in a fire when they were trapped inside a high-rise garment factory in Bangladesh. According to one news report, "Bangladesh has some of the cheapest labor in the world and some of the most deplorable working conditions."**

5 Which claims support the speaker's argument? Choose **all** that apply.

A. We have production standards and inspections in this country to make sure products are safe.

B. News reports of unsafe Chinese products, including seafood, pet food, toys, and tires, have raised concerns among Americans about the quality of Chinese imports.

C. It may be frustrating if a cheap necklace breaks soon after you get it home due to shoddy workmanship.

D. Even American-made products get recalled sometimes.

E. Since 2001, trade with China has increased rapidly, and, according to one expert, this has caused "a dramatic loss of 2.4 million U.S. jobs, including high-tech jobs."

F. Taxes are one way our government raises the money it needs to keep running, but foreign companies that export their goods to America do not pay U.S. taxes.

6 What was the speaker's purpose in giving the presentation? Was the presentation effective? How well did the presentation achieve its purpose? Cite details, reasons, and evidence from your notes to support your answer.

Write your answer on the lines below.

_____

_____

_____

_____

_____

_____

_____

_____

_____

_____

_____

_____

_____

_____

Listen to the passage your teacher reads aloud and study the photograph and caption. Take notes on the central ideas and supporting details in the space below. Then answer the questions.

Athletes who participate in high school sports are more likely to be cheered on by a marching band than are athletes on club sports teams.

Notes

Answer the questions.

1 In a few sentences, summarize the key ideas of the presentation your own words.

_____

_____

_____

_____

2 Which sentences from the presentation **best** support the idea that club sports keep athletes from having equal opportunities? Choose **all** that apply.

A. Sports for kids used to mean neighborhood pick-up games and trying out for school teams.

B. Instead, only the most skilled youth athletes are invited to pay a fee to join a team.

C. Club sports exist for nearly every sport, including less popular sports that schools do not include.

D. By participating in clubs, athletes often increase their chances of being noticed by college recruiters, who are the vehicle to college scholarships.

E. Club sports have changed, not ended, high school sports.

F. Club sports have affected various sports differently.

3 Use your notes from the presentation to complete the chart. Include two details to support each benefit or drawback.

Benefits of club teams	Benefits of high school teams
Drawbacks of club teams	**Drawbacks of high school teams**

4 This question has two parts. First, answer Part A. Then, answer Part B.

Part A

Circle the text structure that **best** describes how the presentation was organized.

Text Structures	chronological/sequence
	cause and effect
	problem and solution
	compare and contrast

Part B

Explain how the structure you circled in Part A helped you better understand the main points of the presentation.

_____

_____

_____

5 This question has two parts. First, answer Part A. Then, answer Part B.

Part A

Which excerpt from the passage do the photograph and caption **best** clarify?

A. As the importance of club sports increases, the issue of equal opportunity becomes more prominent.

B. Club sports have changed, not ended, high school sports.

C. Supporters claim that high school teams offer youth a sense of belonging to something larger than themselves.

D. The possibility of enjoying participation still exists for students who may not be the best athletes.

Part B

Explain how the photograph and caption help you better understand the excerpt you chose in Part A.

_____

_____

_____

Listen to the passage your teacher reads aloud and study the graph. Take notes on the presentation in the space below. Then answer the questions.

Percentages of Fourth Grade Students
Who Scored Proficient on the Florida
Comprehensive Assessment Test

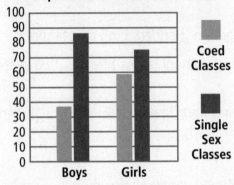

Source: National Association for Single-Sex Public Education

Notes

Answer the questions.

6 This question has two parts. First, answer Part A. Then, answer Part B.

Part A

Identify the speaker, intended audience, and motive of the presentation by circling the correct choice in each column.

Speaker	Audience	Motive
a student	parents	social
a teacher	teachers	commercial
a parent	students	political

Part B

Explain how the motive you circled in Part A reflects the speaker's claim.

_____

_____

7 Using your notes, write one piece of evidence from the presentation that supports each of the speaker's reasons for the claim below.

A. Students in single-sex classes perform better than those in coeducational classes.

_____

_____

B. Single-sex classes would be successful since they would be only for students who choose them.

_____

_____

C. Students in single-sex classes are actually *more* likely to stretch beyond traditional roles.

_____

_____

8 The following question has two parts. First, answer Part A. Then, answer Part B.

Part A

Underline the analogy in this excerpt from the presentation.

> **Students know how they learn best. Some do better on homework while listening to music, while others do better in silence. Our parents and teachers choose who they want to work with, so why shouldn't we be able to choose who we learn with?**

Part B

Which **best** states the inference being made in the analogy?

A. Parents, teachers, and students all make similar kinds of decisions.

B. Students do better on homework when they listen to music.

C. Doing homework and listening to music require similar skills.

D. Choosing who to work with and who to learn with are similar kinds of decisions.

9 The following question has two parts. First, answer Part A. Then, answer Part B.

Part A

Which **best** summarizes an opposing argument from the presentation?

A. Single-sex classes are not popular with everyone.

B. Single-sex classes maintain traditional roles of boys and girls.

C. Teachers can customize strategies so they work with either sex.

D. Students are willing to take more risks in single-sex classes.

Part B

Use your notes to briefly describe how the speaker rebuts the opposing argument you chose in Part A.

PERFORMANCE TASK

Use your notes to write an essay that evaluates the presentation. How sound and effective was the argument? How well did the presentation achieve its purpose? What changes or additions might the speaker make to strengthen the validity of the argument? Conclude your essay by stating whether or not you found the presentation convincing and explain why. Use details, reasons, and evidence from your notes to support your answer.

Write your answer on the lines provided.

_____

_____

_____

_____

_____

_____

_____

_____

_____

_____

_____

_____

_____

_____

_____

_____

GLOSSARY

academic vocabulary terms used in content-specific areas, such as social studies, mathematics, or science (Lesson 9)

act the main divisions of a drama or play (Lesson 3)

adage an old saying that expresses an accepted truth about life; also called *proverb* (Lesson 3)

adjective clause a clause that modifies a noun or a pronoun (Lesson 17)

adjective phrase a phrase that usually appears after a noun or a pronoun that it modifies (Lesson 17)

adverb clause a clause that modifies a verb, an adjective, or another adverb (Lesson 17)

adverb phrase a phrase that tells when, where, how, why, or to what extent (Lesson 17)

affix a letter or group of letters placed at the beginning or end of a word to create a new word and meaning (Lesson 5)

alliteration the repetition of an initial consonant sound (Lesson 2)

allusion a reference to another work, such as the Bible or mythology (Lesson 2)

analogy a comparison that shows a relationship between two sets of things; also a type of figurative language that makes a comparison between things that are seemingly different—such as "Fish is to water as bird is to air" (Lesson 19)

analyze to compare and contrast two texts (Lesson 4)

antiquated language the language that was used in the past (Lesson 3)

antonyms words that have the opposite meanings (Lesson 10)

argument support for an author's position using logical reasoning and evidence; an attempt to convince, or persuade, others to think or act in a certain way; also called *persuasive writing* (Lessons 6, 16)

article a common form of nonfiction (Lesson 5)

aside a comment by a character in a play to the audience but not to the other characters (Lesson 3)

author's bias a preconceived and often unfair feeling that an author has for or against something (Lesson 6)

author's purpose the main reason an author has for writing a text, most commonly to inform, to entertain, or to persuade (Lesson 5)

ballad a short poem that tells a story, composed of stanzas of 2 to 4 lines and a refrain that repeats (Lesson 2)

bandwagon appeal implies that "everyone is doing it" (Lesson 6)

bias a preconceived and often unfair feeling that an author has for or against something (Lesson 6)

biography a true story of a person's life (Lesson 5)

body the text of an argument in which a writer develops the position her or she presents in the thesis statement (Lesson 15)

bulleted list a list that highlights key facts or presents a list of information, in which each item begins with a bullet (•) (Lesson 5)

caption the text that explains a photograph or a graphic feature; usually a phrase or sentence (Lesson 5)

cast of characters a list of the performers in a drama or play (Lesson 3)

categories information that is divided according to groups (Lesson 9)

cause something that brings about an effect or a result (Lesson 7)

cause-and-effect structure a text organization common in technical texts in which the author relates two or more events by examining what happened and why (Lesson 5)

central idea see *main idea*

character a person, an animal, or an object that takes part in the action of a text (Lessons 1, 13)

chronological structure a text organization in which the author organizes details in the order in which they happened; also called *sequence structure* or *chronological order* (Lesson 5)

cite sources to list, usually in a bibliography, the sources—such as books, magazine and encyclopedia articles, and Web sites—that were used to write a text (Lesson 14)

claim the main point that a writer is trying to make in an argument (Lesson 6)

clause a group of words that contains both a subject and a verb (predicate) (Lesson 11)

climax the turning point in a plot when the conflict is at its highest (Lesson 3)

comma the mark of punctuation (,) that represents a pause in a sentence (Lesson 13)

compare to look for similarities between ideas, people, places, events, or passages (Lesson 5)

compare-and-contrast structure a text organization in which the author compares two or more things, ideas, or events to tell how they are similar and different (Lesson 5)

complex sentence a sentence made up of an independent clause and one or more dependent clauses (Lesson 17)

compound sentence a sentence made up of two or more complete thoughts, joined by a comma and a coordinating conjunction such as *and, but, or,* or *so* (Lesson 17)

compound-complex sentence a sentence that has two or more independent clauses and one or more dependent clauses (Lesson 17)

conclusion the end of a piece of writing that restates the claim, summarizes the main points, and makes a concluding statement (Lesson 6)

conflict the main problem in a story that the characters must solve (Lessons 3, 11)

connotation a meaning suggested or implied by a word, separate from its dictionary definition (Lesson 2)

contemporary fiction a genre of writing that takes place in the present day (Lesson 1)

context clue a word or phrase near an unfamiliar word that helps a reader determine what the unknown word means (Lesson 1)

contrast to look for differences between ideas, people, places, events, or passages (Lesson 5)

coordinate adjectives two or more adjectives that are equal in importance, separated by a comma (Lesson 13)

coordinating conjunction a word such as *and, but, or,* or *so* that connects two or more thoughts (Lesson 17)

counterargument the opposite viewpoint of the one given in a text; also called *rebuttal* (Lesson 6)

credible trustworthy and believable, used in relation to the credibility of research sources (Lesson 14)

dangling modifier a word or phrase that causes confusion in a sentence, occurring when the word to be modified is missing from the sentence (Lesson 17)

denotation the dictionary definition of a word (Lesson 2)

dependent clause a group of words that cannot stand alone as a sentence, even if it has a subject and a verb (Lesson 17)

description information that fills in the details of a story and creates a clear picture for the reader (Lesson 13)

detail a fact, statistic, explanation, data, or other evidence that helps to convey the main idea of a text (Lesson 1)

dialogue the lines spoken by characters in a text; a conversation between characters in a text (Lessons 3, 13)

domain-specific vocabulary a word or phrase that has a specific meaning within a particular field of study (Lesson 7)

drafting the second step of the writing process, in which writing actually begins (Lesson 11)

drama a story performed by actors for an audience (Lesson 3)

dramatic irony a situation in which the audience knows more than one or more of the characters (Lesson 3)

draw conclusions to make decisions about a passage based on information from the text, inferences, and prior knowledge (Lesson 1)

editing the fourth step of the writing process, in which writers review the text for mistakes in grammar, usage, and mechanics (Lesson 11)

effect what happens as the result of a cause (Lesson 7)

essay a text in which an author shares his or her outlook or point of view (Lesson 5)

evaluate argument to assess an author's arguments to see if they are relevant and sufficient (Lesson 6)

evidence information an author provides to support the main idea of a text, including examples, research and survey results, statistics, case studies, expert opinions, and direct quotations (Lesson 6)

explanatory text see *informative text*

exposition the text of a drama or story that introduces the characters, setting, plot, and conflict (Lesson 3)

fable a genre of writing that has a moral or lesson (Lesson 1)

falling action the part of a plot that leads to the resolution (Lesson 3)

fiction text that is made up and includes characters, setting, and plot events (Lesson 1)

figurative language a word or phrase that means something other than its dictionary definition, such as a simile, or an idiom; also called *figure of speech* (Lesson 2)

first-person narrator a character in a story who uses the first-person pronouns *I, me, my,* and *our* to comment on events and other characters from his or her point of view (Lesson 1)

flashback a technique in which characters remember earlier events (Lesson 10)

flowchart a graphic feature that uses arrows or connecting lines to show steps in a process or how things relate to one another (Lesson 7)

formal language an approach to writing that uses standard English and avoids slang and casual language (Lesson 11)

free verse a poem that does not follow any rules of rhythm or rhyme (Lesson 2)

generalization makes a general statement that sounds authoritative (Lesson 6)

genre a category of writing, such as historical fiction (Lesson 10)

graphic feature a diagram, model, graph, or table that helps readers locate information quickly in a text (Lesson 5)

haiku a very short poem that has just 3 lines and 17 syllables; usually about nature (Lesson 2)

heading a word or phrase at the top of a section of text that tells the reader what the section is about (Lesson 5)

historical fiction a story based on a real event from the past, or set in a real time and place in the past (Lesson 10)

historical text an informational text that tells about the past (Lesson 7)

idiom a common phrase whose meaning differs from the meaning of the individual words (Lesson 3)

independent clause a group of words that includes a subject and a verb (predicate) and can stand alone as a sentence (Lesson 17)

informal language a type of writing that uses casual, everyday language—such as dialogue (Lesson 11)

informational text a type of writing in which the author provides facts about real-life people and/or events, or explains how to do something; also called *explanatory text* (Lesson 15)

informational presentation a speech, talk, or multimedia display that informs the audience (Lesson 18)

interview shares a person's experiences, ideas, and opinions (Lesson 5)

introduction the beginning of a piece of writing that captures the reader's attention and presents the text's thesis statement, or main idea (Lesson 6)

irrelevant evidence the type of evidence that is not directly connected to a claim—and which can weaken the effectiveness of the author's claim (Lesson 6)

key term an important word in a scientific or technical text (Lesson 8)

lines rows of words in a poem (Lesson 2)

loaded language emotional language, common in first-person texts (Lesson 7)

lyric poem a short poem that is like a song (Lesson 2)

main idea a central message that an author wants to convey about a topic (Lesson 5)

mechanics the technical aspects of writing, including spelling, punctuation, capitalization, and abbreviations (Lesson 11)

metaphor a type of figurative language that compares two things or ideas without using the word *like* or *as* (Lesson 2)

meter a recurring pattern of stressed and unstressed syllables in a poem (Lesson 2)

misplaced modifier a word or phrase that is in the wrong place in a sentence and causes confusion about who is doing an action or what action is being done; also called *dangling modifier* (Lesson 12)

modifier a word or phrase that tells about who is doing an action or what action is being done (Lesson 12)

monologue a speech given by one actor (Lesson 3)

mood the overall atmosphere of a drama (Lesson 3)

motivations the needs and goals of a character, which drive the actions of the plot (Lesson 1)

multiple-meaning word a word that has more than one meaning (Lesson 4)

myth a genre of writing that presents a traditional story from a certain place; may give reasons for how something was created or how something works (Lesson 1)

narrator the person who tells a story (Lesson 1)

narrative the type of writing that describes an event or series of events, which may be true or made up (Lesson 11)

narrative writing the type of writing that develops real or imagined experiences to entertain a reader; always includes characters, a setting, a plot, and a point of view (Lesson 13)

non-coordinate adjective usually the last adjective in a series that is often considered part of a noun, as in *a tall pine tree* (Lesson 17)

nonfiction factual writing about real people, places, events, ideas, and things; often called *informational text* (Lesson 5)

ode a poem that has two or more stanzas with similar structures (Lesson 2)

opinion a view on a certain issue based on a personal judgment; a belief that cannot be proved true (Lesson 6)

opposing argument in a persuasive text, an opposite argument or viewpoint of the one that an author gives; also called *opposing claim* (Lesson 6)

outline a plan or description in which a writer lists the main ideas of an argument, including an introduction, the body, and the conclusion (Lesson 16)

pacing the rate at which the story moves, or is told (Lesson 13)

pamphlet a short booklet that contains information on a topic (Lesson 7)

paraphrase to retell someone else's ideas or information in one's own words (Lesson 14)

part-to-whole structure a text organization that begins with facts and details—the "parts"—followed by the main idea or concept—the "whole" (Lesson 8)

personification a type of figurative language that assigns human qualities to nonliving things (Lesson 2)

persuasive language words and phrases used to affect how a reader thinks or feels (Lesson 6)

persuasive presentation a presentation that attempts to convince, or persuade, the audience to think, feel, or act in a certain way (Lesson 19)

persuasive techniques the ways in which an author tries to create a response from the reader, including bandwagon appeal, propaganda, generalizations, and stereotyping (Lesson 6)

persuasive text the type of writing that attempts to persuade, or convince, readers to accept a certain view or take a specific action, including speeches, arguments, editorials, letters to the editor, and opinion blog posts (Lesson 6)

persuasive writing see *argument*

phrase a group of related words that does not have its own subject and verb (Lesson 11)

plagiarize to copy someone else's writing word for word without giving credit to that person (Lesson 14)

plagiarism the act of taking someone's sentences right from a source without giving the author credit (Lesson 15)

plot the series of events in a story in which the characters try to solve a problem or attain a goal (Lessons 3, 13)

poem a type of writing in which the poet chooses and arranges words to create a strong feeling through meaning, sound, and rhythm (Lesson 2)

poetry a genre of writing that is separated into lines and stanzas in which an author uses sound devices, such as rhyme and rhythm, to create meaning and evoke emotion in the reader (Lesson 2)

point of view the position or outlook from which a speaker tells a story or observes something (Lessons 1, 13)

precise language words that clearly explain the information being presented (Lesson 13)

predicate the part of a sentence that modifies the subject in some way (Lesson 17)

prefix a letter or group of letters added to the beginning of a word to create a new word and meaning (Lesson 5)

prewriting the first step of the writing process, in which writers decide on a topic and subtopics, details, audience, and purpose (Lesson 11)

primary source a journal, manuscript, painting, or other piece of evidence created by someone who was present when an event happened (Lesson 7)

problem-and-solution structure a text organization in which the author states a problem and suggests one or more solutions (Lesson 5)

proofread to check for correct capitalization, punctuation, and spelling (Lesson 17)

propaganda information that is meant to stir up fear in readers (Lesson 6)

proverb an old saying that expresses an accepted truth about life; also called *adage* (Lesson 3)

publishing the final step of the writing process, in which writers make a clean copy of the paper, incorporating changes made in the revising and editing processes (Lesson 11)

purpose see *author's purpose*

quotation the words someone has said, usually appearing within quotation marks (" ") (Lesson 14)

quote to use someone else's words exactly as they were written or spoken—usually placed within quotation marks (" ") (Lesson 14)

reason a statement that tells readers why they should believe a claim (Lesson 6)

rebuttal see *counterargument*

redundancy the inappropriate repetition of ideas (Lesson 17)

refute to oppose an argument (Lessons 6, 16)

relevant clearly related to a topic and supporting a central idea (Lessons 6, 15)

repetition the intentional repeating of words or lines in poetry for a particular effect (Lesson 2)

resolution the way in which a conflict is or is not resolved (Lesson 3)

response to literature a type of writing in which an author makes a claim about one or more literary texts (Lesson 12)

revising the third step of the writing process, in which writers improve their writing by adding facts or details, connect ideas by using transitions, delete repeated or unrelated information, and check the order of details and evidence (Lesson 11)

rhyme the similar ending sounds in a poem (Lesson 2)

rhyme scheme the pattern of end rhymes in a poem that is represented by a sequence of letters, such as *ababcdcd* (Lesson 2)

rhythm a repeated pattern, or "beat," of stressed and unstressed syllables in a line of poetry (Lesson 2)

rising action the part of a plot that leads to the climax (Lesson 3)

root a basic word unit from which other words are formed (Lesson 5)

scene the smaller sections in an act within a drama (Lesson 3)

science fiction a genre of writing about science and technology; may be set in the future or in space (Lesson 1)

scientific text a text that provides information about specialized science topics (Lesson 8)

secondary source something created or written about an event by a person who did not witness the event firsthand (Lesson 7)

sensory details description that appeals to a reader's sense of sight, feel, taste, smell, and sound (Lesson 13)

sentence variation see *varying sentence patterns*

sequence structure a text organization in which the author organizes details in time order; also called *chronological order* or *chronological structure* (Lesson 5)

setting the time and place in a story or drama (Lessons 3, 13)

sidebar a short article, often enclosed within box borders, that appears beside a main article in a magazine or newspaper (Lesson 5)

simile a type of figurative language that compares two things or ideas using *like* or *as* (Lesson 2)

simple sentence a sentence that expresses one complete thought; an independent clause with a subject and verb (predicate) (Lesson 17)

soliloquy a speech in which a character, alone on a stage, reveals his or her thoughts and feelings to him- or herself, but also to the audience (Lesson 3)

sonnet a short poem that has 14 lines, with 10 to 12 syllables per line (Lesson 2)

source a book, person, Web site, etc., that provides information (Lessons 7, 14)

spatial structure a text organization in which things are described in terms of where they are (Lesson 8)

speaker the "voice" of a poem, like the narrator of a story (Lesson 2)

speech an oral presentation of a topic (Lesson 5)

stage directions the directions (a) telling characters how to speak or act or (b) telling how sound, lighting, and props should be used (Lesson 3)

stanza a grouping of lines in a poem—somewhat like a paragraph in prose (Lesson 2)

steps in a process see *sequence structure*

stereotyping a general statement about a group of people (Lesson 6)

structure the way or ways in which information is organized (Lesson 5)

style the words and sentences used in a text, and how they are put together (Lesson 4)

subject-verb agreement the "matching"—or agreement—of a subject and verb in a sentence, in which singular subjects use singular verbs and plural subjects use plural verbs (Lesson 15)

subordinating conjunction a word such as *after, where, because, if, which, or since* that joins a dependent clause and an independent clause (Lesson 17)

suffix a letter or group of letters added to the end of a word to create a new word and meaning (Lesson 5)

summarize to identify the central idea of a text and restate it in one's own words (Lesson 9)

supporting details facts, reasons, examples, statistics, quotations, and other evidence that help convey the main idea of a text (Lesson 5)

supporting paragraphs the paragraphs that provide evidence for the position a writer takes in the thesis statement (Lesson 16)

supporting reasons statements that an author makes to defend a central idea or claim (Lesson 9)

suspense a state of uncertainty an author creates for the reader in order to maintain the reader's interest (Lesson 10)

symbol a picture or letter that represents a word or idea; an object that stands for something else (Lessons 3, 8)

symbolism a type of figurative language that uses an image or a symbol to stand for something else (Lesson 2)

synonyms words that have almost the same meaning (Lesson 10)

technical text a text that provides detailed information about a technical subject, often about how to do something (Lesson 8)

textbook a book that gives factual information about a topic (Lesson 5)

text feature a format used to present information in an organized manner (Lesson 5)

text structure the way a text is organized, such as by sequence, cause and effect, or comparing and contrasting (Lesson 7)

theme the central message that an author wants to convey to readers (Lesson 3)

thesis statement a sentence that states the central idea, claim, or main point to be made in a piece of writing (Lesson 15)

third-person limited narrator the narrator in a story who describes the experiences of one character in the third person, using the character's name and the third-person pronoun *he, she,* or *they* (Lesson 1)

third-person omniscient narrator the narrator in a story who knows everything about the characters, events, and setting of the story (Lesson 1)

timeline a graphic that shows a sequence of events in the order the events happened (Lesson 7)

tone the attitude or mood that a poem or drama creates for the reader or viewer (Lesson 2)

topic what a piece of writing is about (Lesson 10)

topic sentence a sentence stating the topic of a paragraph (Lesson 16)

traits the qualities that a character has, usually revealed through his or her thoughts, dialogue, and actions (Lesson 1)

transition a word or phrase that indicates the passage of time, order of events, or change of setting; also called *transitional words and phrases* (Lesson 13)

varying sentence patterns using different types of sentences—simple, compound, and complex—to make text interesting (Lesson 16)

verbal irony a situation in which a character says the opposite of what he or she really means; intended to make a point or to show sarcasm or humor (Lesson 3)

whole-to-part structure a text organization that begins with a topic sentence or general idea—the "whole"—followed by facts and details—the "parts"—which explain and support that idea (Lesson 8)

word choice the words or phrases selected by an author to convey his or her meaning (Lesson 11)

writing process the process of writing, including prewriting, writing, revising, editing, and publishing (Lesson 11)